Adventures into the Psychic

By Jess Stearn

THE SEEKERS
THE SEARCH FOR THE GIRL WITH THE BLUE EYES
EDGAR CAYCE—THE SLEEPING PROPHET
YOGA, YOUTH, AND REINCARNATION
THE GRAPEVINE
THE DOOR TO THE FUTURE
THE SIXTH MAN
THE WASTED YEARS
SISTERS OF THE NIGHT

Adventures

Coward-McCann, Inc.
New York

into the Psychic

by JESS STEARN

For June, who helped show me the way

Copyright © 1969 by Jess Stearn

Library of Congress Catalog
Card Number: 79-81004

Contents

1

Always a New World

How ridiculous! Not for a moment did I blame an editor at *This Week* magazine in 1965 for omitting that part of the prediction. Certainly, there was nothing illogical about an early marriage for Jacqueline Kennedy. She was youthful, vibrant, glamorous, and very much alone after the assassination of her young President husband. And it was not amiss to suggest that she would marry a foreigner, for she mixed naturally with the international set. But to say that she would be married in two years in the Greek islands—how preposterous!

I could hardly avoid an embarrassed glance at my hostess as psychic Helen Stalls announced, "Jacqueline Kennedy will be married in two years, to a foreigner in the Greek islands." Not even in Greece, but in one of the islands, mind you.

I was not to hear the end of this for some time. Whenever the conversation got onto psychic phenomena, the editor who had scoffed at this prediction would good-naturedly deride my serious involvement with the psychic world.

In October, 1968, only a week or so before the President's widow announced plans to marry Aristotle Onassis on the private island of Scorpios, this editor, discounting an astrological prediction of Richard Nixon's election, remarked grandly, "When Jacqueline Kennedy gets married on the Greek islands, then I'll believe the rest."

Obviously, he would never become a believer. He was not ready to accept the psychic when it contradicted the cold bleak world of logic to which he clung so comfortably.

I could very well understand his skepticism. I had been through it myself, and it took years of research before I could accept what common sense told me was impossible.

How could anybody predict what was going to happen before it happened? It was obviously absurd—and yet, with other predictions as remarkable as the one about Jacqueline Kennedy, Helen Stalls obviously made the impossible possible.

Turning back three years, what other predictions had she made that evening that could not have been the result of logical causal process? There were many, as I thought back, and all made with skeptical witnesses gathered around.

I could recall the scene, as if yesterday, though it had all taken place in June of 1965—putting her a year off on Jacqueline Kennedy's wedding. But then time is often difficult for psychics to pinpoint, functioning as they do in a world in which time and space do not have a conventional context.

The session had got under way after dinner, after the servants cleared the dishes, and our hostess, Mrs. Louise Tinsdale Ansberry, a prominent social figure and public relations counselor, looked inquiringly around the table. The others were a well-known newspaper editor and his wife. They looked on with frozen, uncommitted faces, and my feeling was they would stay unconvinced.

I had heard reports of Helen Stalls' prediction of the Jack Kennedy assassination three days before it occurred, and had myself heard her prediction that a similar tragedy would befall brother Bobby. But I had attributed the latter forecast to an essentially pessimistic nature. Whenever the name came up as a political potential, she would say, "Bobby will never be President of the United States."

Our first meeting had been at the Manhattan home of a friend, Virginia Biddle. Without knowing me, Helen had said, as I walked in, that I was going through a divorce and that my wife's name had four letters, beginning with *J*. She could not quite get the name, but it was a reasonably fair effort for *June*. The Biddle family had been impressed, since Helen had got a number of unlikely things accurate about the children in the family. They had found her helpful in getting ready for problem situations anticipated months ahead.

And so, with this perspective, I now considered Mrs. Stalls' performance at the Ansberry apartment that June evening in 1965. Besides the Jacqueline Kennedy forecast, she predicted that President Johnson would undergo abdominal surgery, then recover, that he would not be a candidate in 1968, that a Republican with the initial *R*, from California, would be elected President, that Adlai Stevenson would die within six weeks, in a public place abroad. There were one or two other prognostications, rather hazy in my mind, as I had left the note-taking to Mrs. Ansberry.

As the predictions materialized, climaxed by the Greek wedding, I strove to recall other details of that memorable evening. There had been nothing unusual about Mrs. Stalls' appearance. She was a tall, angular woman of seventy, who had worked with some success as an office manager and was known by associates for her precise, orderly mind. She would have been the last in a crowd to be taken for anything as exotic as a clairvoyante. She did not publicize her gift, nor did she ever take money for a reading. She accepted, and gave, of her gift, with the calm assurance that it was God-given. She did not invoke spirits or go into trance. She merely closed her eyes, and impressions came.

On this particular evening, she concentrated first on the newspaper editor. She fastened her pale-blue eyes on him briefly, then the lids came down, and she began to speak in a dull monotone.

The editor was a Texan and skeptical, but he smiled politely. His smile vanished, however, when Mrs. Stalls promptly got onto his daughter's current romance. "You're very unhappy about the man," she said. "But don't worry, she will marry somebody completely different, somebody you will approve of." My eyes flashed across the table to my editor friend. He looked relieved, in spite of himself, and asked a question or two relative to the situation. Obviously, Helen Stalls had correctly appraised the problem.

Mrs. Ansberry, who had lived in Washington for years, turned the conversation to the political world. "What," she asked, "lies ahead for President Johnson?"

The psychic brushed a veined hand across her closed eyelids, hesitating briefly. "The President will be very ill this fall. He will have abdominal surgery, but he will recover."

Not for months of course, not until October 8, when Johnson had a gall bladder operation, was this prediction confirmed. But even so the performance was impressive, as the questioning, prodded by Mrs. Ansberry, brought forth a singular response.

"If Mr. Johnson is not going to run, as you indicate," Mrs. Ansberry said, "then who will?"

"It will most likely be Humphrey," referring to the Vice President.

"And who do you see as President?" Mrs. Ansberry insisted.

This time her brow furled into a frown. "It will be a Republican," she said finally.

"But who?"

She shook her head. "All I see is the initial R, but he will be from California and a man of strong religious principles, returning the country to the path of morality."

There was a pause. "It could be Ronald Reagan," Mrs. Ansberry finally said, "or perhaps Richard Nixon."

Mrs. Stalls was not to be baited, psychically. "He will help the country, and the change will be good." Obviously, Mrs. Stalls was Republican-oriented.

A whole channel of association appeared to have opened up. For Mrs. Stalls' subconscious was now roaming down the political corridors of America. "I see another American statesman, as well known as the President." She shielded her closed eyes from the vision apparently streaming through her subconscious. "He will die abroad, unexpectedly, in a public place within six weeks."

She had not mentioned his name, and when prodded could only shake her head.

"Would it help if we mentioned a few names?" Mrs. Ansberry said.

The older woman nodded her gray head.

"Would it be Harry Truman?" Mrs. Ansberry asked.

"No, he is out of things now."

"One of the Kennedys—Teddy or Bobby?"

"Their name does not yet signify as much." This was 1965.

"Walter Reuther?" somebody suggested.

"A statesman," Mrs. Stalls rejoined sharply. "Much better known, almost like the President."

Suddenly a familiar name struck Mrs. Ansberry, a statesman whose name was a household word, a man who might have been President—our distinguished ambassador to the United Nations.

"Would it be Adlai Stevenson?"

The clairvoyante's eyes blinked open, and one could see the sadness in them. "Yes," she sighed, "it is he."

In the busy weeks that followed, the session naturally slipped into the background. But one day in July I was to recall with a jolt one of the most dramatic predictions. I picked up a newspaper and the black headlines stared back. Adlai Stevenson was dead. He had died abroad, in England; in a public place, the streets of London; and quite unexpectedly, of a heart attack. The lapsed time was five weeks.

In the months that followed I was to think often of Mrs. Stalls' predictions, particularly as the Presidential race began to shape up, with three *R*'s, governors George Romney, Nelson Rockefeller and Ronald Reagan, the early front-runners in the Republican picture. Richard Nixon was nowhere in sight.

The personable governor of Michigan had appeared to have the inside track, and Mrs. Stalls, asked about the Republican nominee in a conscious moment, now ventured that it looked like Romney. She was not in anything like a trance at the time, it was a matter-of-fact reply to a matter-of-fact question. And certainly, from all the publicity at the time, it looked like another hit.

But Mrs. Ansberry, not at all psychic, disagreed. Consulting her notes for the evening, she had come up with a discrepancy —Mrs. Stalls had said that a Republican *R* would be from California, and Romney could not begin to stretch that far west.

"Helen Stalls," Mrs. Ansberry decided, "has allowed her conscious to be influenced by the Romney boom, but Romney just *didn't* fit all the specifications she laid down when she was in tune that night."

Ronald Reagan appeared the logical choice, though Nixon also qualified, as the *R* was applicable, psychically, to either the first or last name.

Obviously, psychics, like anybody else, are influenced by the constant barrage of impressions from the external world. Only through meditation, through detached concentration, facilitated by cards, tea leaves, crystal balls, or any other resort they can devise, are they able at times to ward off these distracting effusions.

In January of 1966, Mrs. Stalls again gave a startling demonstration of her uncanny skills, this time before a group which included skeptical professors, the Broadway composer Alan Jay Lerner, the socially prominent Mrs. Jeane Murray Vanderbilt, muralist Buell Mullen, and myself. Mrs. Stalls concentrated on Lerner, the most active of the group.

"You are writing a new play, is that not right?" she said.

Lerner nodded noncommittally.

"I see you using a number of old characters, maybe five of them, in this new production."

Lerner was amused. "That's right."

Mrs. Stalls' face took on a faraway look. "You are deeply concerned about Susan. Stop worrying, she will be all right."

The lyricist's jaw dropped. "Susan is my daughter," he said weakly, "and I have been concerned about her."

The scattered impressions continued to flow through her. "You have not been getting along with one of your collaborators," she said, "and you will work with somebody else."

Lerner nodded, seeming to know what she was talking about.

Coolly then, she launched into a detailed discussion of Lerner's business activities, including the initials of several confidential associates. As she got the name Lenox, Lerner, wagging his head, disclosed that one of these men was in Lenox, Massachusetts. "Fantastic," he said, "and they say that *On a Clear Day* (his musical, *On a Clear Day You Can See Forever*) is far fetched."

Unfortunately, or perhaps fortunately, the psychic gift cannot always be invoked at will, even by professionals. But a flash of psychic insight may come out of the blue at any time.

One day, the late Mary Talley, who once presided at Cerruti's Restaurant in New York, felt an irresistible impulse to phone an old friend, steel tycoon Rudolph Boyko. As a psychic consultant, she knew Boyko was planning to set up an organization in Israel, with his scientist brother, Hugo, to salvage that tiny country's desert wastelands. "I have a premonition," she said bluntly, "that Hugo will have a heart attack. Do what you have to right away."

Boyko repeated the conversation to his wife, Rhoda, and decided to fly to Israel right away. He was greeted at the airport by his brother, and saw with secret relief that Hugo had never looked better. The two men worked tirelessly together for weeks, and before Rudolph Boyko returned to America, a project to irrigate the Negev with seawater was well launched. Hugo saw him off, and again Rudolph remarked on how well his brother seemed. He had never appeared more vigorous, or in better spirits.

In New York, Rudolph Boyko philosophized gratefully that psychics can't always be right. And then the news came. Brother Hugo had suffered a severe heart attack and was hospitalized.

As I rummaged about the psychic world, I was singularly unimpressed by physical phenomena—the blowing of trumpets by dead spirits, the levitation of live bodies, the lifting and turning of tabletops with the fingertips. Without some bearing on the mainstream of life, the psychic became no more valid than a magician's bag of tricks. Without spiritual motivation, without the design to help people, as Christ Himself had had two thousand years ago, it was all meaningless. I was reminded of the ancient Indian tale of the young man who went off to study the mystic. Some fourteen years later he returned, and anxious to demonstrate his learning, turned to a brother and said, "Let us go down to the river, and I will show you what I have learned."

At the riverbank, he climbed down to the water, and began, as his brother watched quizzically, to walk across the surface of the water, returning in the same way. "Look, brother," he said, "I can walk across the river."

Strangely, the brother did not appear impressed.

"Come with me," he said, and walked down the river's edge to the dock a short distance away. He boarded a ferry and was quickly whisked across the river.

"You see, brother," he said, "you have gone through so much to achieve what I can do for a penny."

The practice of the psychic was at its highest when people were being helped through its proper function. In Hollywood, I encountered a pretty twenty-five-year-old actress whose whole life had been changed through a psychometric reading by the Dutch psychic Peter Hurkos, who became celebrated when he was officially employed by the State of Massachusetts in the Boston Strangler case.

The reading had been expensive, since the psychic machine that was Hurkos put a businesslike price on his generous gift. The psychic, holding a ring that had been the girl's since she was a child, proceeded to get his uniquely vivid impressions. He had never seen the girl before, nor had she given her full name. And so she was quite unprepared for the personal drama that followed.

"You had a baby when you were seventeen," he remarked boldly, "and gave it out for adoption because you were not married at the time."

She began to tremble in spite of herself.

"This boy," he went on, "is now in Phoenix, Arizona, and is in good hands." She had given the child up to a maternity agency, without ever knowing what had happened to it. "It is in the home of professional people, who love it as their own."

He regarded her speculatively. "You have been troubled with a guilt complex since giving up the child. You should not blame yourself. You made the only choice you could, for the good of your child."

A weight seemed to leave her. He had got every detail of her accouchement so precisely that she could not see how he could be wrong about anything else.

But this was only the beginning. Pointing to his own jaw, he said, "Get that filling taken care of, or it will give you trouble."

The filling had dropped out only the day before. One week later, as she sat in the dentist's chair, he advised her she would have lost the tooth had she waited any longer.

Next, Hurkos told her that the house she lived in was under police surveillance because of two shady characters who had been using the place, without her knowledge, as a drop for drugs. He advised her to move. She was able to recognize the two persons he was talking about, and could discern the police lookout for herself, once apprised of it. She moved that month to another house, and cut off her association with the precious pair Hurkos had described.

"And none too soon," she recalled with a tiny shudder.

There had been other predictions, which had not yet had time to be fulfilled. She was to be happily married in eighteen months (six months had already elapsed) and her career as an actress was to tilt forward at approximately the same time.

She left the reading with a singing heart. "I lost my guilt," she said, "and found hope."

Sometimes hope—and a wound—are inflicted at the same time, without even the psychic understanding all the issues involved, as only the result appears, not the events leading up to the result. For instance, reading for young Duane Perelli of Oak Ridge, New Jersey, just inducted into the military service, psychic Maya Perez predicted he would be home in less than a year.

"Impossible," Perelli said, "I'm in for three years."

His brother, Marine Lance Corporal Keith Perelli, was already in the thick of the fighting in Vietnam.

Some few months later word came, not about Duane, but Keith. He had been killed in action before Con Thien in Vietnam. Found on his body was a mud-stained Bible with the underlined passage: "Do not be afraid of those who kill the body but cannot kill the soul; rather be afraid of God, who can kill both body and soul in hell."

Within a short time of Keith's death on September 24, 1967 —nine months after his induction—Duane was mustered out of service, as the only surviving son in a war-stricken family.

The psychic area is as broad as humanity itself. Its scope includes every conceivable activity of man, from marriage to politics to commercial enterprises. For instance, searching the hand of promoter Edward White, psychic palmist Marie Welt, of New York's Fifth Avenue Hotel, said with a puzzled frown of a man she had never seen before:

"I see you making money out of the ground very shortly."

White gave a start, and his wife and another couple exchanged smiles.

White pursued the matter. "What do you see specifically?" Marie renewed her concentration. "Could it be uranium?" she said finally. "Anyway, that's what I see."

Four months later, in December of 1967, the White mining interests hit uranium in upper Canada. "I called the new company Weegee," White said with a smile, "because it sort of came in on a ouija board."

In the area of romance, a dominant interest of the psychic-bent, many sensitives, as psychics and mediums so often style themselves, have helped many troubled by the love bug. The English-born Laura Park Mangiameli of Metuchen, New Jersey, consulted by a confused bachelor who could not understand why his ladylove was not responding adequately, was able to advise that there was another suitor in the background, whose suit was then preeminent. She suggested he hang on, as that relationship would founder, and he would then make the desired impression.

And so it worked out.

The psychic is hardly in the same category as mathematics or chemistry, for what is foreseen does not always occur. When this happens, the psychic may fall back on the excuse that individual prayer has altered the course of events, or that God's will, previously inscrutable, has shifted. It is my own feeling that the psychic may merely be wrong. Even in more substantial fields, it is next to impossible for the most gifted statesman, mathematician, physician, or jurist to be always right. It is truly human to err, since prejudices, inequities, emotional disturbances, and minor ailments often appear to affect the rhythmical flow of the subconscious.

Like everybody else, psychics have their good and bad days. Helen Stalls, over the years, had a remarkable accuracy quotient. But when upset or ill, she was not quite on point. That night at the Ansberry apartment in New York was an obvious reflection of a clear mind and spirit. This, I felt, would have been the evening to have asked anything and got the proper reply.

Like myself, our hostess, Mrs. Ansberry, a most practical

person, was solidly impressed as one unique event after another materialized with time. And when I wrote her subsequently in New York for confirmation of my own recollection of the evening, she even added to the picture as I had recalled it, pointing up a prediction that I had felt too absurd to even consider at the time.

"You forgot," she wrote, "one of Helen's predictions—that one of the Nixon family was going to marry one of the Eisenhowers."

Her letter arrived in California, where I was working, even as Julie Nixon, the President-elect's daughter, and young David Eisenhower, the former President's grandson, were preparing for their wedding.

As with other remarkable predictions, the Helen Stalls' forecasts pose the problem of where this power comes from and how the information is dredged up. I have heard some, like the astrologer Dane Rhudyar, say that these impressions are gleaned from the subconscious of the subject or from a subconscious awareness of events already in motion. It is an interesting concept, but it does not explain the Nixon election, which was certainly not in motion in 1965, three years after Nixon had lost the California gubernatorial race and taken himself out of politics. As recently as 1967, at a dinner sponsored by Rockefeller-Javits Republicans in New York, Nixon's political stock was so low that party leaders in New York decided not to have a dais rather than be embarrassed by having him on it. Only Nixon, apparently, held any hope of one day being President, and though this was an essential factor, as we were to see in the summer and fall of 1968, it did not in itself constitute an event in motion.

There are more plausible theories. The mystic Edgar Cayce seemed gifted with a universal mind, which seemingly drew on a subconscious register of everything that had ever happened or was going to happen. A Kentucky physician, Dr. Wesley Ketchum, who used Cayce to diagnose ailments and prescribe cures, explained Cayce's powers in terms that might be applied to other psychics: "Cayce's mind has the power to interpret what it acquires from the subconscious mind of other individuals. The subconscious mind forgets nothing. The conscious mind receives the impressions from without and transfers all thoughts to the subconscious, where they remain even though the conscious be destroyed." Long before Dr. Carl Gustave Jung theorized about the collective unconscious, Cayce was presumably tuned into the knowledge possessed by endless millions of subconscious minds.

But Cayce, like other psychics, believed himself able to visualize the past, present, and future because of a God-given gift to help others—preparing them for eventualities they might not otherwise be ready for.

The psychic quality is apparently universal, though more active in some than others. Nearly all of us, the psychic researchers tell us, have varying, if infrequent, psychic impressions, which we dismiss as coincidence or else suppress for fear of ridicule. And yet the animals, considerably less complex than man, constantly reveal an inexplicable sixth sense: The dog howls at his master's death before this death is otherwise known; the cat, taken blindfolded or in a sack by car to an unfamiliar place, finds its way home by foot fifty miles over unfamiliar terrain; the ants build stronger mounds before a harsh winter; and fish swallow pebbles to sink to a safe depth before a hurricane strikes. All are psychic.

There are many aspects to man's sixth sense. What we think of as intuition or imagination, even a mere hunch, often reflects the psychic force at work. No psychic could have been more remarkably prophetic than Jules Verne, the French author of *Twenty Thousand Leagues Under the Sea* and *From the Earth to the Moon.* More than a hundred years ago, he predicted that the United States would be the first nation to travel to the moon, shooting *three* men into space from a launching pad in *Florida,* not far from Cape Kennedy, at a speed of *25,000 miles* an hour.

The psychic force has worked in many ways. A mother, in the midst of making dinner, swayed at the stove as she saw her boy wounded at the battlefront thousands of miles away, and twenty-four hours later he was hit by a sniper's bullet. In the thick of life, many fighting men quietly knew when and how they were to die—the poet Rupert Brooke, so lyrically fatalistic in World War I, and an unsung, but not unmourned, teen-ager in Vietnam. A scientist like Einstein "mystically"—in his own words—visualized an abstract principle he had no way of proving at the point of inspiration, but which an atomic explosion later demonstrated as one of the great universal truths. A Leonardo da Vinci drew models of airplanes, helicopters, and submarines that did not materialize for another five hundred years, and a Victorian railroad magnate, Chauncey Depew, half dozing on his back porch, pictured himself making a nominating speech for Teddy Roosevelt for governor, a vision subsequently confirmed when he was introduced at a nominating convention by a politician he had never seen before except in his dream.

After nearly every major disaster—a train wreck, the crash of a big airliner, the sinking of a ship—the reports of life saving premonitions seem to stream in. There were so many of these reports after the "unsinkable" *Titanic* hit an iceberg and sank in 1912, with a loss of fifteen hundred lives, that one wag ghoulishly quipped that more people had been saved by the *Titanic* than lost by it. But it seems at times, as the Good Book says, that coming events cast their shadow before them. All that is required, apparently, is a sensitive human antenna to pick up the microwave of the future.

This psychic sense seems to flow through the subconscious mind, leaving the conscious to cope with the routine problems of life. Dr. F. Regis Riesenman, Washington psychiatrist and psychic researcher, who once employed Hurkos to solve a Virginia murder case, expressed the view that this latent power could not be invoked at will, except by a gifted few, but was galvanized as the need arose, when the ordinary reasoning processes were subdued. "It came during the sleep state," as Riesenman saw it, "at the point of death, under hypnosis, in the stress of fear, or even when completely relaxed." It is interwoven in the everyday fabric of life, with all its pain, joy, tragedy, and hope.

The incidents are endless. While a posse of hundreds was combing the tangled underbrush of a Long Island park in August, 1962, for three-year-old Stephen Papol, one of the searching party, Mrs. Rosemarie Finger, had what she called a hunch.

"I have a feeling, feminine intuition, if you like," she told her skeptical husband, "that we'll find the boy near Parking Field Three." This was a mile from the search area, and across a main highway from where the child had disappeared. The husband reluctantly tagging along, they drove to the designated parking lot, and there, at the edge of the lot, in a junglelike undergrowth, they found a whimpering child, covered with scratches and insect bites. It was little Stevie.

Acceptance of the psychic poses obvious philosophical problems. I was not able to seriously consider it myself until 1952, when a psychic I had never seen before, in an impromptu reading, picked out that I had recently gone through a divorce and was now planning to marry a blond, blue-eyed girl. This girl, she said, I would not only not marry, but would not see again. And so it turned out, against all logic, and through no doing of my own. She also pinpointed my writing career, and described the girl I would marry—some seven or eight years hence. And so it was, along with other predictions contrary to my own will and judgment at the time.

In the years that followed this experience, I came to note the experiences of others, including the motion-picture actress Grace Kelly, who told me that the late clairvoyante Rava, in New York, had foreseen her meteoric career in every detail, but had missed on one personal point. "She saw me," Miss Kelly said, "becoming a princess one day."

To accept the psychic, it is not only essential to become aware of its potential, but of the potential of man himself. It is as boundless as the universe in which he lives and of which he is an integral part. It moves around him just as he moves around in it. All he has to do is concentrate on God's purpose for him, on a God who is not an old man with whiskers sitting in judgment in the clouds, but who is all of creation, an infinite force reflected in man's own capacity for infinity.

We all seek the infinite in our own way. My own Yoga exercises and meditations appear to confirm my kinship to the infinite about me. At Concord, Massachusetts, the home of Thoreau and Emerson, where I studied with the ephemeral Marcia Moore, I began to sense the orderly pattern of the universe and man's orderly processes even in the midst of apparent disorder. The seasons come and go in orderly regimen; in roughly the same order man is born, mates, struggles and dies. There is a strong kinship between human life and plant and animal life;

all belong with one another because all belong in the same universe—each in its place.

As I proceeded with my Yoga, studying with other teachers —Blanche DeVries in Nyack, New York, and Clara Spring in Hollywood, California—I had ample opportunity to meditate on the wisdom of the East and its placid acceptance of the paranormal.

With each class the seed thought varied, but the meditation was up to the meditator. "Thou art without beginning," says the Upanishad, "Because thou art infinite, Thou from whom all worlds are born."

Man is not only what he eats, but the product of even more vitalizing food, the food of inspired thought:

> There is nothing I can give you
> Which you have not;
> But there is much, very much, that
> While I cannot give it, you can take.
> No Heaven can come to us unless our hearts
> Find rest in today. Take Heaven!
> No place lies in the future which is not hidden
> In this present instant. Take peace.

The inspired monk Fra Giovanni, like the holy man of the East, recognized that the future is spread out in space, ready for the human instruments to make it materialize. How else can a psychic foresee the future, unless it is there to be seen? The Frenchman Tardieu has postulated that it is not the present that influences the future, but the future that forms the present. In other words, since the future is set, an unfolding of events that will assure that future is inevitable.

And so what of free will?

How much free will did millions of Americans have in World War II as they were trundled off to different parts of the globe? Life and death move on inexorably, and we can do little to affect them; very few plans launched by man have concluded as he intended. But as man reacts to events, events beyond his control, so he finds happiness or sorrow. "We cannot halt the rain," a wise man said, "but we can carry an umbrella."

Perhaps we can not turn away adversity and pain, but we can endure them and still savor life, if we believe in a divinely orderly process.

2

Coming Events

Tragic as it was, the assassination of John Fitzgerald Kennedy, as one of the most widely prophesied events of the century, electrified millions into a sudden awareness of the psychic.

The shadow of the impending death was so long on the land that people everywhere were dreaming and talking about it in whispers. The feeling was so spontaneous that it defied normal explanation of cause and effect—of logic itself. There was a strange eerieness about the brooding atmosphere that appeared to be building up to the climactic event. The Los Angeles *Times* reported that in the highly vibrating Los Angeles area, fifteen minutes before President Kennedy was shot, a telephone company supervisor at nearby Oxnard overheard a woman caller whisper:

"The President is going to be killed."

The call was intercepted by a General Telephone Company office at 1:10 P.M. EST. The fatal shooting occurred shortly after 1:25 P.M. EST.

The call was reported to the police, but only after the President had been shot. A company executive explained that the supervisor had been listening in because of trouble on the line. "The caller kept dialing although her call was connected. Then she started whispering, 'The President is going to be killed.' " It was impossible to trace the call, and the chances were it would have been only one intuitive old lady giving her hunch to another.

The Kennedy slaying, even more than the similar assassination of Abraham Lincoln a hundred years before, was a classic example of the Biblical principle that coming events cast their shadows before them. Not only did scores of psychics and astrologers predict the gallant young President's violent death, but a host of private individuals, many of them distinguished, many uttering their warnings publicly, raised their voices to forestall an assassination which appeared as inevitable as Julius Caesar's at the Ides of March. Just as Caesar overrode foreboding dreams and brooding aspects to proceed to the Senate and his death, so, too, did Kennedy ignore warnings that would have kept him from Dallas that fateful November 22 of 1963.

The President, a sensitive man with a quick intuitive grasp, believed, as had Lincoln, in his own destiny, good or bad. Therefore, he was not ready to listen when Adlai Stevenson, attacked in Dallas a short time before, urged Presidential advisers to get Kennedy to call off his Dallas visit.

Obviously, if he would not listen to trusted advisers, he would not heed psychics. In June, 1963, London sensitive John Pendragon, in Britain's *Fate* magazine, sent this prophetic message across the sea: "The President may make powerful enemies among his own people, and I would not rule out the possibility of an attempted assassination or worse if he is caught off his guard. There may be a strange turning of the Wheel of Fate, for it is just a century ago that the American Civil War was raging with unabated fury and that President Lincoln was shot by a madman in April, 1865."

As the event approached, Pendragon became increasingly concerned by ominous vibrations, and finally, unable to contain his premonitions, he took the liberty of writing the President in the White House four weeks before the event: "I am becoming deeply concerned for your physical safety and would respectfully urge you to strengthen your bodyguard, especially when you are in streets and other public places."

There was a sense of real danger in the air—it was almost tangible. Two weeks before the event, as the shadows closed in on the young President, evangelist Billy Graham was beginning to develop grave forebodings. Governor John B. Connally of Texas, who was to become more involved than he knew, had visited Graham in his Houston hotel room and described his misgivings about the President's projected trip to Texas.

As Graham thought about it, he became so perturbed that he attempted to head off the President's tour and made an abortive effort to contact Kennedy through an emissary. "I had such a strong premonition that the President should not go to Texas that I tried unsuccessfully to reach him through Senator Smathers [Florida Democrat]," Graham said. "The Senator said the President would get in touch with me later on. I wanted to talk to the President, but it occurred to me that it might sound ridiculous to him, so I dropped the idea."

The most publicized prediction about the President's assassination was by no means the most precise or dramatic. However, it happened to have been widely reported months before the event, in my book, *The Door to the Future,* which was serialized in newspapers around the country. And since the publication date was March, 1963, its authenticity could hardly be questioned. With a jolt, I watched television commentators flash the book on the screen, saying somberly, "In this book there was a prediction of the President's death."

Actually, the prediction, by Washington realtor Jeane Dixon, had been first published about an anonymous President, in *Parade,* a magazine supplement, in 1956. I used it only to establish that Mrs. Dixon had not picked Nixon to be President in 1960, as a forgetful writer, newspaperman Jack Anderson, had skeptically insisted. The *Parade* article spoke for itself: "As for the 1960 election, Mrs. Dixon thinks it will be dominated by labor and won by a Democrat. But he will be assassinated or die in office, though not necessarily in his first term."

Mrs. Dixon had actually been much more specific in one Kennedy prognostication. However, I had decided it might be too inflammatory, and had not used it. But I still recall the prediction as if it were made yesterday, instead of September, 1961, two years before Kennedy was shot down in Dallas. We were in Mrs. Dixon's Washington home—not far from the White House—and Mrs. Dixon, with a frown, was studying the crystal ball on a table between us. She pointed to what she said was a shadow in the lower portion of the gleaming ball. "I see no way out for the President," she said solemnly. "He is completely hemmed in by the dark shadow. There is no escape for him."

Then she looked up at me with the sad dark eyes that reflected her mood, and said in dirgelike tones, "I see only one term for the President and he will not finish out that term."

Even without her enjoinder to confidence, I would not have thought for a moment of using so specific a prediction about a living President. Even if taken seriously—or perhaps especially if taken seriously—it would clearly be a breach of taste and public policy.

Subsequently, as the event approached, she was even more precise. Toward the close of 1962, in my quarters at Washington's Fairfax Hotel, she pointed to "dark shadows" at the bottom of her crystal. I saw nothing myself, but the thought struck me that we see with our brain, not our eyes. And it could very well have been only in Mrs. Dixon's subconscious that the shadow existed. "I saw the same darkness with Hitler before his violent death," Mrs. Dixon said.

She looked up from her crystal with a somber glance. "President Kennedy," she said, "will meet with a violent end toward the end of his third year in office."

I was to think of this prediction often in the next months. And on the day of the assassination, not quite a year later, I was walking through the streets of mid-Manhattan and noticed a handful of people clustered around a car radio. I knew—knew with a sudden twinge—that the President had been shot and killed.

The first scattered radio reports gave no indication of the seriousness of his injury, but the overwhelming trend of the predictions had prepared me for the worst.

The unusual validation marking the predictions of the Kennedy assassination gave many skeptics pause. For with the predictions came a wealth of detail which defied the laws of coincidence. Obviously, through the law of averages, some predictions are bound to materialize—whether of death, marriage, plane crashes, earthquakes. However, nobody could have logically anticipated the events forecast by psychic Helen Stalls before a distinguished audience of churchmen and professional and business people in the Manhattan home of distinguished muralist Buell Mullen three days before the assassination.

The group, rightfully dubious, had been invited to witness a demonstration by an amateur psychic. The spiritual Mrs. Stalls had never given a reading for money, for she felt that her gift, however it worked, was a manifestation of God's power working through her. She found her reward in helping people.

As usual, she sat down quietly, brushed back her lank hair, and closed her eyes. No more than the people sitting about her did she know what was going to come through her.

Suddenly, as the circle regarded her skeptically, she clapped her hands to her head, crying, "I hear three shots—oh, my head hurts so, I can't bear it. President Kennedy is going to be assassinated."

There were expressive shrugs among the skeptical. But three days later the President was dead. Helen Stalls had apparently previewed the fated assassination.

Despite all the underground predictions, the general public was blissfully unaware of the portended event. Many psychics felt the urge to communicate their presentiments to responsible authorities, but they were sensible enough to know they would go unheeded—if they did not, indeed, bring an investigation down on their own heads.

The late Florence Psychic (Florence Light Sternfels) of Edgewater, New Jersey, had several premonitions of Kennedy's death. A week before the assassination she told Mrs. Jean Calabrese of Cresskill, New Jersey, of her fears. Mrs. Calabrese had never met Florence before, but had heard of her talent for finding lost articles. She was not impressed.

Two days later, Florence was reading for Mrs. Dolly Sohm, of Cliffside Park, New Jersey, who had first gone to her a month before to locate a leather belt with some sentimental value. Florence had closed her eyes, described the woman's house, and told Mrs. Sohm that she would find her belt in a closet under her husband's trousers. Florence had said, as Mrs. Sohm gaped, "Now let me run through your house with you for a moment." She had described various pieces of furniture, their positions and their designs, and she was right.

And then, as she was concentrating on the leather buckle, she had suddenly looked up and said, "You poor child. You have had two shocks. Your house burned down recently, and you hit a baby in a carriage with your car." She held up a bony finger. "But it wasn't your fault, the mother just ran out with the carriage between two cars."

Mrs. Sohm, jaw hanging, could hardly wait to get home to see whether Florence was as right about the belt as about the other things. She pawed through her husband's closet, saw the dark trousers Florence had described, lifted them off a hanger, and there, lo and behold, was the missing belt.

Now Mrs. Sohm had come to ask about a blouse that had apparently vanished. But in calling on Florence, she discovered that the psychic was strangely distracted. She kept mumbling to herself, and didn't seem to hear what Mrs. Sohm was saying. The phone rang, and Florence told her caller, "I have something of great importance for the Army and the Navy intelligence. I would like to sit down with them and tell them what I see."

Then she turned back to Mrs. Sohm and a solemn expression darkened her face. "I don't like to see President Kennedy going to Texas; he will be shot if he goes there."

All over the country, people with some special interest in the President were the repositories of ominous dreams, as troubling as they were prophetic. The dreams, for some reason, seemed to become more vivid, more detailed, as the event approached. In many instances the dreamers discussed the dreams almost immediately afterward, not knowing what to do about them.

Why did these particular dreams visit these particular people? Dr. Regis Riesenman, the eminent psychic researcher, has suggested that approaching tragedies or holocausts, such as the *Titanic* disaster, build up their own peculiar prophetic aura, described as odic force. And it is this force that presumably triggers the prophetic dream, vision, or impression. In the Kennedy case, inquiry revealed that virtually all of the dreamers had some sentimental attachment to the young President.

The mystic Cayce, examining the subconscious function with his own remarkable subconscious, felt that the dream was probably the most perfect clairvoyant expression. In sleep, the conscious is dormant, cut off, and the subconscious becomes a clear channel for the intuitive faculty. All through history, since Joseph's interpretation of the Pharaoh's seven-fat-seven-lean-year dream, there have been notably prophetic dreams. Plutarch told of Calpurnia's dream, in which she saw Caesar murdered, but, like the soothsayers who foresaw his murder, she was unable to dissuade her imperial husband from his rendezvous with death.

In a haunting dream, which he described to his Cabinet, Abraham Lincoln saw his own body lying in state in the White House.

The dreamers often have other psychic experiences, and presumably have more sensitive subconsciouses than the average. Jenc Lowry, modeling in New York as Jackie Joyce, came from Mount Ary, North Carolina, and in her family had the reputation of being psychic. As a child she had a nervous flutter in her stomach before certain events, and the flutter would persist until the event occurred. There was no recognizable pattern to her extrasensory experiences. They came as premonitory flutters, or in dreams in vivid color—the apparent touchstone of precognitive dreams.

From modeling, Jenc Lowry went into saleswork and became the only woman salesman of steam construction cranes in the country. But whether a child in North Carolina, a model in Manhattan, or a crane salesman in New Jersey, the premonitory flutters continued.

Because of the nature of her dreams, she had the feeling that the gift might be hers as a warning for others. In 1947 in Atlantic City, Jackie dreamed that she saw her brother, Walter Lowry, and his small daughter strolling together in Mount Ary. In her dream they came to a cemetery. The father swung open the gate and took a long look at a row of newly planted trees and tiny tombstones. He sighed heavily as his eyes fell on the child, who had been crying. She suddenly stopped her weeping.

Jackie woke the next morning, weary and achy, with a terrible feeling of apprehension. Her dream was so realistic that she had to mention it to someone. She was modeling then, and she called her agent, Saxe Holzworth in New York, and a friend, Herbert Loup.

A few days later she got back to New York and found a message waiting. It was from her brother Walter. "Our baby," it said, "smothered during the night." The baby had apparently died as she was dreaming about her.

While working subsequently for the Skylift Corporation of Elizabeth, New Jersey, she twice visualized accidents in which people were killed or injured. Both times a nervous flutter stopped after the anticipated event occurred.

In view of all her dreams and premonitions, the dream about Kennedy, when it came, was no surprise to Jackie Joyce and her immediate circle—for even back in her native North Carolina she had been known as the Blond Witch.

The Kennedy dream occurred in December of 1960, after the President's election and before the inaugural. As with her other clairvoyant dreams, this was in vivid color. "The first thing I saw was former President Eisenhower making a speech; his face was full of sorrow, and surrounding him was a battery of microphones."

As she stood watching Eisenhower, the scene merged with the picture of a man lying on a narrow table, such as one sees in an operating room. At first she couldn't distinguish the features, but as she kept watching intently, she finally recognized him. It was President Kennedy, and he was lying quite still. The table was at a slope, and people were hovering over him. His features were bulging and his face was turning darker and darker. It was almost purple. "His lips got thick," she recalled, "and every feature changed as I watched him. I knew he had been shot, and he was in sore straits, but I kept telling myself there was no picture of a coffin so he can't be dead."

On her awakening, the dream would not fade. It grew even stronger during the day and she felt she had to talk about it. She discussed it with Holzworth, Frank DeLuca, her employer, and a sister in Clifton, New Jersey. She was afraid now that the President was going to be shot.

She had no impression of time, but there was a feeling that it would be in his first term. Gradually the dream faded away. But when it was announced three years later that Kennedy was going to Dallas, she abruptly felt that old familiar flutter in the stomach. She told a friend that the President should not be allowed to go to Texas because he would be shot there. On the day of the assassination she slept late, having been restless most of the night.

She was awakened by a jangling phone. She looked sleepily at her night-table clock. It was after one, and it was her boss, DeLuca. All he said was, "Your dream came true. The President was shot."

The flutter in her stomach was gone. She rushed to the television set and turned it on. "The first person I saw was President Eisenhower. He was at a conference. His face was clouded with shock and sorrow. And he was expressing his deep shock.

There were microphones on all sides of him." Her dream had come true in striking detail.

In an equally singular case, a beautiful undergraduate at Berkeley's University of California was particularly drawn to the youthful President who had a special charisma for the young. She had even involved herself in the Kennedy election campaign, having made a preelection poll of the Berkeley-Oakland area which gave Kennedy a hairline margin. As a crusading liberal, whose family was associated with the pro-Kennedy Americans for Democratic Action, Aubrey Degnan Beauvais' shiny-eyed partisanship for the charmer in the White House never faltered.

Before the dream in which she was to see her hero hospitalized, Aubrey, like Jackie Joyce, had a number of psychic experiences, establishing her subconscious as a better than average channel. Once, while touring Egypt with her mother, she was haunted by a strange familiarity as she strode through a Cairo marketplace and correctly anticipated the scene as she turned a corner—a bazaar never consciously seen before, in a city she had never been in before.

She had many dreams in color, and kept a pencil and pad at her bedside to record them the moment she got up. On the night of November 2, 1963, in New York City, where she was then living, Aubrey Beauvais had the most upsetting dream of her life. In the dream, a voice told her to warn the President of his imminent danger. The nature of the danger was not clear, but as the voice faded out Aubrey saw herself turning into the White House. And there in a corridor, in a building she had actually never been in, she encountered a guard with nondescript features. He seemed to be patrolling the hallway. The voice now returned to her dream, describing the guard as "Kennedy's timekeeper," and then "Kennedy's watchman." She had the hazy impression that he was really a Secret Service operator. He was carrying a gold watch, clock size, which read 2 P.M. "He wanted to stop me, but somehow I pushed past him," she recalled, "and then I passed through a series of corridors, doors and smaller hallways, into a large rectangular room—much of it covered in yellow."

Aubrey had been a hospital aide, and her father was a doctor, so she was familiar with hospital procedures. "As I saw the

President for the first time," she recalled, "he was lying on what appeared to be a hospital bed; it was iron-framed and had a thick mattress. He was lying on his back, his body tilted at the angle at which a person is normally placed in shock. His head was tilted up, his knees were hunched up by the tilt of the lower part of the bed. His bed was surrounded by chairs, perhaps two dozen of them, with people sitting in them." She recognized none of these people, but all appeared worried.

"An oxygen tent, of plastic, transparent design, was hanging over the upper frame of the bed, but had not been placed over his face, though this appeared to be imminent. The atmosphere in the room deepened to one of great alarm. And then the time-keeper appeared. He announced somebody had stolen his way into the White House and had to be gotten out."

In her dream, Aubrey suddenly found herself sitting in a chair around the President's bed. As she looked about apprehensively, the President turned his head and regarded her blankly.

At this point, most of the people got up to leave, and Aubrey saw the President was going to be left alone. He had obviously been injured and was receiving treatment for shock, but she saw no wound or blood. That ended the dream. When Aubrey awoke that morning at about 8 o'clock, she felt strangely troubled. She kept seeing that sloping hospital bed, with the President on it, and the big watch at 2 P.M.

Nearly two weeks later, on November 14, after flying from New York to the Bahamas for a holiday with her parents, she was still brooding oppressively over the dream. She told her mother about it, also some others—her aunt and uncle, and a friend, all of New York. They listened without, of course, having any suggestions. Oddly, even then, she did not realize the full significance of her dream.

All that week her dark mood prevailed. On the day of the assassination, at 1:30 P.M., she was walking down to the docks when she saw some people clustered intently around an outside radio, but she did not stop to inquire. She got home a half hour later, and the phone rang. It was a friend saying that Kennedy had been killed. Her eye happened to fall on the clock. It was 2 P.M., exactly.

She felt curiously empty. A warning had been given her, and

she had done nothing with it. "I felt personally responsible," she said, "because I did not fully recognize the purport of my dream. Obviously, I could not have stopped the President from going to Dallas, but I would have felt better for the effort."

Ironically, the day before the assassination she had picked up *The Door to the Future* but stopped reading just before the chapter dealing with the Jeane Dixon prediction. The night of the assassination, rather sadly, she returned to the book. She read on a few pages, and then bolted upright in her chair. There it was on page 28: "A Democrat will be elected President in 1960 with the aid of labor, and he will die or be assassinated in office."

Had she read this twenty-four hours earlier, it would have crystallized her own fears—and she would have acted.

Jack Kennedy had been well aware of the prevailing predictions. Some, like novelist Taylor Caldwell's and Pendragon's, had come to the White House and been routinely acknowledged. Even before he was President, as he toured the country electioneering, Kennedy was made aware of an astrological forecast concerning the death in office of United States Presidents elected at intervals of twenty years, beginning back in 1840.

"The Presidents elected at these twenty-year intervals," a newsman told him with a smile, "supposedly are jinxed in office."

The candidate flashed the famous Kennedy grin. "I'm the one to break the jinx," he said.

In office, he lived boldly. Despite the uncertain times, he dared the crowds, saying a President should be able to go anywhere in his own land, unafraid. And so he went to Dallas, where Adlai Stevenson had been roughed up only a short time before. Even then a premonition may have been weighing heavily on his mind. Changing his normal pattern, he had gone to Confession that Friday before he took off for Dallas, and he was hence in a state of grace. He had made his peace with his conscience—and his God.

Kennedy frequently discussed his fatalistic philosophy with intimates. He was a student of Lincoln and had something of his mystique, though their outer personalities and backgrounds were manifestly different. His favorite poem was Alan Seeger's "I

Have a Rendezvous with Death," and his wife, Jacqueline, had memorized it so she could recite it on request. It was read by actor Fredric March as a memoriam at the Democratic National Convention in 1964:

> I have a rendezvous with death.
> At some disputed barricade at midnight
> In some flaming town
> When Spring trips north again this year.

The President's widow had bitter-sweet memories. "He was always moved by the poignancy of young men dying," she said. And he was also struck by the prophetic quality of Seeger's verse, for Seeger died, as he knew he would, in World War I.

Ironically, that day of horror began with a strangely prophetic conversation in a Fort Worth, Texas, hotel. On that fateful morning, the President, his wife, and an aide, Kenneth O'Donnell, had been discussing the risks in public appearances.

"According to O'Donnell," a report disclosed, "the President commented, 'If anybody really wanted to shoot the President of the United States, it was not a very difficult job—all one had to do was get on a high building some day with a telescopic rifle and there was nothing anybody could do to defend against such an attempt.' "

That was the last the President had to say on the subject, before Oswald fired from a high window, with a rifle with a telescopic sight.

After his death, there were numerous indications of his own foreboding about dying in the White House. Ten days after the assassination, Washington columnist Drew Pearson disclosed a prescient conversation between Kennedy and cabinet minister Arthur Goldberg.

"John F. Kennedy," Pearson wrote, "seemed to have a strange premonition he would not last out his term.

"A little over a year ago when Justice Felix Frankfurter retired from the Supreme Court, Kennedy had a soul-searching conversation with Secretary of Labor Arthur Goldberg to whom he offered Frankfurter's place on the Supreme Court. Goldberg had been doing a masterful job as Secretary of Labor. As a former labor attorney, he had the confidence of labor unions and was able to get them to settle serious labor difficulties which previously had disrupted the nation.

"It was obvious that Kennedy hated to lose him.

" 'It's like cutting off my right arm to have you go,' the President told his Secretary of Labor.

" 'I'm perfectly willing to stay on for another opening,' Goldberg told him. 'I'll take my chances on other opportunities. You'll probably appoint a majority of the court before you're finished.' "

But the President demurred. Looking out the window and away from Goldberg, he said:

" 'I don't know that another opportunity will present itself.' "

"Then after a pause he added: 'And you'll be here a long time after I'm gone.' "

Even the stars were against him. The idea of a Presidential jinx at twenty-year intervals was born of an astrological aspect which became operative in 1840 and will continue until 1980. This is a Jupiter-Saturn conjunction, to which astrologers have linked the death of Presidents in twenty-year elective cycles. In New York City, shortly after Kennedy's 1960 election, astrologer Mary G. Harter pointed out that every Chief Executive chosen since Harrison, in 1840, had been succeeded by a Vice President through death in office—Lincoln, in 1860; Garfield, 1880; McKinley, 1900; Harding, 1920; Franklin Roosevelt, 1940; and Kennedy, 1960.

"We hope it fails this period of tenure," she told an astrologers' convention at Long Beach, California, "but all were replaced during their terms by Vice Presidents."

The broadest of the astrological predictions foreshadowing Kennedy's election and death was made by David Williams, an electrical engineer who was manager of cable purchases for New York's Consolidated Edison Co. Williams got interested in astrology through studying the effects of the planets on economic cycles. In 1960, remembering the governing Jupiter-Saturn conjunction, and noting certain unfavorable aspects in John Kennedy's natal chart, he decided that a Kennedy victory was more likely to fulfill the ominous Jupiter-Saturn cycle.

"It was obvious from Nixon's chart," Williams said, "that his prospects of longevity were superior to Kennedy's."

Williams' prediction of Kennedy's election—and death in office—was made on August 4, 1960, shortly after Kennedy's nomination. The prediction was written down, then signed by seven witnesses, six of them scoffing brother executives at Consolidated Edison. The other was Joseph Fried, president of the Mackay Construction Co., on whose pleasure cruiser the forecast was made. Knowing of Williams' predilection for astrology, the group had jestingly asked whom the stars foresaw in the White House. Williams, having already plotted the Kennedy horoscope, responded confidently, "I see Kennedy winning the election, but he will die in office and will be succeeded by Johnson."

The others laughed in good-natured derision. "Now we got you," they said. "Write it down."

Still laughing, they witnessed his statement with the jocular comments, "I heard it," and "I heard it too."

After Kennedy's death, I questioned the seven about the circumstances of the prediction, of which I had a photostated copy. Some were sheepish, others marveled, but none scoffed now at astrology, nor did they write it off to coincidence. "I just don't know what to make of it," was the burden of comment.

No prediction is valid research material, of course, unless it has been noted before the event. Out of consideration for the niceties, little was said about most of the Kennedy predictions at the time they were made. Astrologer Sydney Omarr, for instance, dwelling on the Saturn-Jupiter conjunction, had predicted John Kennedy's violent death months ahead to Los Angeles newsman Bill Kennedy. In the summer of 1963, lunching with reporter Ray Irwin of *Editor & Publisher,* the newspaper trade bible, Omarr again mentioned his Kennedy prediction but said he would not want it published before the event as he might be criticized for bad taste.

Irwin listened politely.

"All right," he said, "but if it happens as you say, I will remember and write about it."

He was as good as his word—after the event.

After John Kennedy's tragic death, many in the psychic field felt that brother Bobby's was almost inevitable, and Bobby, curiously, shared this view. He constantly evaded security precautions, feeling they served no useful purpose. For he, too, had a premonition of an untimely end. He plunged headlong into things, hurling caution to the wind. There was nothing he would not do. He ran treacherous rapids, scaled dangerous mountain peaks and, disregarding the circumstances of his brother's death, exposed himself recklessly to uncertain crowds. Friends frequently teased him on the risks he took, and he would tease them back.

After Jack's death, Bobby and a Kennedy family friend, Alan Jay Lerner, author of *Camelot* and *My Fair Lady,* were engaged in a discussion of the rough life. With customary prankishness, Bobby was goading Lerner, a schoolmate of Jack's at Choate and Harvard, about joining one of his excursions. He made no impression on the songwriter.

"Listen," Lerner said, "I went through the war, and that was excitement enough for me." He chuckled. "When I turned forty, I changed my religion. I turned coward."

He regarded Bobby quizzically. "I don't see any sense to running around risking your life playing games."

Kennedy's mood suddenly changed. "It really doesn't make any difference. I am convinced this family is jinxed."

Lerner looked at him incredulously. "You really don't believe that?"

Bobby shrugged. "There's no doubt of it. We're jinxed."

Two brothers and a sister had already died violently, another sister had been born retarded. But there was undoubtedly more to it than that. Bobby, closest to his President brother, had doubtless shared that brother's darkest presentiments.

Bobby's death, like Jack's, was foreshadowed. The New York astrologer, Maria Crummere, had foreseen the event as inevitable, and told Mrs. Louise Ansberry about it some weeks before it occurred. There was even a historic parallel. Not long before Bobby was fatally shot, one observer compared the two Kennedys to the Gracchi brothers of ancient Rome—wealthy aristocrats who favored the masses and were cut down years apart as they were bidding for power, the younger as he strove to finish the work of the older.

In Los Angeles, a well-known amateur psychic, Hollywood hair stylist Eddie Crispell, had apparently tuned into Bobby Kennedy's odic vibrations as Jeane Dixon had tuned into John

Kennedy's—with dramatic spontaneity, without any particular thought to the Kennedys.

Eddie's forecast was well documented. One day in February, 1968, the phone in her busy shop rang, and it was commentator Regis Philbin of the Joey Bishop television show, calling for an appointment for a haircut.

How this would have triggered a premonition of an assassination, it was hard to say. But in any case, the people in the shop suddenly heard the boss blurting out, "Oh, my God, Regis, Bobby Kennedy is going to be shot."

The following day Eddie repeated her prediction to Steve Lengel, a television producer. On May 26, as the event of June 4, 1968, was casting a definite shadow, she told various people on a Metro Goldwyn Mayer set at Tucson, Arizona, that Bobby's assassination was drawing close. Ironically, the movie was titled *Heaven with a Gun.*

Bobby Kennedy's assassination was not as closely pinpointed as the President's, though I had myself heard one dramatic prediction only a few days before this tragic occurrence—by a business woman, who had years before foreseen John Kennedy's violent end. In the Manhattan home of attorney Helen Borgia, a small group, including Clarissa Aiken, Boston writer and former wife of essayist Conrad Aiken, were sitting around the television watching the California debate between Robert Kennedy and his primary rival, Senator Eugene McCarthy. With one exception, the viewers were adherents of Senator McCarthy, and as the program inconclusively faded out, they expressed concern that Kennedy had overshadowed their man and would win the Democratic nomination at Chicago.

As the conversation proceeded in this vein, the business woman finally cut in. "You don't have to think about Bobby Kennedy being President," she said somberly. "He will die soon like his brother did."

There was an abashed silence, and then somebody said lightly, to relieve the atmosphere, "Oh, you are always making predictions."

The woman rejoined quietly, "He will never make it and neither will McCarthy, but for a different reason."

I now remembered her prediction about John Kennedy years before.

"Where does it all come from?" I asked.

She knew exactly what I meant.

"God decides," she said simply. "Man proposeth, God disposeth—"

As the Englishman Pendragon had suggested, the death of John Kennedy seemed to round out a Wheel of Fate that had begun with Abraham Lincoln. There were many striking similarities in the Kennedy and Lincoln assassinations. Both were engaged in the battle for Civil Rights for the Negro; both assassinations occurred on Friday, accompanied by lax protective measures; each was shot in the head as his wife looked on; and Kennedy's assassination occurred on the hundredth anniversary of Lincoln's Emancipation Proclamation. Just as Lincoln had been warned against exposing himself in the theater, Kennedy had been warned against Dallas.

There were other apparent coincidences. Both had Vice Presidents named Johnson who had served in the Senate, and the second Johnson, Lyndon, was the first Southerner to become President since the first Johnson, Andrew, similarly became President. Lincoln's assassin, John Wilkes Booth, was born in 1839, and Lee Harvey Oswald in 1939. Booth shot Lincoln in a theater and ran to a warehouse; Oswald shot Kennedy from a warehouse and ran to a theater. Both were gunned down before trial. Lincoln and Kennedy each lost two children, one before the White House, one while President. Kennedy had a secretary named Lincoln, and Lincoln one named Kennedy.

Carrying the parallels further, Andrew Johnson was born in 1808 and Lyndon Johnson in 1908. The names Lyndon Johnson and Andrew Johnson each contain thirteen letters, those of John Wilkes Booth and Lee Harvey Oswald, fifteen letters. Each President in his thirties married a twenty-four-year-old brunette who spoke French fluently. Both were minority Presidents. Both were first elected to Congress in forty-seven, a hundred years apart; both lost the Vice Presidential nomination in fifty-six, four years before the Presidential nomination; both had close relatives as ambassadors to England—Kennedy his father, Joseph P. Kennedy, Lincoln his son, Robert.

As for Oswald and Booth, was there any foreknowledge of their roles? When Oswald was twelve, a psychiatric report listed him potentially dangerous and said he could kill. But this was

more analytical than prophetic, unless one credited the psychiatrist with an intuition he did not recognize himself. Perhaps,
as more becomes known about Oswald, his role will be pinpointed. Meanwhile, there is some evidence that Booth's was
foreshadowed. As far back as 1840, as baby Wilkes lay in his
crib, Mary Anne Booth had a terrible premonition that her
child would one day inflict a terrible evil on his country. Recalling her mother's vision, Asia Booth in 1852, thirteen years before brother Wilkes fired the fatal shot, prophetically wrote:

> Tiny, innocent, white baby hand,
> What force, what power is at your command,
> For evil or good?
> My God, let me see what this hand shall do.
> In the silent years we are tending to.

And then the outcry from a mother's heavy heart.

> The flame up-lept
> Like a wave of blood
> An avenging arm crept into shape,
> And the country shone out in the flame,
> Which fading resolved into her boy's own name.

As a schoolboy, Wilkes had his palm read by a traveling
gypsy. Cowering from the boy as she examined his hand, the
gypsy shuddered, as the boy laughed wildly. "I've never seen a
worse hand, and I wish I hadn't seen it. All I can tell you is that
you'll die young and make a bad end."

Meanwhile, the other character in the drama that was to
unfold in a single tragic meeting had his first presentiment before entering the White House. On leaving Springfield for Washington in 1860, Lincoln sadly told friends that he would not be
back—alive.

In the White House, Lincoln's whole nature was agonized by
a bitter turn of events which found this most Christian of men
sending tens of thousands of young men off to death. He was
afflicted, too, by personal tragedy. A son, Willie, his only play-
ful reprieve from the grim mission of preserving the Union, was
taken from him in the White House. And, thereafter, he became
ever more melancholy. After Willie's death, reported artist

Francis B. Carpenter, who went everywhere with the President as he studied his features for a memorable portrait, the President underwent a spiritual transformation. He seemed to become more sensitively attuned to the other world, as his own numbed spirit reached out for his departed son. Mrs. Lincoln, not always mentally stable, had also suffered greatly. As political friends of the time confirmed, she clandestinely brought spiritualists into the White House through whom she hoped to communicate with her son. There is evidence, supported by Carpenter, that the Great Emancipator sat in on these seances. One of the mediums, Nettie Colburn Maynard of White Plains, New York, was later to describe her sessions at the White House. These apparently had no small effect on the sixteenth President.

On one occasion, Mrs. Maynard, or a spirit voice—believed by some present to be strangely like that of Daniel Webster— urged the harassed President not to delay issuing the controversial Emancipation Proclamation beyond the New Year. Lincoln was told to stand firm and "fearlessly perform the work and fulfill the task for which he had been raised up by an overruling Providence."

On another occasion, Nettie had still another major message for the troubled Commander-in-Chief. A voice speaking through her said that "a very precarious state of affairs" existed at the front, where General Hooker had just taken command. The Army was pictured as totally demoralized, with insubordination rife and regiments threatening to desert.

Lincoln, the account went, listened intently, his head in his hands. "You seem to understand the situation," he observed mildly. "Can you point out the remedy?"

Nettie Maynard, or the spirit, if you like, replied: "Yes, if you have the courage to use it."

The President smiled wanly. "Try me."

"Go in person to the front," he was told, "taking only your wife and family, inquire into the grievances, show yourself the father of your people. . . . It will unite the soldiers as one man."

Lincoln smiled thinly when the medium forecast his reelection at a time critics were demanding he resign for the good of the country.

Before Nettie Maynard left the White House that night, Congressman Daniel Somes of Maine, an intimate of the President, cautioned her to be discreetly silent, "until sufficient time has elapsed to remove condemnatory criticism" of the President.

The next day, Nettie was thrilled to see the headline in the Washington *Gazette*: "President is about to visit the Army of the Potomac." He was taking only his family on this morale-building tour.

The last reported meeting between the medium and the President occurred shortly after the President's reelection. The young woman gravely contemplated the man she thought was the greatest Christian since Jesus Christ. "What they [the spirits] predicted for you has come to pass. But they also reaffirm that the shadow they have spoken of still hangs over you."

The President made an impatient gesture. "Yes, I know. I have letters all over the country from mediums warning me against some dreadful plot against my life." A melancholy expression clouded his countenance. "Well, Miss Nettie," he said resignedly, "I shall live till my work is done, and no earthly power can prevent it."

That, she knew, was the last she would ever see of the Great Martyr.

But the President was to receive his own special message. As he communed increasingly with the mystical universe around him, the President found his dreamworld was becoming even more of a reality than the everyday world around him. His dreams, often fitful, often disturbing, came on vividly before the great crises that appeared to be bleeding the nation to death. Finally, there was the ultimate dream, not before any great battle, as before, but with the bloody war at last won, the Ship of State safely moored.

The dream had been so real that, on waking, Lincoln turned to the Bible for reassurance. And he found none. Wherever he turned there was an allusion to dreams consistent with his own somber thoughts. Just a few days before his assassination, still troubled and uneasy, he described the dream to astounded cabinet members: "There seemed to be a death-like stillness about me. Then I heard subdued sobs, as if a number of people were weeping. I thought I left my bed and wandered downstairs. There the silence was broken by the same pitiful sobbing, but the mourners were invisible. I went from room to room, no living person was in sight, but the same mournful sounds of distress met me as I passed along. It was light in all the rooms, every object was familiar to me; but where were all the people who were grieving as if their hearts would break? . . . Determined to find the cause of a state of things so mysterious and so shocking, I kept on until I arrived at the East Room. There I met with a sickening surprise. Before me was a catafalque, on which rested a corpse wrapped in funeral vestment. Around it were stationed soldiers who were acting as guards; and there was a throng of people, some gazing mournfully upon the corpse, whose face was covered, others weeping pitifully. 'Who is dead in the White House?' I demanded of one of the soldiers. 'The President,' was his answer. 'He was killed by an assassin.' "

3

Looking It Over

Television moderator Regis Philbin was not terribly impressed by psychic Eddie Crispell's spontaneous forecast of the Bobby Kennedy assassination. "A lot of people," he said, "had an idea Bobby Kennedy was going to be killed. It was almost in the air."

Actually, Philbin was more impressed by a far less spectacular prediction that Eddie Crispell had made for him. In 1965 in San Diego, where Philbin had a local television program, Miss Crispell had predicted that he would in a short time transfer to a network show. When Philbin received an offer as a temporary replacement for the nationally syndicated Joe Pyne TV show, he felt Miss Crispell's forecast had thus materialized.

"Oh, no," Eddie Crispell said, "another show will be offered you, a network show, that's what I see, and in a very short time."

Within a week or so, Regis Philbin received an offer to become the commentator on the Joey Bishop show.

There is no comparing the predictions in terms of broad impact—and no comparing the impact on Regis Philbin. "Before you can accept the psychic," he said, "a psychic prediction must happen to you."

Philbin's observation summarizes the attitude of skeptics everywhere. How can anyone tune into a future not yet in motion? One can conceivably understand telepathy—a radiolike receptor receiving thought waves from a mind on a similar wave length—or clairvoyance, in which some antennalike faculty picks up events as they transpire. But future events— weeks, months, even years ahead—that is something else again. For if the future can be foretold, that future is presumably out there waiting. And what does that do to free will? It leaves only the freedom to react freely to events.

In any investigation of psychic phenomena, the researcher has to be pragmatic, deciding whether in its realization the prediction transcended all laws of probability. What were the odds of Helen Stalls' "guessing" that Jacqueline Kennedy would be married in the Greek islands? It was obviously outside the scope of coincidence, probability, or chance—neither Lloyds nor Las Vegas would have made book on it. There was just no chance of its happening.

In a pragmatic posture, the researcher must discard his own limiting prejudices and judge each prognostication on its merit. The fact that Helen Stalls or Jeane Dixon or Peter Hurkos have made incorrect predictions—as they have—does not reflect on other predictions not logically drawn. For as one psychic researcher observed, "It takes only one white crow to establish that all crows aren't black."

In predicting Adlai Stevenson's death, Jacqueline Kennedy's unexpected marriage, Lyndon Johnson's abdominal surgery, and the Presidential election of a Republican with the initial R from California in 1968—all at one session—Mrs. Stalls certainly manifested a high degree of extrasensory perception. However, like writers, artists, lawyers, doctors, stenographers, no psychic is always at her best. She may be troubled, ill, distracted, or the motivating factor may not be sound. Vanity or cupidity may impair the spiritual force of the subconscious, minimizing its powers.

No psychic can honestly claim infallibility, though some, with overweening egos, have tried. The Dutchman, Peter Hurkos, prided himself on being right 80 percent of the time; I have never checked Jeane Dixon's average, but have known her to be wrong often, as when she predicted De Gaulle's assassination and told friends, shortly before President Kennedy's assassination, that Lyndon Johnson was through politically. Ironically, she had misread one of her own visions, interpreting a vision of the Vice Presidential doorplate being taken off Johnson's office door to mean that he would be purged. Had she coupled this vision with that of Kennedy's murder, she would, logically, have come to an entirely different conclusion. But Mrs. Dixon's logic was obviously not up to her ESP in this case.

Remarkable when right, even the most remarkable psychics are occasionally wrong. At a small dinner party, one turned to a young lady and said solemnly: "You must be concerned about your father. He has only three more months. He will be dead in three months."

It was quite a shock for the young lady. Nevertheless, two years later, the father was still very much alive in Atlanta, Georgia. Had the psychic caught the vibrations of somebody else in the room? And even so, how can one trust a power so manifestly unpredictable at times?

But, in all fairness, I have observed others deliver warnings on a dozen occasions that would have been helpful had the individual heeded these warnings. Once, in 1966, Helen Stalls was reading at my home for two friends—socialite Susan Burden, cofounder of the Paraphernalia shops, and fashion model Joan Scott—when pretty twenty-two-year-old Sharon Lewis, helping with drug research for my book, *The Seekers,* unexpectedly stopped by.

The psychic was having an *on* day. She had tuned in startlingly to the private situations of the recently divorced Mrs. Burden, and of Joan Scott, estranged from her husband. She even advised what had gone wrong. She picked out their respective children, described their personalities and idiosyncrasies so accurately that both young women were obviously fascinated.

Sharon Lewis was watching, intrigued, and finally asked, "Can you tell me anything?"

Mrs. Stalls pushed back a hank of gray hair and regarded the girl for what seemed an eternal moment. Then she brushed a bony hand over her eyes, and said with a sigh, "You must be careful, my dear. I see very bad company about you—you must change your friends."

Sharon looked up brightly. "Oh, you must see my sister," she said. "I am very concerned about the people she's going out with."

The psychic shook her head wearily. "It is not your sister I see. Please heed my words."

I looked around the room; Mrs. Burden and Joan Scott had obviously got the same message I had. Their faces were solemn, and they were looking at Sharon curiously.

The psychic now took the girl's hands. "You are very young and beautiful, my dear," she said, "and you must not tease people—they get very angry."

Sharon laughed gaily. "Oh, I like to play with people sometimes. It doesn't mean anything."

The psychic regarded her somberly. "But they don't always realize it, child."

As Sharon Lewis left, Mrs. Stalls followed her to the door. Standing there with Sharon, she again took the girl's hands and said earnestly, "Please be careful, and do watch the company you keep."

Sharon again laughed and politely thanked the older woman.

As the door closed on the girl, Mrs. Stalls turned to us with a heavy sigh. "I see darkness about that poor child. I only hope she listens." She stared ahead blankly for several minutes, unable to continue her reading, and then shook her head ominously. "I see nothing for her."

The incident hung over me like a pall for days, and then gradually diminished as I put my mind to new things. The episode had practically faded out of my consciousness when I was awakened two weeks later by a phone call from Joe Russell, a Broadway publicist, who had first introduced me to Sharon, saying she might help me with my research.

Now, as I listened drowsily, Joe Russell's voice rasped, "Did you see the morning papers?"

"No," I said sleepily, and then quickly roused myself as my own subconscious rang an alarm.

"Is it Sharon?" I asked.

His voice came back dourly. "How did you know?"

"Well, you introduced me to her," I explained rather inconsequentially.

I went out and got the papers. There on the front page of the New York *Daily News* was a photograph of Sharon Lewis. She had been found dead in an empty lot in Long Island. Police theorized that she had been given an overdose of drugs and was then thrown from a car. It was a sorry end for the beautiful girl with the bright smile—who laughed at bad company.

The next day, as I sat brooding about the unfathomable quirks of fate, the phone rang. It was Joan Scott. Her voice was taut. "I couldn't sleep all night," she said, "after recognizing the girl in the papers." She shivered at the other end of the line. "How horrible to think Helen Stalls saw all this and had to carry it around with her."

I had not thought of it this way before. My thoughts had been more of the girl, whose whole life had been before her.

I could sense Joan hesitating over the wire.

"Do you think," she finally asked, "that if she had listened to Helen Stalls she would be alive today?"

I could only shrug. "I don't know how Helen could see it, if it wasn't there to be seen."

She seemed relieved, but not much. "That poor girl," she said, "never having a chance. I feel so sorry for her."

And so had Helen Stalls—two weeks earlier.

From observation, I concluded that when they were right, psychics were very, very right. Their predictions came in accurate clusters, reflecting a keen state of sensitivity. But, conversely, on an off day, for whatever reason, they seemed to miss on one point after another. Consequently, I felt that psychics who could accurately peer into an individual's past were most likely to be accurate in foretelling future events. This is an indication that the vagrant subconscious is apparently well tuned in—the past, present, and future usually merging out of the same psychic bottle.

As some have warned, it can be dangerous to run one's life by astrology or clairvoyance, which may be even more fallible at times than one's own judgment. Still, the professional psychic is usually consistent enough to be of general practical value in evaluating the authenticity of phenomena. For in the spontaneous unfolding of life, not in trifling laboratory experiments, lies the evidence that defies explanation by the five senses—in the solution of a crime, the finding of a body, the anticipation of events—and it is all fully documented in the natural course of human affairs. Sometimes, it is like watching a goldfish bowl. On January 3, 1967, psychic Irene Hughes of Chicago had forecast in a column for community newspapers that the Windy

City would have an unprecedented snowfall between January 26 and 29. The snow fell as Mrs. Hughes had predicted—more than two feet, in fact—and Irene Hughes' local fame as a prophet soared. On the 29th of January, blocked off from the Chicago airport, I had entrained from Kansas City for the snowbound city to keep a television engagement on the Irv Kupcinet Show. As I arrived at the depot, the paralyzed metropolis had just begun to dig itself out. Traffic was possible only along the main thoroughfares, and the roads to and from the airport were still blocked with high snowdrifts, though, hopefully, the first planes would leave on February 1.

That first evening in Chicago, before going on the Kup Show, I was visited by the psychic Mrs. Hughes who acquainted me for the first time with her prediction of an unprecedented blizzard. I was not terribly impressed by predictions after the event.

Mrs. Hughes took no offense.

"If you intend to leave town," she said seriously, "you should get away in the next couple of days, by February 1."

"Why is that?" I asked.

She smiled. "Because on February 1, it will start snowing again, and though not as heavily, it will still tie everything up again."

That evening, I mentioned the Irene Hughes' prediction to a publisher's representative in Chicago, Marilew Kogan, and asked her to make a plane reservation the morning of February 1.

She shrugged unbelievingly. "Where is all the snow coming from? There just can't be any more left in the heavens."

Nevertheless, she made the reservation, and passed on the Hughes' prediction to Irv Kupcinet, who, besides his weekly television chore, wrote a daily column for the Chicago *Sun-Times*.

On the morning of February 1, with flights barely resumed, I cheerfully headed out of the snowbound city for New York. By Herculean efforts, the highway to the airport had been cleared and the runways scraped clean. I got to New York without incident, and the next morning checked the newspapers. Poor, suffering Chicago had had another five or six inches of snow, and the airport was again closed off. I had got out just in time, thanks to Irene Hughes.

The Hughes' prediction, recalled before the event by Kupcinet, was chronicled after the event in the Kupcinet column, and overnight Mrs. Hughes became a front-page personality. The columnist sardonically suggested that perhaps Mrs. Hughes should be employed as a forecaster instead of the Weather Bureau. She was certainly more accurate.

In other, more consequential ways, the psychic force makes itself felt. I have witnessed attempts by Peter Hurkos and the eccentric Florence Psychic to solve crimes at the request of the police, and have researched others, including Holland's amazing Gerard Croiset, so it was no surprise to hear of a very strange case of psychic sleuthing in the very unstrange state of Georgia.

It all began when Mrs. Jane Coats disappeared from her home in suburban Atlanta. Her sister, Evelyn Stowers, could not banish an uneasy sense of disaster. Christmas was approaching, and Evelyn had spoken to her sister the day before her disappearance about presents for the three Coats children. Jane gave no indication in this conversation of clearing out, but Jane Coats' husband told police that his wife had tired of the marriage and had skipped out with two thousand dollars. But Evelyn Stowers would not believe it. "My sister," she said, "would never leave the children. She was so happy dreaming up plans for their Christmas together."

The disappearance was reported to DeKalb County police by Miss Stowers in November, 1958. Two detectives were routinely assigned to the case. But there was nothing suspicious, and the investigation lagged. While not claiming any psychic powers herself, Evelyn Stowers did fall back on her feminine intuition to record her belief that her sister had been the victim of foul play. She haunted police headquarters, trying to egg these worthies on, and carried pictures and descriptions to the Atlanta newspapers, asking editors to run them so that somebody, somewhere, might possibly identify Jane. She even toured the Coats' neighborhood, talking to neighbors in the slim hope somebody might have a clue.

With no lead in sight, she eagerly agreed when an aunt suggested they consult a psychic who had reputedly helped locate lost articles, including misplaced jewelry—and people. And so they traveled to the seer's home in Stone Mountain, a few miles north of Atlanta, for a reading with Mrs. Josephine Pittman.

At first sight, Mrs. Pittman was not terribly impressive. She looked like a middle-aged housewife. But as she peered off into space broodingly, her eyes held a faraway gaze, as though visualizing a chain of passing events. And then, looking up at the two women, she spoke slowly as if it were all happening in front of her.

"Your sister," she said with a sigh, "is no longer living. Her body is lying in a shallow grave beside a new road not far from where she lived. There is a bridge under construction nearby."

And how had Jane Coats died?

Mrs. Pittman's face darkened. "She was murdered, brutally strangled with a cord, and then carried to her grave."

Electrified, Miss Stowers plied the psychic with questions.

Yes, the body would be found, and there was even a prediction how this would occur. As the two women listened in wonder bordering on disbelief, Mrs. Pittman said softly, "A little animal with a sharp nose and pointed ears will lead the way to the body."

There was further description of the grave site, a small body of water that was neither lake nor river, a thick clump of trees. There was even a description of the missing housewife's attire, indicating she may have been attacked in her sleep or else spirited away and assaulted. This description heightened Evelyn Stowers' suspicions. "She saw my sister, at the time of her death, dressed in night clothes with a bedcover wrapped around her."

When she left the house on Stone Mountain, Evelyn had no way of knowing whether a single thing that Mrs. Pittman had said was in the least accurate. However, she did carry away the conviction that the psychic had somehow tuned into the events she had described, and nothing was to be lost in checking her story. So, continuing her own investigation based on the Pittman report, she began searching for terrain that fitted the psychic's description. Meanwhile, because of Evelyn's activities, the police heard reports of Mrs. Pittman's revelations, and decided that this sort of quackery, upsetting people needlessly, would have to stop. And so they decided to call on Mrs. Pittman.

"We knew that what she had told the family had upset them terribly," said DeKalb County Detective B. S. Ivey, "and we went out to Stone Mountain to tell Mrs. Pittman to cut it out."

The woman was at home, rocking coolly in a chair when they arrived. She listened calmly to Ivey and his superior officer, Detective Captain T. L. Wayne, then said quietly, looking the officers squarely in the eye: "I told them the truth."

Sardonically, the officers asked when the woman's body would be found.

She thought a moment. "If not in January, it will be in mid-March."

January came and went, and there was no sign of Mrs. Coats' body anywhere. But on March 19, 1959, construction work was resumed after the long winter layoff on a section of highway in northern DeKalb County. During the noon luncheon break, workmen observed two opossums fighting on the dirt ramp of a bridge for which the men were laying the foundations. As they noticed the men, the possums fled. The men, drawing closer to see what the animals had been fighting over, noticed a crude but familiar object jutting out of the dirt. It was the mangled remains of a human hand—a woman's hand, and this was what the possum—"a little animal with a sharp nose and pointed ears"—had led them to.

The workmen scooped out the dirt around the hand and soon the remains of a body, badly decomposed by time and moisture, began to emerge. Though the remnants were unrecognizable, an autopsy revealed that the victim had been strangled. "In my opinion," reported Dr. Herman Jones of the Georgia Crime Laboratory, "she died from strangulation or suffocation from a cord being wrapped around her neck." And he might have added, tightened about her neck.

The body was in night clothing, as Mrs. Pittman had foreseen—tattered shreds of green pajamas, a blue housecoat, all wrapped together in a burial shroud, a plaid bedspread. There was little Mrs. Pittman had missed. She had even foreseen the pools of water—from the recent thaws—around the shallow grave and a grovelike clump of trees along the highway right of way.

The husband Coats was now a prime suspect, but he remained stubborn to the end. He denied that the undistinguishable remains were those of his missing wife, and who should know better than he? But Miss Stowers, an avenging angel, identified engagement and wedding rings found near the body, that the killer had foolishly overlooked. They had dropped off as the flesh rotted away. The blue housecoat was the clincher. Evelyn had given this to her sister only the year before.

Coats was arrested and held for murder. Three months later, protesting his innocence, he went on trial. The evidence was overwhelming, particularly when the missing motivation was supplied. Coats, it developed, had been seeing another woman just before his wife's convenient disappearance. He was found guilty and sentenced to life imprisonment.

Ironically, not once during the trial was the name mentioned of the woman who had revealed in the first place that there was a crime. But Mrs. Josephine Pittman did not care about that. As she wrote later, shortly before her death, she didn't like publicity. It brought too many people to her mousetrap on Stone Mountain.

Just as the late Mrs. Pittman intriguingly turned into the lifestream of people she had no way of knowing, so has the course of many lives been so accurately predicted that the lives themselves are testimonials to the validity not only of the individual psychic but of psychic phenomena in general. In a rather remarkable illustration of the susceptibility of human beings to prophetic trends, the life and vicissitudes of actor John Conte have been mirrored over the years in the predictions of three different psychics. The first prediction, of marriage, came at a dinner party at a New York apartment, with a dozen people in the room.

The psychic, Maya Perez of New York and Los Angeles, contemplating a girl with red hair sitting at a distance from Conte, advised her abruptly, "I see you getting married in the next four to six weeks. You will not expect it yourself, but it will be decided on impulse. You will be on a Southern trip at the time."

The girl, smiling unbelievingly, drawled in Southern style, "It's all news to me."

Madam Perez next turned to Conte. "Do you know an *H?*" she asked, picking out an initial.

Conte shook his head absently, but suddenly recalling his dinner partner, Miss Harris, he nodded vigorously.

Still using initials, the psychic proceeded. "I see you making a trip soon to an *F* and a *G*." Then she gave a little gasp. "Do you know you're going to be married—and soon?"

Actor Conte shrugged indifferently.

"And what's more," Madam Perez said, "I see you going out to California for one show, but you will stay and do better than ever before."

Five weeks later, Miss Harris and Conte, having known each other but a few weeks, were married in Folkeston, Georgia, just across the line from Florida, where they had been visiting over the Christmas holidays. "When we left for Florida," Conte said later, "all we were thinking about was Christmas, but suddenly it seemed like a good idea, and we got married in Georgia because there was no waiting there—not because of Maya Perez."

A few weeks later, Conte flew from New York to California for a minor television role, expecting to return shortly. Unexpectedly, he drew a part in the motion picture *The Man with the Golden Arm,* and subsequently became the celebrated host on television's *Matinee Theatre.*

Conte's life appeared to be rolling along splendidly a few years later when I visited him in Beverly Hills. But one night after dinner at the Conte home, where Madam Perez was also a guest, I had an intimation that not all would be well. Madam Perez drew me aside and whispered confidentially, "I don't like the vibrations," she said. "John's marriage won't last unless we pray for him."

I suggested she pray hard but did not communicate this implied prediction of a breakup to the actor, who seemed sublimely happy at the time.

With all the prayers, the marriage foundered in two years, and since marriages, particularly in Hollywood, are constantly breaking up, the presentiment was hardly calculated to make a psychic believer out of the skeptical.

Conte's marriage and career were already on the shoals when he consulted Hollywood's Lucille Joy about his problems. She was able to offer him that priceless ingredient—hope. She saw him proceeding to New York for a part in a stage play, and though he was painfully low on cash, she predicted a sudden windfall. "When you leave for New York, you will be offered six hundred dollars. Take it."

As he was drearily heading off for Los Angeles' International Airport with a hundred dollars in his wallet, actor Conte had a caller—his elderly, indigent mother. She gave him a fierce maternal hug, kissed him, and then pressed something into his hand. He opened his palm, and his eyes boggled. There, astoundingly, unpredictably, impossibly, were five 100-dollar bills.

On the plane, now strangely comforted, he recollected the rest of the prediction, indeed the major portion—that after a relatively brief low spot, he would enter the most successful fourteen years of his life.

Separated from wife and children, jobless, this had been difficult for him to accept. But now he wondered—after all, Lucille Joy had been magically correct about the rest.

In New York the actor's career backed and filled. Nothing very sensational, merely a road show with actresses Joan Hackett and Linda Darnell.

In California, he again pursued his career, with nothing solid in the offing. And then one night, quite by chance, Conte was read by still another psychic, Los Angeles' Maxine Bell. This maternally aspected sensitive, who also dealt in astrology, told Conte that within three weeks, through an ex-wife, he would meet a petite brunette; he would marry her, and she would help him reestablish himself. Within the predicted period, Conte met the fabulously successful business woman, Sirpuhe Philobosian. They were introduced by Marilyn Maxwell, his first wife. They were married shortly thereafter, in 1965. By 1968, he had acquired, with his wife, the multimillion-dollar El Mirador Hotel in Palm Springs, one of the nation's showplaces, a Palm Springs television station affiliated with National Broadcasting Company, and he was again a host on a nationally syndicated television show, which took place right in his backyard—the grounds of the luxurious El Mirador.

As predicted, he was in the most successful phase of his career.

Knowing the predicted future, many still seem unable to avoid it. And still others, even after one prediction after another has materialized, refuse to accept them as anything but coincidence. Not long after sensitive Maya Perez first read for me in 1952, she read also for a young Greenwich, Connecticut, socialite, Barbara Williams.

"You are interested in a young man in Japan," she told the twenty-year-old girl.

The girl's jaw dropped, but she retorted, "I am not."

"He is not a Japanese," the psychic went on, but an American." She frowned. "I see him very clearly, he's blond and fair, and well built." She raised her eyebrows. "He's in the service, but a professional man." She eyed the girl quizzically. "Do you know anybody like that?"

The girl nodded shortly, glancing briefly across the table at me. "Yes, but I just broke off the engagement."

Still frowning, Maya Perez said, "Well, this young man is so concerned about the relationship that he's planning to fly here. He'll be here before you know it."

Miss Williams shrugged indifferently.

Madam Perez laughed. "Well, you're going to marry this man—and have four children."

Barbara Williams laughed scornfully, utterly disenchanted with her first psychic reading. But a few weeks later I ran into her on the streets of New York, arm in arm, with a young blond man of military bearing, who had flown in unexpectedly from Japan. And less than a year later she married Flight Surgeon Cadvan Griffiths, on his return from Japan to an American base.

Seven years later, when the Griffiths already had three children, I invited them for a psychic evening with the selfsame Maya Perez, now visiting from California. There were about a dozen in the room, most of them unbelievers, and none more unbelieving than Dr. Griffiths, then a successful plastic surgeon at Bellevue and Columbia Presbyterian Hospitals. Madam Perez had read for several in the room, and then came to the former Barbara Williams, whom she obviously did not recall from that one brief meeting years before.

As the group looked on amused, Madam Perez said, "I see you having a child soon." She drew a hand across her abdomen. "I see some trouble in this area, but it will be all right."

It sounded ominous to me, but Dr. Griffiths, sitting next to me, scoffed, "Barbara just can't have another child."

Meanwhile, Mrs. Griffiths, more a believer because of her previous experience, remonstrated mildly, "I don't expect another child."

Madam Perez gave her an even smile.

"You are pregnant right now," she said, "whether you know it or not."

Dr. Griffiths turned to me. "Where do you get these people?"

I shrugged, a bit discomfited, but realizing that even the best psychic was not always correct.

The reading continued.

"I see you living in California," Madam Perez was now saying, "and your daughter (the oldest child, Bonnie) will be in the movies."

By now, even Mrs. Griffiths was smiling tolerantly, and the doctor had dismissed the reading as a farce. "I have no intention of leaving New York," he cut in.

The evening appeared to be a psychic bust.

But about a week later, Barbara Griffiths phoned and said, "Guess what? I'm pregnant."

I was to think of the rest of the prediction months later when Mrs. Griffiths entered Columbia Presbyterian Hospital in New York to have her child.

I had not heard anything, and then one day I phoned the hospital. Dr. Griffiths answered. A child, Chester (my godson, as a matter of fact), had been born, and the mother was now out of danger. "We almost lost her," Dr. Griffiths said in a tight voice. "If it hadn't been for my colleagues who served around the clock, I don't know what would have happened."

A Caesarean operation had been performed, the surgeons cutting skillfully through the abdominal area the psychic had pinpointed that night at my apartment.

There was one little afterlude. Two years later, through an unexpected development, the young plastic surgeon severed hospital ties in New York and established practice in Beverly Hills, California, completing the picture drawn by the psychic against all logic.

And daughter Bonnie, what of her? Through an actor friend, Bill Lundigan, the ten-year-old girl appeared in a movie, *The Way West,* starring Kirk Douglas, shortly after the Griffiths family moved to California.

Despite it all, Dr. Griffiths remained an unbeliever, not ready to accept the unacceptable. However, he did relent sufficiently to have Madam Perez in his Beverly Hills home to entertain some friends. "Purely amusement," he said.

One of those present was a medical associate, obviously another unbeliever, the medical profession not being very imaginative at best. This doctor watched with some amusement, as Madam Perez sidled next to him on a couch and began her reading. But as she proceeded, the smile quickly vanished.

"I see you meeting with two men," she said, "to discuss the possibility of acquiring a sanitarium in Switzerland."

Dr. Griffiths, listening, shrugged expressively. It was obviously news to him.

The doctor friend remained noncommittally silent. But when I next saw Griffiths a few days later, he gave me a quizzical look. "You know," he said, "my associate was quite irked with me because of that evening?"

"Why was that?" I asked.

Dr. Griffiths shook his head. "He thought I had told Maya Perez about the Swiss hospital, but I knew nothing about it."

It was my turn to be quizzical. "How do you think she got it?" I asked.

Obviously she had come by it psychically, just as she had foreseen everything else for him and his wife. But how and why it had come through to her, nobody could say for sure. Another man of medicine, distinguished Nobel Prize winner Alexis Carrel, observed in *Man the Unknown*: "The facts of prediction of the future lead us to the threshold of an unknown world. They seem to point to a psychic principle capable of evolving outside the limits of the body."

And this search for the unknown keeps many delving into the spiritual and the psychic, hopefully the same thing.

Actress Mae West, exploring spiritualism itself in the hope of finding a greater meaning to life, had about lost faith in the spiritual when she heard of the Reverend Jack Kelly, Welsh-born head of Buffalo's nondenominational Universalist Church. Knowing she was a conspicuous target for charlatans, the actress commissioned a business associate, James A. Timony, to observe Kelly as he demonstrated one night in a Los Angeles auditorium.

Timony was accompanied by Joe Stanley, an ex-fighter.

They had just seated themselves in the hall when Kelly, standing blindfolded on the platform, said: "I get the name of S—." He rattled off a polysyllabled, ordinarily unpronounceable Polish name. Stanley, whom Timony had thought of Italian extraction, suddenly turned pale. "That's my family name," he said, almost in awe.

Kelly was now ready with a message from a man with that name, and pointing to the dumbfounded Stanley, he said, "The father of this man is here with information for his son. He wants him to know that he was killed and his body thrown into the water. It was not an accident."

Timony turned curiously to his companion. The effect on Joe Stanley was remarkable. The blood had completely drained from his face, leaving it the color and texture of starch, and he had broken into a cold sweat. Shaking his head, he turned to Timony, and in a hoarse whisper disclosed that his father's body had indeed been found in the water, as the spiritualist said, but that the family had always thought that he had drowned naturally. Since the incident had occurred years before, there was no way of checking it for murder now.

But Timony was impressed, and so was Mae West when she got his report. Kelly was promptly summoned to the star's Santa Monica home for a seance. Medium Kelly encouraged the group, invited by the actress to ask whatever was on their minds. Since the time was October, 1941, the European war and possible American inclusion were very much in everyone's thoughts. Mae West spoke for the room when she inquired, "Will we get into the war?"

Kelly hesitated but a moment. Cocking a hand to his ear, as if listening to a private communication, he replied in a resonant voice: "There will be a surprise attack on Honolulu within three months by Japan."

There was a slight rustle in the room, nothing more. It seemed a ridiculously provocative statement, designed to capture the attention of the moment.

Another question followed: "How long will the war last?"

"From five to six years."

It was hard for anyone to conceive at that time that beleaguered England could hold out alone that long. And then

Kelly calmly added: "President Roosevelt will not live out his fourth term."

The wiseacres in the room exchanged sly glances. Kelly was killing Roosevelt off in a fourth term, when FDR was now in the first year of a third term. But the psychic had impressed at least one person—Mae West. She found herself responding to Kelly's quiet assurance.

"Will we win the war if we get into it?" she asked.

The spiritualist held his head to one side, as though better to hear the voices that hovered around him. "Yes," he said finally, "America and England together will win the war."

Mae West consulted Kelly repeatedly and remained impressed. "He used absolutely no gimmicks," she said, "no gadgets and no assistants." A theatrical expert herself, often working with improvised props, she had studied his technique closely. "Sometimes before beginning he would say, 'If you hear any voices or whisperings around me, pay no attention to them.'" She was beginning to seriously ponder the other side. "He was definitely not a ventriloquist," she said. "The source had to come from outside the room."

The friendship continued happily for many years before Mae West was to have direct recourse to the Reverend Kelly's remarkable powers. Mae's sister, Beverly, a Good Samaritan, had become innocently involved with the law by harboring a stranger who identified himself as a friend of her parents in Brooklyn. The man stayed briefly, and then one day disappeared as mysteriously as he had arrived. Shortly thereafter, the Los Angeles police called on the West home. The stranger innocently befriended was wanted back East for killing his wife. All Beverly could do was tell detectives the man had come and gone. It was hard for them to believe that she would take in a perfect stranger, and they obviously considered the eternal triangle.

Distressed, Mae decided to call Kelly and ask if he knew where the fugitive was. She turned to the detectives. "Do you mind if I call a friend in Buffalo? He might be able to help us."

They shrugged indifferently. So Mae West picked up the phone and put through a long-distance call. As Kelly came to the phone, she started to explain why she was calling. But Kelly, immediately grasping the situation from twenty-five hundred miles away, quickly interrupted.

"The man the police are looking for was arrested twenty minutes ago."

Mae West had not even mentioned the police.

She thanked Kelly, and limply hung up the receiver. And then turning to the detectives, who had been looking at her as if she were mad, she repeated what Kelly had said. "He says we can stop looking."

Naturally disbelieving, a detective put through a call to police headquarters. As they watched him, a curious transformation occurred. First, an expression of disbelief, then of wonder, stole over his face. Slowly he returned the phone to its cradle. "Our man was arrested in San Diego a half hour ago; the teletype just came in."

Whereas almost anybody might have a presentiment of an extrasensory nature at some time, the quality that sets professional psychics apart is their apparent ability to invoke their subconscious at will. Ever intrigued, I have watched as Hurkos, Marie Welt, the late Mary Talley, Maude Robinson, Helen Stalls, Margaret Shelford, Arthur Ford, and others have magically shed one personality for another.

The professional is invariably a good "cold" reader, paid to produce whether the muse comes or not. When the subconscious flags, many fall back on psychology or perception, and some will even stoop to drawing out the guileless and feeding the answers back to them. However, the reliable, when not at their best, will take a day or two off and then, subconsciously refreshed, return to the psychic fray.

Each psychic has his own way. When *Door to the Future* was published, the Washington seeress, Jeane Dixon, appeared on the Long John Nebel all-night WOR radio show with me. Not considering Mrs. Dixon a cold reader who could turn on at will, I had suggested that Long John also include Maya Perez, who had given me my first psychic reading.

As expected, Mrs. Dixon had little to communicate spontaneously. But Madam Perez, prodded by an irrepressible Long John, rose grandly to the psychic occasion.

When the radio interviewer skeptically inquired what she foresaw, she rejoined with spirit: "I see you leaving WOR and going to a larger station at three times the money."

Long John laughed incredulously.

"First of all," he scoffed on the air, "there is no larger station, and second of all, I intend remaining right here, where I have been happily located for years."

Madam Perez sniffed. "Just remember what I told you, and it will be all right."

As Long John regarded her with a wry smile, she suddenly frowned. "You know, John," she said, "I see somebody with a heart condition around you, somebody close."

Long John shook his head. "Not that I know of," he said shortly.

The psychic continued to frown. "Are you sure? I see it very clearly."

"I have no idea what you're talking about," he said shortly.

And so, on the air at least, it ended in a hopeless impasse. But two weeks later, Long John stopped by my New York apartment briefly, and I suggested he stay on for dinner.

"I have to get going," he said. "You know my wife had a heart attack a few weeks ago at a friend's house, and I have to get over there, because we can't move her as yet."

Sometime thereafter, the popular Long John, experiencing contractual problems with Station WOR, transferred his talents to a larger, more prestigious broadcasting concern, the New York City outlet of the National Broadcasting Company—at a starting salary three times what he had been getting before!

The psychic gift, mysterious as it seems, has a way of developing, even unacknowledged by the owner. Working his way through a North Carolina medical school, Spencer Thornton demonstrated his talents as a mentalist. He would read minds, achieve feats of memory, do number tricks and, of course, card tricks. He didn't pretend to be psychic, and curiously, it never occurred to him that he had some subconscious flair. Some of his tricks were so impressive that audiences thought he was surely psychic, but the budding young doctor knew better. Yet away from his demonstrations, he was beginning to have unaccountable experiences. He was able to send his wife visual signals, and she would purchase something at a store that he had visualized, without quite knowing why she had done so.

In time, he began predicting newspaper headlines, days and weeks ahead, and sporting events. He was often challenged, and as often made good. But prophets having small honor in their hometown, as the Bible tells us, a Nashville television station challenged Thornton, now a practicing physician in that city, to pick the winners of the upcoming Kentucky Derby.

The year was 1959, it was the last week of April, and the favorites of the current classic were the great Sword Dancer and First Landing.

Thornton picked up the gauntlet. "I'll try," he said. "Who's running?"

He had never picked a horse before or, for that matter, seen a race. But he had a strong feeling that he could tune in by just scanning the list of entries, as he had once picked a Miss America, Mary Ann Mobley of Mississippi.

The race was scheduled for May 2, a Saturday. Thornton made his selection on April 28, four days before. And he predicted not only the winner, but the place and show horses as well. Nobody else knew what he had designated, and meticulous protocol was observed to rule out collusion. This was to be an experiment in spontaneous ESP, transcending anything that could be possibly achieved in any college laboratory by any smug parapsychologist checking out the paranormal to suit himself.

Before impeccable witnesses, including pillars of the Nashville banking world, the slip with Thornton's selections was sealed, unread, in an envelope, notarized, and put in a vault of Nashville's Third National Bank. Only a combination of three keys could open the vault, and they were held by two vice presidents of the bank and the vault custodian. On the Monday after the race, May 4, 1959, the bankers opened the vault. With photographers and newsmen, Thornton waited in a chamber outside the vault as Granville Bourne, a bank vice president, pushed his hand into the safe deposit box and removed the envelope with the unbroken seal. As Bourne broke open the envelope and scanned the slip, his eyes seemed ready to pop. Silently, he handed the slip to the banker next to him. It was his turn to blink. And no wonder. Thornton had not only picked the first three horses in order, but had called the closeness of the race precisely and named as winner a horse which didn't figure to win.

"Tomy Lee in a photo finish; Sword Dancer second; First Landing, third."

In Nashville's banking circles, Thornton was a ninety-day wonder. "There was no way in the world for that slip to have been altered in any way," banker Granville Bourne assured me. "I walked into the vault and, with the custodian standing there, turned one of the keys that opened the safe. The envelope was not out of my hands at any time before I opened and read it."

It gave this solid banker, with an international reputation, serious pause about the metaphysical. He invited Thornton and his wife to dinner, hoping that he would get to know more about the man and his methods. But there was no method other than the psychic, and this was not in a banker's lexicon. "To this day, though I have thought about it often," Bourne marveled, "I don't know how he did it. But there was no chance of a trick, that I know."

4

Getting to Be Psychic

"Do you think there is a common psychic denominator?" the major asked.

"Everybody has some psychic potential," I responded, "some more than others, and it may be developed through meditation and awareness of the power itself."

He frowned uncertainly.

"What I am saying," I hastened to explain, "is that as we know about something, as we become conscious of it, as we think about it, we allow it to take form."

Major Aiken was a practical man, and for that reason, perhaps, had been chosen by the Air Force to determine whether psychics could be trained, as astronauts are, to perform a specific mission in the Space Age. "When we land on other planets, as we will one day," the major said soberly, "there may be only one practical way of communicating from this planet—by telepathy."

The major had a long way to go. "We haven't yet found how to cultivate this power," he said, "but we hope one day to find a common denominator in the psychic personality that we can isolate and develop—once we know how."

From a Texas missile base, the major's quest had taken him to Virginia Beach, where he pored over the documented wonders of America's greatest mystic, Edgar Cayce. He had toured the college laboratories, where, with Zenor cards and other gadgets such as encephalographs, the erudite professors, their heads perversely turned from what was happening right in front of their eyes, had established extrasensory perception to their own pedantic satisfaction.

The major had not been particularly impressed by routine experiments at Duke University and elsewhere, and for that matter, neither had I. "If they are presuming to be scientific," I pointed out, "all they are proving when somebody anticipates correctly whether cards are circles or squares is that that person could anticipate these cards with unusual accuracy.

Like myself, the major had been far more impressed by phenomena which played a tangible role in the dynamics of living. In Boston, where he had visited the Massachusetts Institute of Technology, the major had a strange psychic encounter that had convinced him, as no experiment could, that the ability to prognosticate was as real as man's power to resurrect the past at will. On a casual sightseeing stroll, the major had wandered down a dingy side street near the center of Boston. In front of a dreary walkup he noticed a sign heralding the presence of one who could tell the past, present, and future. Out of curiosity, he ambled into the building and was greeted by the prototype of all fortune-tellers. The figure that met his eyes was indeed unimpressive: her face was seamed and lined, her hair straggled over her eyes, her fingernails were broken and her hands gnarled. But the eyes that looked out at him watchfully were sharp and contemplative.

The major, telling her nothing of himself, regarded the woman with secret skepticism as she brought out a deck of battered playing cards. As elementary as his research had been, the major knew these cards were mere catalysts, pinpointing the powers of concentration, blocking off the conscious and clearing the subconscious mind for psychic impressions.

But the old woman, spreading out the cards, spoke with demonic conviction. "You are planning to leave for the Southwest, but you will not go there right away. You will make several unexpected stops first."

The major smiled to himself. In his pocket were orders to fly back to his Texas base.

The fortune-teller continued with easy assurance. "You will

go to Ohio, Michigan, even Indiana, before you finally depart for home."

Even though he had not expected much, the major was disappointed. He had been privately hoping, even in this inauspicious atmosphere, for some dramatic confirmation of ESP. In Virginia Beach he had been impressed by documented reports of Edgar Cayce's amazing ability to "go to sleep" and tell people he had never seen of ailments for which he correctly prescribed. He had read about Peter Hurkos, Jeane Dixon, and others, but now, bowing out the door, he had new misgivings about the psychic.

"Just remember what I told you," the woman said, apparently reading his mind.

At his hotel there was a telegram waiting for the major. It was from his superiors. His plans had been changed. Instead of getting back to Texas right away, he was being asked to go to Columbus, Ohio, there to discuss experiments in ESP.

In Ohio, unexpectedly, he was notified of another change in itinerary; he was to go to the University of Michigan, at Ann Arbor. He was there a while, and was preparing to leave for home when he realized almost sadly that the fortune-teller had finally gone wrong. There were no telegrams, no messages sidetracking him this time. And then, just as he was heading for the airport, there was a long-distance phone call. He picked up the phone, spoke a few minutes, and when he finally rang off there was a dazed look in his eyes. The call was from Texas. The major had been ordered to stop off, enroute, at the University of Indiana, in Bloomington. The fortune-teller had been right in every respect.

It was nothing of great moment, this prediction that had been fulfilled so dramatically, and yet it revealed, within its own narrow framework, that the future was foreseeable—and that some people, unaccountably, had special insight into that future.

Having had virtually every major event of my own life predicted in detail—marriage, divorce, success, failure—I have often wondered where the psychic power has its genesis, and why some are more gifted this way than others. The good professional psychic, whether functioning with palms, crystal ball, cards, or tea leaves, has to be correct some 80 percent of the time at least, to impress or influence. And this power necessarily has to be invoked at will, at the convenience of the subject, regardless of how psychic the psychic feels at the moment.

Accordingly, many psychics who operate very well under their own conditions are reluctant to put unnecessary burdens on themselves. The psychic machine Peter Hurkos, able to do psychic tricks at will, nevertheless refused to be tested at Duke University, arousing the ire of Dr. Joseph B. Rhine, one-time psychologist head of the widely publicized ESP laboratory there. While Rhine was consequently ready to classify Hurkos as a fraud, others less scientifically oriented pointed out that Hurkos had obviously chosen wisely.

"It would be like bringing down a Hemingway or a Steinbeck," a Hurkos defender said, "putting an encephalograph on his head, surrounding him with students and professors with pencils and pads, and then telling him to write a novel."

Obviously, the subconscious, the source of creative inspiration, can not shine when conscious thinking—annoyance, elation, anger, fear—distractingly intrudes into a clear channel.

In exposing myself more and more to the psychic world, I became aware, in time, of increasing intuitive impressions, once dismissed as reportorial perception. However, though they began in dribs and drabs, there was no accounting for these impressions without relating them to some unknown psychic force. I was obviously average, psychically. And yet as the average person becomes aware of his intuitiveness, his psychic experiences seem to increase. In my case, I would think of people I hadn't seen or thought of for years and then run into them on the street. I would pick up the phone to call somebody, and that person would be calling me. I began to anticipate what people were going to say—an obnoxious habit.

My first experience in picking names out of the air, so to speak, occurred while I was researching *The Door to the Future* and constantly brushing up against psychics like the dead Cayce, Arthur Ford, Spencer Thornton, and the like. Two young acquaintances, newspaperman Jon Bradshaw and a Texan friend, Albert Briggs, called on me, and Briggs mentioned the various colleges away from home that he attended. "My family," he chuckled, "liked keeping me away."

I asked what boarding school he had been to.

"I didn't go to one," he replied, "though my mother had."

"I suppose she went to Ward-Belmont," I said, without thinking.

My young guest regarded me uneasily over his Scotch and water. "That was quite a coincidence," he said finally, "your guessing her school in Nashville, Tennessee, and it being closed for years, too."

Young Bradshaw mentioned the name of a pretty model but could not remember her agency.

"Would it be Foster-Ferguson?" I inquired.

It was his turn to smile uncomfortably.

It was apparently a lucky hit, even though the agency was a relatively obscure one.

This facility I had seemed to develop with time and increasing absorption in the psychic. One evening, in Altadena, California, I was dining at the home of Jack O'Leary, Doubleday's Western manager. O'Leary mentioned that he had spurned an offer to transfer to New York, and that, regardless of any promotion, he would never make such a move. He turned fondly to his wife, Helen. "We love California, and wouldn't leave for anything."

As O'Leary's wife smiled agreement, I found myself saying rather rudely, "You will not only move to New York, but you will make that move in six months."

O'Leary smiled tolerantly. "Is that psychic?"

I returned his smile. "Wait and see."

The weeks passed into months. I left California for New York and completely forgot my prediction, a bit of a social blooper at best. And then one day, a postcard arrived from O'Leary in California—my first communication from him. "You and your predictions," it said. "I start working in New York in another month." Our meeting had been five months before.

What had happened to change O'Leary's mind, I don't know. However, as usual, the psychic force, disregarding cause and effect, cuts through logic, through every unseen eventuality to the illogical outcome.

I often get mail reminding me of some prediction or impression I've forgotten. In September, 1968, I received an announcement of an exhibition of paintings by the artist Momoko, at the Nicholas Roerich Museum in New York City. I scanned it curiously, not having the slightest idea who Momoko was. And then my eyes fell on a paragraph scrawled in red ink: "Your prediction about the breakthrough for my art career came true, even as far as the exact time period of two years. Remember?"

It was signed Malia Phillips, with Momoko in parentheses. Of course, I remembered now. Malia Phillips was a lovely young woman, a dancer—not a professional artist then—who had been painting because of her love for this form of expression. She had been discouraged at her apparent lack of progress in this side career, and I had spoken optimistically, giving her the encouragement she obviously required. She had recalled the time element, which was more than I had, because of course it was more important to her.

More amusingly, there was a note from Anne Gehman, the pretty young psychic reader in the spiritualist community of Cassadaga, Florida, not far from Orlando. When I had last visited her, two years before in 1966, she had been contemplating marriage to a man she had been seeing for some time. Tired and overworked, she had not been up to giving a reading at that time, so I offered to give her one. It had begun as a joke, but as I proceeded I had an unexpected impression that she would never marry this man. "You will marry somebody you have not yet met," I said, and supplied a description of the groom-to-be.

I had no idea whether I was right or wrong, nor did it seem to matter much, as Anne Gehman, from the amused look on her face, was certainly not taking me seriously. And yet I now had before me a note dated September 24, 1968, from the same Anne Gehman: "I married a man of the description you gave whom at the time I did not know and we are very happy."

I have no way of knowing how wrong I may have been elsewhere, for these people would obviously not write. Yet, there was a certain conviction about these impressions which were very different from my impressions as a reporter, a conviction so strong it was at times embarrassing.

One evening, at the Manhattan apartment of commentator Virginia Woodruff, the conversation had turned to the psychic when an attractive blond girl I had never seen before abruptly asked: "Are you the writer who wrote *The Sixth Man*? If so, it is the only one of your books I have read."

I looked appraisingly at this beautiful girl who appeared no more than twenty years old, then said without thinking about it: "I know why you read this particular book on homosexuality."

"Why?" she asked, almost challengingly.

"Because you were married to a man whose sexuality you had grave doubts about."

She blinked, and I looked at her left hand. There was no ring there.

"How long was I married?" she asked.

"Two years."

She drew her breath in sharply. "Exactly. I married a day before my birthday, and left two years later, a day before my birthday."

She regarded me quizzically, and then demanded: "Why did the marriage break up?"

"Your husband was on drugs," I said.

She shook her head. "No, it was his drinking. That's what made me wonder about him. He was always bellied up to some bar with the boys, while I sat home alone."

I did not give up easily. "I am sure he was on drugs," I said.

A neighbor, Earl Peed, was following the exchange curiously, but the girl seemed completely unaware of anybody else.

"Well," she conceded, "he was on marijuana, but that wasn't the problem."

Problem or not, she had taken to hiding the marijuana he left around so he could no longer smoke it as needed.

The girl now regarded me squarely. "All right," she said, "before I came down from Boston, I spelled my name one way, and now I spell it another. Tell me, which is which."

I already knew her name, phonetically. Quickly, I gave two spellings, the antithesis of what might have been expected, since she had simplified the spelling on becoming an actress.

Oddly, this impressed her more than anything else I had said. She slumped into a nearby chair and took a deep breath. "It's scary," she said with a shiver.

Before she left I made a date with her to discuss the drug problem, as I was still researching the subject.

The following week I contacted her by telephone.

"I can have lunch," she said, "but I'll have to find a sitter for my son."

"Is he four years old?" I asked.

There was a brief pause at the other end of the line. "Four and a half," she said.

We met for lunch as planned.

"Apparently," I said, "you got a sitter for Philip."

She looked at me strangely. "How did you know his name was Philip?"

I shrugged, puzzled myself. "You must have mentioned it."

She shook her head. "Not on your life. I never mentioned his name to you—and nobody at that party would know it."

She seemed oddly upset. "You must be able to see right through me," she said.

It was my turn to shake my head. "I am really not very psychic. I get occasional impressions and you are apparently a clear channel for these impressions."

We made another date, but even as we made it, I knew it wouldn't be kept. When I phoned to confirm the date later that week, a nondescript voice said the girl had been unexpectedly called out of town. I understood. Nobody likes to live in a goldfish bowl.

Generally, psychics have little standing in the community, and skeptics sardonically ask why, if they are so psychic, they haven't become wealthy through predictably playing the market, or the horses. The answer is obvious. The psychic works exclusively through the subconscious mind, and thinking on a conscious level—fear, anger, greed—only blocks off the subconscious. The desire for gain is very much a conscious thought.

However, when not directly involved, many psychics have accurately foreseen the results of gambling events. Dr. Spencer Thornton, as we saw, picked the first three horses in the 1959 Kentucky Derby, and Edgar Cayce not only made a fortune for some Wall Streeters but correctly forecast the market crash in October, 1929, the Depression, and the economic upswing in 1933. Only recently followers of Cayce made large sums by buying up land in the Virginia Beach area, which, thirty years ago, he predicted would peak off in 1968.

As one relaxes, the subconscious appears to be at its best.

And with this relaxed feeling comes sublime confidence. In Detroit during the height of the baseball race in the summer of 1968, I appeared together with Alan Alda, star of the movie, *The Paper Lion,* on the Jack McCarthy radio show. The conversation, from ESP, naturally got onto the pennant race. The Detroit Tigers, though front-runners, were in a losing streak and floundering. Host McCarthy commented sourly that it looked like the Tigers were in their familiar tailspin.

I expressed an opposing view.

"Is that a psychic prediction?" McCarthy twitted me.

"Detroit," I replied on the air, "will win the pennant and beat the Cardinals in the World Series."

I was to have misgivings about this prediction when Detroit tottered on the brink of defeat, down three games to one in the October classic. Watching on TV, I wondered how I had gone wrong. I had felt so sure of myself—and the Tigers. And then, amazingly, the hopelessly outclassed Tigers rallied, even beating St. Louis' unbeatable Bob Gibson in the decisive seventh game.

Testing, I tried to consciously invoke the subconscious. But I was rarely ever right when the impressions didn't come spontaneously. Still, hardly a day passed that I didn't get some psychic impression.

One afternoon late in the summer of 1968, the phone in my New York apartment rang, and a feminine voice said in an uncertain treble, "This is Lisa, Lisa M—. Do you remember me?"

The name rang no chord.

"We met through Jeane Dixon in Washington seven years ago," the voice said. "I was the girl she had befriended and made certain predictions about."

While not remembering the exact incident, I now recalled the girl and the fact that she had been a protégée of the Washington seeress. However, the meeting had had such little impact at the time that I could not even recall what she looked like.

She turned up an hour or two later, a comely young woman of twenty-five, whom I recognized instantly.

"I suppose," I said, "a lot has happened to you."

She nodded noncommittally.

"Are you married?"

She shook her head. "No, I never married."

I gave her a curious look. For some reason her remark had triggered a spontaneous impression. "You have married," I said mildly, "and your marriage was annulled."

She looked up sharply. "You must have been talking to Jeane Dixon."

I hadn't spoken to Mrs. Dixon in years.

"Then somebody told you."

I smiled. "I haven't heard your name in seven years."

She refused to be convinced. "What else do you get?" she demanded.

"You were his third wife, and he has already gone on to a fourth."

Her eyes bugged. "You had to be talking to Jeane, or somebody else," she said. "And what's more," she added, "his fourth marriage has already broken up."

She paused, eying me suspiciously. "How old is he?"

"Twenty-seven," I said.

She laughed triumphantly. "Twenty-eight."

She seemed halfway convinced, but she was still checking.

"Who was he?" she asked.

"A young Maryland socialite," I said, without thinking.

With an exclamation, she picked up a huge handbag, riffled through it, and then came up with a worn newspaper clipping. It was an announcement that she, Lisa, had just wed—a young Maryland socialite."

She put the clipping away, shaking her head. She had one last question.

"Why did the marriage break up?"

I hesitated. "No one person is wholly to blame."

She squirmed in her chair. "But there was one very special reason for my leaving him."

"Oh, that's a different matter."

"But what was it?"

"You were upset that he wouldn't work."

She clapped her hands. "Exactly."

And so the door closed on Lisa and her problems, without quite answering my own problem—the nature of psychic development.

I was sure, as I thought about it, that my Yoga experience, begun the spring of 1964 and culminating in *Yoga, Youth and Reincarnation,* had served to open certain psychic centers. Almost imperceptibly I had felt a oneness with the universe around me. At Concord I had laughed when my Guru, Marcia Moore, hesitated to exterminate the insects plaguing our exercises, but later, with a laugh, I found myself carefully brushing similar insects out of my hair instead of swatting them into oblivion. Life, I was beginning to believe, is an orderly, continuous cycle in which everything has its place. And just as the movements of the planets are predictable, so, too, apparently, are the life processes of the mortals who, as parts of the whole, certainly have no properties greater than that whole.

All great psychics, from Cayce to Norfolk's Maude Robinson, have felt they were instruments of God and their power flowed through them because of God's will. To tune in, they merged the infinity discovered within themselves with the infinity outside them, and this they call God.

How does this increased awareness of God, of a God not only Creator but Creation, affect the latent psychic sense, that genetic legacy which protected primitive man back in the jungle days when he had to know what was lurking in the dark corners of a cave or be extinguished?

Now death is lurking as never before, man for the first time having the technical know-how to wipe himself out with the very nuclear force that rightfully used could bless his every day. Has a psychic milieu been developing to help man resolve the problems the intellect has failed at? Is it a manifestation of God's power that will one day fully awaken man to the presence of his Maker, and to his purpose in achieving the ends of that Maker—perfection within himself?

Only when we are spiritually attuned does this psychic development become apparent, whether the person is a professional psychic or one with only occasional flashes of intuition. Conversely, where psychics had a true gift, I had seen this gift diminish, even disappear, through greed or vanity. One of the best known psychics, priding herself on not taking money for her readings, nevertheless made a fortune through commercial enterprises which stemmed out of the publicity she had so assiduously cultivated. She constantly strove for the limelight with predictions calculated to gain her attention, but she was wrong so often that she only undermined confidence in herself and the psychic field, generally.

Another misled psychic, an excellent "cold" reader, read a book about Edgar Cayce and began to fancy herself a healer. Instead of giving people the psychic readings they wanted, she announced loftily that she was no fortune-teller, and she prattled along to great lengths about her own spirituality while her clients sat squirming impatiently, to hear their own problems analyzed.

On the other hand, there were psychics like Maude Robinson, Hollywood's Bill Corrado and Ashakan, Helen Stalls, in Jupiter, Florida, and Maria Bleikers, in New York, who have given freely of themselves in trying to guide the troubled through a future so often clearly foreseen. As they grow older, sensitives such as palm-reader Marie Welt in New York and Eloise Page in Cassadaga, Florida, seem to become even more spiritually acute because of their motivation to help people. A clergyman, concerned that so many of the girls in his flock were consulting Marie Welt, turned his collar around and called on her himself. After the reading, he held out his hand with a smile, and revealed himself. "I know now why they come to you," he said. "You make them feel better."

In the Far East the psychic is taken for granted. It is considered neither surprising nor noteworthy that certain people can foresee the future. Have there not always been prophets in the great lands of antiquity, and is there not a Book of Prophets in the Bible, presumably followed by the Western world? In the great subcontinent of India there have been mystics and gurus ever since tradition began, and these have undoubtedly had a role in the recognition of an inexorable fate in the affairs of man. The gurus are teachers, and they work often with yoga —the yoga of the mind and spirit as well as the body. In man's becoming unified within himself and then communing with a unified world, they teach, lies the seed for the development of the spiritual and its subconscious channel. The whole Yoga discipline, as I know myself, seems geared to this development. In the deep breathing and concentration, there seems to be a subtle exchange of secrets with the unbounded universe. The universe presumably has no secrets for those who understand how it works. And yet not knowing fully, just having a glimpse at times, is enough to sharpen and hone a faculty that seems capable of peering ahead. Precognition, or prevision, is obviously a part of the natural universe, but like the principles of electricity and aerodynamics, it did not gain substance until man was ready to use it. The pillows of air keeping heavier-than-air-craft afloat were certainly a reality long before the Wright Brothers sent their first glider into the air. And electricity, even now not completely understood, was discovered only recently by Faraday, Davy, Ben Franklin, and Edison, though it obviously has been an inherent force in nature since the first caveman struggled to stay warm. In conceding that some people do have the gift to foretell the future, Dr. Alexis Carrel, though scientifically oriented, philosophically asserted that when man does find out how this phenomenon works he will one day solve the riddle of the universe.

In practical concentration or meditation, certain cosmic laws are assertedly revealed even when the object of the meditation itself is of the finite, like flying or electricity. The great teacher Prasad Shastri, stressing that man must rid himself of false ego to see the world clearly, relevantly observed: "Professor Yukawa, the Japanese physicist who won the Nobel Prize for physics for his prediction of the particle called the meson, said that the new idea came to him when he was alone, late at night, and he had passed into a state of meditation on the problem. Newton, too, passed into meditation states in which he was totally insensible to the world around him, and many artists speak of such experiences as the source of their inspiration."

To meditate, involving the subconscious, it is helpful to plant certain seed thoughts. Meditate on peace of mind or on the true unlimited self, through musing, perhaps, on Christ's words: "Before Abraham was, I am," and "I and the Father are one."

Another seed thought, stirring subconscious visualization, may be the lives of the sages—Socrates, Confucius, and Mohammed. Some visualize Christ with his disciples, and others hone their subconscious by meditating on dreams. "In the dream," said Shastri, "our hopes of wealth and fears of destruction will never be realized because they are unreal. By deep meditation we should understand this is true of the waking world also."

To directly stir the psychic centers, Shastri urged the novice to calm the mind with deep breathing, to close the eyes gently and concentrate on a pencil of light down the center of the body, meanwhile pressing a forefinger on the pineal or third eye, downward to the navel, using the sensation as an aid to visualization.

All this sounded like so many brave words until it began to work for me as it had for others. As I meditated, I began to realize truths I should have known long before. I could work best, think best, see most clearly, only when concentrating on effort and not results. "One who can be indifferent to success or failure," said the Swami Pavitrananda, "is usually calm and serene; and it is obvious that such a person will work better—especially during a crisis—than one who is always in feverish anxiety about the result."

In a state of serenity, I have noticed, the psychic power flourishes best. The successful psychics are generally calm to the point of stolidity, with a few exceptions. But their gift usually manifests itself early in life. Visualization, breathing, and concentration are for the average person who wishes to develop. There was little doubt in my Yoga teacher's mind as to how to develop the ordinary paranormal or psychic quality. Marcia Moore had seen many develop this way, and felt she had developed herself. "Concentrate on the third eye as you deep breathe," Marcia counseled, "and you will find the electrical energy—the Kundalini—mustered in breathing rushing to this pineal center after a while. In time, as you concentrate, you will notice a tingling sensation, indicating pulsating energy and budding psychic power."

After a few weeks of this, I noted a slight buzz between my eyes, then a whirring sound. I began to get premonitions, and looking at a couple who seemed perfectly happy, I found myself thinking, "They will be divorced in two years." It was not altogether pleasant, particularly when the prediction materialized—for the couple was my guru, Marcia, and her astrologer husband, Louis Acker.

Believing in the psychic apparently made me more psychic. Certainly, it made me more receptive, through establishing a closer rapport.

I am apparently a clear channel for mystics. Sensitive Maya Perez foretold accurately that my third book (*The Sixth Man*) would be a best seller, when I had not yet written a book; palmist Marie Welt, in the lounge of Manhattan's Fifth Avenue Hotel, foresaw my Edgar Cayce book, *The Sleeping Prophet,* going to Number Two on the New York *Times* best-seller list. In Norfolk, Virginia, the dean of readers, Maude Robinson, guided me through a ticklish situation by telephone, telling me at every step what the other parties to a transaction would do, and when. I was on the long-distance phone with her when she mentioned a name and said, "He is trying to contact you now, even as we are talking."

As I hung up, the phone rang. It was the person whose name she had mentioned.

How can I help but be impressed as I recall an amazingly precise reading from Marie Welt, before witnesses, years ago when I was a newspaper reporter in New York? I had written one book at this stage, and because of its indifferent success, artistically and commercially, I had abandoned a career in book writing. So I was very much unimpressed when this psychic palm-reader, playing her tiny flashlight on my hand, looked up with a frown and said, "Are you thinking of writing a book?"

"Hardly," I said.

She kept scrutinizing my hand.

"Well," she said finally, looking me in the eye, "a publisher will phone you in two days and ask you to write a book." She held up two fingers. "Not three days, or a week, but two days, remember that."

The project, she went on, would hit a snag, but after some delay this book would be written and would dramatically alter my career, eventually taking me out of the newspaper business.

As I recall, I was rather embarrassed for Marie in front of my friends.

"Never mind," she said peremptorily, "you will come back and tell me I was right."

Two days later, I walked into my newspaper office, and

found a message on my desk. A Mr. Tom Payne had called from Avon Publications, and would call back. Even as I was reading, the unknown Payne rang up again.

"You have no idea why I am calling you," he began.

"Oh, yes, I have," I said lightly, "you want me to write a book."

There was a pause, and then Payne said, "How did you know that?"

"I was only kidding," I said, not wanting to get into it.

"Well, that's exactly right," he said.

The book was to be on juvenile delinquency and the rehabilitation of street gangs by the New York City Youth Board. Mine had been one of five names suggested by Board directors. But I had been the only one Tom Payne had telephoned.

I felt rather flattered. "I suppose you read some of my newspaper articles on delinquency."

"No," he said dryly. "I never heard of you before." He had no idea why he had picked me.

We became good friends before our discussions were over. However, the project did hit a snag, as predicted, when the publishers, a paperback concern, felt the market for a delinquency book had been saturated by the current success of *The Blackboard Jungle.* Moreover, I failed to see how a paperback book, however well received, could affect my career or raise it to a new dimension.

In the next few months, I saw Tom socially a few times, and then one day he phoned rather excitedly and asked if I would care to do the book for Doubleday & Co., the largest publisher of trade books in the country.

"What do you have to do with Doubleday?" I asked.

"They're in the same building," he said, "and I just happened to mention the idea we had discussed."

Lee Barker, the executive editor of Doubleday, had asked Payne to arrange a meeting.

Out of that session with Barker came not only the delinquency book, *The Wasted Years,* but a succession of books on various subjects, the next being *The Sixth Man,* a study in homosexuality, which became a best seller and took me out of a newspaper job after twenty years.

How had Marie Welt seen all this? Certainly, there was no

perception involved. Obviously there is a tide in the affairs of men as predictable as the tides themselves. Does not the Bible say that the stars ordain and "thy days are numbered like the hairs of thine head"? Had not the Greatest Life Ever Lived been foretold by the ancient prophets of Israel? And had not Christ Himself announce that He had come to live and die by that prophecy? "No man taketh it [my life] from me, but I lay it down of myself. I have power to lay it down, and I have power to take it again. This commandment have I received of my Father."

Had He not said that Peter would reject Him before the cock crowed thrice? At the well, when the woman denied being married, had He not told her that she had married not once but five times? And when, marveling, she asked how He told her this, He explained so that she would know who He was and who had sent Him. What He had done, with faith in the Father —the eternal Father of man—others could do. And perhaps this is how it all works.

I have not met anybody more spiritually motivated than Maude Robinson. She contemplated people with problems compassionately, saying: "The Lord is my shepherd, I shall not want. He leadeth me into green pastures . . . he restoreth my soul . . . I will fear no evil: for thou art with me; thy rod and thy staff they comfort me."

But the psychic denominator is by no means exclusively spiritual. Many creative people—artists, writers, politicians, inventors—drawing inspiration from a fertile subconscious, also may be psychically in tune. H. G. Wells long ago imagined a war between planets, and saw men moving about easily in space; Heinrich Heine foretold, a hundred years before it took place, the onslaught of a Hitler Germany on a mesmerized humanity; in a 1967 issue of *This Week* magazine, as editor Charles Robbins pointed out, novelist Taylor Caldwell predicted that the leading Negro civil rights leader would be assassinated in the spring of the following year. Martin Luther King's tragic end made it clear whom she meant.

For me, casually at dinner, Miss Caldwell predicted my greatest success would be a novel.

Since my work was exclusively nonfiction, it seemed hardly likely.

Two months later, I was discussing with my editor a newspaper story I had covered years before. A curious gleam came into his eyes.

"Why not do it as a novel?" he suggested.

"But I've never written a novel," I demurred.

"Just write it like any other book."

And so, unexpectedly (except for Taylor Caldwell), I signed for my first novel.

The psychic is inexplicable. I have heard of people who visualized accidents before they happened. In one instance, a mother hurriedly left a bridge game for home, at a flutter of concern for her infant daughter, tended by a trusted baby-sitter. She dashed into the child's room, where the baby appeared to be slumbering peacefully, reached into its mouth, and removed an open safety pin from its palate. "My stomach," she said, "told me something was wrong."

It is hard to tell whether people are psychic by looking at them. Hollywood actress Julie Parrish looked like an angel, but friends knew her as a witch. When strange predatory males phoned the blond beauty, she would frequently disconcert them by describing what they looked like and what they were wearing. They invariably hung up quickly.

At times, Miss Parrish's psychic gift had considerably more practical value. In the summer of 1966, she was riding along Santa Monica Boulevard in Los Angeles with actor Frank Alesia. Suddenly she asked Alesia to pull the car to a curb and exclaimed: "There has been an accident, and I must meditate to help the person in distress."

While Alesia sat dumbfounded, the actress closed her eyes and sent her thoughts astrally to the scene of the disturbance. She finally looked up with a solemn smile. "Drive on a few blocks," she said, "we'll come to the scene."

Alesia uneasily drove on without a word. A half dozen blocks farther along at an intersection, they spotted a crowd gathered around a young man sprawled out on the sidewalk. Some were yanking at his arms, others at his legs. One man had the youth's mouth open and was trying to find his tongue. He was having a seizure of *grand mal*—epilepsy.

As Alesia started to climb out of the car, Julie Parrish put a restraining hand on his arm. "There are too many people out there now. Let me send him a message. He needs to know that someone loves and wants to help him."

Again Julie closed her eyes, and Alesia could barely hear her murmur. "Relax and know that you are loved, and you will be made well and whole again." Julie had made her prayer to God, in keeping with what Christ said of man's being able to work miracles through faith in the Father.

At this instant, Alesia recalled, the young man began to stir and then got up and looked dazedly around. He was apparently completely recovered. The crowd scattered, and Alesia and his good witch drove off.

Alesia never felt quite the same about the lovely girl. "I regard her now with awe. For as I live and breathe, she communicated with that fellow she had never seen before, and helped him without his even knowing it." This was their first date and he never dated her again.

More recently, in October, 1968, Miss Parrish was driving late at night from Palm Springs to Los Angeles with an actress friend, Timothy Blake. Several miles west of the desert resort, she found she was low on gas. Instead of going ahead a few miles to a gas station on the main highway, she decided on an impulse to return to Palm Springs, miles out of her way, and fill up. On another impulse, driving through Palm Springs, she took a side street, approaching a dilapidated old hotel which she had mentioned earlier in the evening for no particular reason.

Outside the hotel, they saw a man on a window ledge, and a woman inside the window, screaming for help.

The man called down to the girls. "Don't pay any attention to her, she's had a few drinks."

"Don't believe him," the woman cried. "He's trying to break in."

But Julie already knew why she had come back for gas. As with the epileptic, she had got the message of another human being in need.

She drove to a nearby phone booth, called the police, and then as they arrived and took the interloper away, she quietly sped off into the night, after gassing up. Her ESP had done a good night's work.

Can the psychic be tested in the trivial, as in the great events?

Palmist Marie Welt foresaw minor as well as major turns with the same clarity. In September of 1967, planning to take off for California, I called on my psychic friend at the Fifth Avenue Hotel cocktail lounge.

She took my hand, squeezed the thumb and mound of Venus, and scanned the network of tiny lines, as she had a dozen times before.

"I see you going to California," she said, "and real soon."

I nodded. "Tell me something I don't know."

She smiled. "I have to get on track first."

She kept looking at my hand and squeezing it, then finally glanced up with a frown. "I see you doing some articles for your old paper, the New York *Daily News*."

I shook my head. "Not in a million years."

Again she smiled. "I wouldn't be that sure if I were you. I see them calling you in three weeks."

"But I'll be in California."

"They'll call you there."

I laughed, disbelievingly. After seventeen years with the *News,* I had left seven years before. "If they wouldn't call when I was only a few blocks away, why call when I'm three thousand miles away?"

"You're going to hear from them in three weeks." She almost flung my hand down in annoyance at my lack of confidence. "And what's more, you'll do the articles."

The following week I flew out to California and settled in the Beverly Hills home of friends, the Cadvan Griffiths, who were in Europe. Only my editor knew where I was, and the telephone was unlisted.

Busy as I was, I had not given any thought to the prediction, when, not quite three weeks later, the phone woke me at seven one Friday morning. It was, of course, only ten in New York City.

A curt, crisp, metallic voice announced: "Just a moment, Mr. Barger will be with you."

Half asleep, I thought he had said Barker, and when a new voice came on, I said, "Hello, Lee," thinking it was Lee Barker, my editor at Doubleday.

"This is Floyd Barger," the voice corrected.

Floyd Barger was an old newspaper associate, whom I

hadn't heard from in years. He had recently been named managing editor of the New York *News*. But still, why would he be calling me across a continent, going to the trouble of getting my unlisted number?

Barger didn't keep me in the dark long.

"Did you read about Bishop Pike communicating with his dead son?"

I had seen a news story about a Toronto television show on which spiritualist Arthur Ford had claimed spirit contact with Pike's son, a suicide victim.

"I read something about it," I said rather vaguely.

"What do you think of people communicating with the dead?"

"I don't know whether they do or don't."

"You're not a believer then?"

"I'd have to know more about it."

"Well, then," Barger said, with a grunt of satisfaction, "would you do a couple of articles about Pike and this whole area—objectively, of course?"

By coincidence, I was planning to spend that weekend in Santa Barbara, about a hundred miles north of Los Angeles, and Pike, I recalled, was in Santa Barbara at the Center for the Study of Democratic Institutions.

I agreed to contact Pike and get back to Barger by Monday. And so we left it.

In Santa Barbara I spent a day with Bishop Pike, and discussed the episode of his son Jim. It had struck me as strange that a twenty-two-year-old with everything to live for—health, social position, youth, intelligence, tradition—should have reached such a point of despair that he would fling away all life had to offer.

I had a feeling there was more to it than had been reported, and that young Pike had been under stress when he went out and bought a gun and killed himself.

As we faced each other across a table, I asked the father: "Was your son on drugs at the time of his death?"

The bishop toyed with a fork.

"Why do you say that?" he asked.

"An intuitive feeling."

He blinked a moment. "Yes," he sighed, "but I wish you wouldn't mention it now, as I would like to handle it myself in my own story." The youth, like so many of the young, had been experimenting with psychedelic drugs, trying to find himself, and when he bought the gun he was under their influence. "They should have known better than to sell a gun to anybody in his condition," the bishop said.

The spirit-communication story, which the bishop subsequently wrote a book about, involved three different mediums. It required more checking and delving than I was ready to do at the time.

Back in Beverly Hills, on Monday, I decided not to do the story, and was preparing to call New York when the telephone rang. It was Barger. I was half through my apologies when he interrupted to say, "I wasn't calling about Pike."

His voice took on a quizzical note. "Did you see the story about a BOAC plane crashing in the Mediterranean with sixty-six dead?"

I had caught the headlines only.

"Anyway," he rushed on, "a woman in New Jersey, an Elizabeth housewife, awakened with a premonition that her husband and daughter had crashed on this plane bound for Cyprus—an hour before the airline had the news." Before they had flown off, she had tried to talk them out of the flight.

"What do you think about that?" Barger said. "Can people foresee the future?"

"There is no question of this," I said. "It has been proven again and again, and the chief basis for skepticism is a lack of information. As a matter of fact," I added, "just before I came out here, a psychic in New York told me that I was going to write a series of articles for the *News* in three weeks."

Barger laughed uncertainly, apparently not thinking I was serious or hoping I wasn't.

"Will you do a couple of articles on predictions for your old paper?" he asked.

That day, I wired into the *Daily News* office the first of the articles Marie Welt had said I would agree to write, in three weeks' time. The first article headed page 2, on October 16, 1967, and was titled, "Shadows of Impending Doom," with the subtitle, "How Our Psychic Sense Warns Us." The second ran the following day. It concluded with Marie Welt's prediction, and an accolade to a truly remarkable psychic: "Last week, the phone rang early in Beverly Hills and I picked it up drowsily. It was an editor of the *News,* whom I hadn't seen for years. This series is the result."

5

Cayce's Castor Oil Packs

Shortly after the turn of the century, some sixty years ago, a youthful Edgar Cayce fascinated some of the medical doctors in Christian County, Kentucky, with his remarkable ability to correctly diagnose the symptoms of a patient he had never seen and then effectively prescribe a cure.

Cayce felt that for every human disorder there was a panacea in plant or animal life and in right thinking.

Behind the scenes, for years, he worked with Dr. Wesley Ketchum, an ambitious young general practitioner from north of the Ohio River, and helped make this "damyankee" an outstanding success. Ketchum, still alive, living in Southern California, used Cayce on his most difficult cases, and this strange association, unique in medical annals, ended only when Cayce felt the pressure on him to be too great.

By and large, the medical profession has never accepted the "psychic doctor" or his thousands of successful physical readings, maintaining the rigidly closed mind for which it is justly renowned.

In *The Sleeping Prophet,* I mentioned a young, relatively open-minded member of the Harvard medical faculty, who had closely examined Cayce readings of the so-called incurable diseases—multiple sclerosis, epilepsy, leukemia, and cancer—and tried to formulate some basic conception of Cayce remedies.

In my report I pointed out that the Harvard man, after studying various cases out of the files at Virginia Beach, neither vouched for nor recommended treatment outlined by Cayce. And when I subsequently met this researcher months later in Boston, he protested good-naturedly, "You claimed more for Edgar Cayce than I did."

"How was that?" I asked, feeling I had claimed nothing in reviewing the Harvard man's survey.

"Cayce," he said, "was right one hundred percent of the time in his diagnoses, but he was correct only half the time in his cures."

I looked at the doctor almost in disbelief.

"That's far more than I would claim for Cayce," I said finally. "Do you know of any diagnostician who can make a similar claim?"

"And as for the cures," I added, "everybody dies sometime of one thing or the other, even doctors and writers, and it is remarkable that Cayce had that many cures among disorders normally listed as incurable."

During his lifetime, Cayce was constantly belittled by doctors who made no effort to examine his work or check his readings with people who had actually been helped. During Cayce's latter period in Virginia Beach, a group of Norfolk, Virginia, doctors approached Cayce's personal physician, Dr. Robert Woodhouse, the dean of Virginia Beach medics, and inquired sharply about the quack in their midst practicing medicine without a license.

Dr. Woodhouse only laughed.

"I told these doctors," he recalled, "not to worry about Cayce; he was no competition for them. Whatever he was doing came from some other source that neither we nor he, for that matter, knew anything about."

Cayce seems to have gained greater recognition among the healing fraternity after his death, than he ever did in life. His insistence on osteopathic adjustments, once decried as the ultimate in quackery, has become more acceptable with the years as the osteopaths themselves have earned acceptance. And many of the therapists, osteopaths, and medical practitioners who have researched his readings have become articulate advocates of Cayce after successfully applying his remedies to cases they have conventionally diagnosed.

Through as bizarre an event as any Cayce himself participated in, a medical research project based on the Cayce readings was established posthumously through the contribution of a wealthy Connecticut woman helped by the dead Cayce after the living doctors she knew couldn't help her.

Gratefully, this woman made possible a research project headed by Dr. William O. McGarey, a prominent Phoenix, Arizona, physician, who has already reported remarkable cures for many different ailments with the warm castor oil packs so often recommended by the sleeping Cayce.

"Cayce," McGarey observed, "implied in all his readings that the method he was using required patience in application, persistence always and a consistency of use. Without these he implied that the healing would not come. It is the philosophy of the readings that healing brought to the individual in the manner that he saw advisable was a healing of the whole person— body, mind and soul. Anything less than this would always be short of the mark."

McGarey was struck by the fact that Cayce recommended the external use of castor oil, the Palma Christi (hand of Christ) of antiquity, for some fifty different illnesses. "I saw literally hundreds of instances," the doctor pointed out, "where such packs were advised for conditions of the body that seemed not to be in any way related to each other. Yet they were given the same therapy."

Castor oil was an important ingredient in folk medicine, but the medical profession long ago stopped using it for anything but internal purposes. Long after Cayce had died, Dr. D. C. Jarvis, in his controversial, best-selling book on folk medicine in Vermont, listed the topical uses of castor oil, among them its use in removing warts, healing a body ulcer, reducing irritation of the conjunctiva of the eye, stimulating growth of hair in small children, relieving aching feet, corns, and calluses, and removing disfiguring blemishes, such as liver spots on the hands, papillomas of the skin, and pigmented moles on the face and elsewhere.

McGarey conceded that "folk medicine is not the usual

area of information to draw from in medical literature because it does not have the sanction of the scientific method." However, if castor oil worked, McGarey was not only curious about how it worked, but was ready and willing to try it on patients who did not react to orthodox therapy. Certainly, it should do no harm.

For my own part, I had seen how it worked on myself. Having a painful nodule on my right ear, diagnosed by medical friends as actinic keratosis, a possible prelude to skin cancer, I dabbed it with a smidgin of castor oil morning and night. In three weeks the pealike protuberance had granulated and fallen off, and there was no need to resort to even minor surgery, as the doctors had advised. And so while it should not have worked, it apparently had, and all the learned arguments to the contrary would not alter the fact of obvious cause and effect.

"When a therapy has been used for many years without ill effect," McGarey observed, "then it is time to take that therapy and find out no longer *if* it will work, but instead *why* it works, and what perhaps happens in the body when it does its job."

The castor oil packs applied to the abdomen apparently stimulate the liver, increasing the lymphatic flow which Cayce saw as vital to health and well-being. The packs were often followed by olive oil taken internally as part of an obvious cleansing process. McGarey briefly quoted from a Cayce reading to indicate the type of physiological activity that was expected:

"How long should the castor oil pack be kept up and how often?" was asked for an ailing ten-year-old.

"Keep up packs," Cayce replied, "until the corrections and the lesions in this area [obstructions] are broken up. These should be taken by periods, three days at a time, an hour each day. Follow same with two teaspoonfuls of olive oil. We wish to clear the alimentary canal and keep it clear. After the packs have been given for three days, skip a week, and then give them again."

A four-year-old boy with an obviously dissimilar illness was given a similar Cayce prescription, along with specific directions:

"Apply castor oil packs over the liver area about one hour

each day for two days, then give internally two teaspoonfuls of olive oil after the second day. Apply the castor oil pack with at least three thicknesses of flannel, saturated with the castor oil, and then apply the electric pad over same. This should stir the liver into activity. These are what is needed to remove the tendency for strep."

McGarey picked out the case of a sixty-three-year-old woman told by Cayce that her difficulty was in large part caused by a malfunction of the liver. "In Cayce's terminology," McGarey elaborated, "she was told that the right lobe of the liver was causing distress to the pancreas and the spleen, while the liver as a whole was causing distress to the kidneys and bladder, the lungs, heart and assimilating system [this undoubtedly being the stomach and small intestines]."

In other words, Cayce saw an interrelation of nearly all the vital organs of the body in this instance of bodily dis-ease.

The doctor analyzed the probable impact of the treatment: "Treatment consisted first of castor oil packs. This would indicate that Cayce, in his unconscious state, 'saw' the necessity of improving the condition of the liver before anything else would or perhaps could be done. And thus is seen implied one of the functions of the castor oil packs—an enhancement of the function of the liver, not only in its ability to be the great detoxifying organ of the body, but also in its beneficial effect to the surrounding organs rather than being as dross and a distress to them.

"Cayce," McGarey sought to explain, "seemingly approached the human body from within, looking at it intimately, seeing it function, even to the manner in which one nerve cell bridges the gap to its synaptic partner, and seeing the substance which allows this to happen. He was able to see the symptoms in a body, and what we might call a disease process coming into being from a single source."

Not having Cayce's apparent X-ray vision, McGarey conceded it might be difficult to find medically the same cause that Cayce hit upon psychically, as science had no device to judge the sensitivity of each and every cell in the body.

Regardless of where symptoms cropped up, Cayce saw the origins of much physical and mental distress in the relationship of the spinal cord to the sympathetic ganglia or nerve complexes. These were described by him as lesions, resulting from injury or depletion of the system in certain foodstuffs or nutritional needs, or even from emotional stress.

The lesion, not the cause but a result of the underlying fault, in turn prompts additional symptoms. "In the beginning," said Cayce in a reading for an ailing thirty-five-year-old man, "in the cause or seat of the trouble, we find there was that in the system that produced a depletion to the physical resistance. During this period there was an injury, or a subluxation, to the ninth and tenth dorsal vertebrae. In the recuperation, in ease, the body formed a lesion to meet the needs of the conditions."

From observing Cayce at long range, and his own cases at short range, McGarey tried to form a picture of how it all hung together. Just as man is not an island, the organs of the human body do not stand alone. "The philosophy of function in the human body, as became gradually apparent in Cayce," the doctor pointed out, "would have us understand that these lesions which are formed then become the etiology (causative agency) of other troubles throughout the body, through imperfect transmission of impulses from the higher brain center to the general areas of the internal workings of the body which are controlled autonomically by the ganglia (a mass of nervous tissue containing nerve cells, external to the brain or spinal cord) which are thus affected."

McGarey noted that when liver function was affected, coordination between the liver and the kidney in elimination might perhaps become a problem: "The patient may then develop irritation without evidence of infection. Through the disturbance to the liver, the digestion may be affected, and then in quick order the assimilation of needed food qualities is limited, the energies of the body suffer, and the nervous system is affected through the lack of substances given to the lymphatic, and subsequent inadequate lymphocytes, and again the "globular" substance (created in Peyer's Patches). This substance is necessary to form a contact between these two systems [autonomic and cerebrospinal], and lack of proper contact brings sometimes physical disorders, sometimes mental derangement that varies from very mild to critically serious."

Cayce, as a spiritual source, went farther than any physician, even an extraordinary one, in analyzing this relationship.

"Cayce," McGarey observed without comment, "infers that this lack of contact is a true lack of relationship (in one cell or millions of them) between the physical consciousness and the 'soul and spirit forces,' which we may perhaps call the unconscious mind."

"What happened a few months ago during the headache," a thirty-eight-year-old woman once asked Cayce, "when something seemed to pop in my head, since which time the attacks haven't seemed as severe?"

"There is the coordination between the nerve systems," Cayce characteristically replied, "at the area where the medulla oblongata enters the lower portion of the brain. At that period when there was such a severe attack, there was the breaking of a lesion in the abdominal area. This sounded through the sympathetic nervous system, producing the condition in the head itself."

Apparently, relief could also occur spontaneously without castor oil.

If Cayce was correct, the castor oil packs applied abdominally directly affected the lymphatic vessels of the intestinal canal that are called lacteals because of their appearance and function.

In a reading for a fifty-year-old man, Cayce identified the lacteals as:

"That portion that makes for the ability of the system to take from the food values and prepare same in the manner in which same may be used to revivify, revitalize, recharge the system itself."

This is quite an order for any part of the body, and if true, it would explain why the castor oil packs, stimulating this area, had a general salutary effect on the system as a whole, thus beneficially affecting different conditions which seemed to have no relationship to each other.

In one of his more remarkable readings, Cayce, with no conscious knowledge of medicine or biology, in speaking of the lymph nodules found in the intestines, made oblique reference to Peyer's Patches (named for Johann Conrad Peyer, a Swiss anatomist), which were deleted from recent physiology textbooks as so little was known of their function.

Yet Cayce, in a reading for a thirty-four-year-old male, clarified the function of these patches or glands that, to McGarey's knowledge, had never before been touched upon:

"Now in the physical forces of the body (as seen and understood in the nervous systems of the body), there are those glands that secrete fluids in the nerve channels themselves."

As McGarey saw it, the substance apparently produced in Peyer's Patches became a part of the lymphocytes and was carried through the bloodstream to areas where electrical contact was made between the autonomic and the cerebrospinal nervous systems.

In the last reading he ever gave, for a sixty-six-year-old man, Cayce enlarged on his concept of the function these Peyer's Patches might perform in the body; it was interwoven like a vast, complex network in which the whole was no stronger than the weakest link—explaining the possibility of a breakdown at any point.

"These congestions caused in the trachea," Cayce began, "the conditions in the heart activity, the pressure is near normal at most times. When there is over-exercise physically, or especially of the mental forces, as of worry or anxiety, to be sure it calls on the necessity of these emunctory (excretory) activities, or those patches that are called by a man's name. These are then lessened in their number and thus make a quickening, or an anxiety, causing the flow of blood in the heart, as an organ, to dilate."

After the X-ray diagnosis came the remedy, with its remarkable appraisal of the secret workings of the body:

"In making administrations to supply those glandular centers which supply to these patches, or the emunctories, add those in the B-complex or the riboflavid, the necessary elements in each portion of the B-vitamin forces. For the excess use of salines to flush or to cleanse the colon has reduced in blood more of that which causes that plasm. Thus the inabilities of those centers, those patches through which there are the areas of the lymph circulation, are such as to cause ofttimes a state of disintegration. In these patches, then, there is a lack of sufficient globular forces to cause the coagulation in the flow of the lymph, or that portion of same which is the leucocyte, or the sticky portion in the blood is not sufficient to make perfect contact between sympathetic and cerebrospinal activities of the body."

For an open-minded researcher such as McGarey, the physiological possibilities suggested by the reading were electrifying: "Perfect contact between the sympathetic and cerebrospinal nervous systems made possible through substances created in these small patches of lymphatic tissue in the mucosal surface of the small intestine—a concept which is indeed exciting."

There were other points of possible significance: "The comment that physical or mental stress puts a stress on these areas leads one to wonder if worry or loss of sleep couldn't bring on a nervous prostration of sorts through this particular mechanism. There is also a warning relative to the excessive use of saline enemata, which also seems to be significant."

The castor oil packs apparently affected such a broad spectrum of disease that sometimes, in mistakenly treating one disease, the unguided layman cleared up an entirely different disorder. A member of the Cayce-sponsored Association for Research and Enlightenment in Virginia Beach, whose wife had developed cervical cysts at the uterine opening, reported the clearing up of these cysts (as confirmed by a physician), through use of the ARE file of Cayce readings on cysts. There was only one slight oversight. The treatment, castor oil packs, for the cervical cysts, had been erroneously drawn from the file on cystitis.

Cayce, with his irrepressible humor, would have undoubtedly had a hearty laugh over this happy boner. But he might also have philosophized pertinently, as he did once for a forty-seven-year-old man:

"For what is the source of all healing for human ills? From whence doth the body receive life, light or immortality? That the body as an active force is the result of spirit and mind, these coordinating and cooperating, enables the entity to bring forth in the experience that which may be used (castor oil, for instance). Each soul has with its power that to use which may make it at one with creative forces or God. These are the sources from which life, light and the activity of the body, mind and soul may manifest in whatever may be the active source or principle in the mind of the individual entity."

Had it not been for my own personal experience with castor

oil and actinic keratosis, even with all of Cayce's—and Mc-Garey's—documentation, I would have found it difficult to accept the still inexplicable—if eloquently hypothesized—impact of the packs on so many different ailments.

Still, there was no gainsaying McGarey's explicit reports, with a name and address for each patient and a name for every treated condition—here, bursitis, an inflammation of the shoulder joint; there, arthritis; here, a sprained arm and there, a broken foot or unsightly warts. And all the treatments worked.

In the pragmatic interest, I quote from a McGarey case report, recorded at his Phoenix office:

"A sixty-four-year-old pool maintenance man dropped a sixty-seven-pound drum on the toes of his right foot, causing what showed in X ray to be a fracture of the tuft of the great toe and a fracture of the distal phalanx of the second toe. There was much pain associated with the injury, and motion of any sort or pressure to either toe was painful. Examination showed swelling of both toes with redness and a subungual hematoma (under-the-nail swelling of blood) on the great toe. The nail was not removed because of the trauma already present and the fracture. The tissues of the great toe were markedly injured with much swelling. Diagnosis, of course, was subungual hematoma secondary to fracture of tuft of great toe.

"Treatment consisted of castor oil pack to the great toe and the second toe twice daily for an hour and a half, to be continued for two weeks. The patient was given only a soft slipper to wear on the affected foot and told not to bear weight. The tenderness subsided rapidly. The hema was gone in seven days, the patient was wearing his own shoes in ten days, at which time all tenderness was gone, and he was discharged in fourteen days, asymptomatic and with all swelling and tenderness gone."

Now an arm sprain:

"A seventeen-year-old female high school senior was seen in the office complaining of pain in her left arm as a result of injuring it during Physical Education Class earlier that day. She explained that she was doing pull-ups when she suddenly experienced a sharp pain, with rapid appearance of swelling in the left forearm. Examination revealed swelling and marked tenderness in left forearm just distal to the antecubital space in the area of the insertion of the biceps muscle at the tubercle of the radius and the deep fascia of the forearm. Diagnosis was made of sprain of the left biceps muscles at its radial insertion.

"Only treatment suggested was application of a castor oil pack over the entire proximal half of the left forearm and the elbow daily, this to be left on all night long, and worn as much during the day as possible. The patient was seen in three days and she stated that there had been a gradual disappearance of the swelling and pain. Examination showed all tenderness to be gone and all swelling subsided. She was discharged from care."

And now for warts:

"A forty-year-old married secretary was seen with common warts on her right index finger that had been present for several months. The largest was eight mm in diameter. Diagnosis was verruca vulgaris, right finger.

"These were treated by applying a band-aid to the warts on the finger, the bandage portion being first soaked in castor oil. This was worn continuously, being changed once or twice a day for a period of two months. At the end of that period of time, the warts had completely disappeared."

And uterine difficulties:

"A twenty-five-year-old housewife, two and a half months pregnant, was seen in our office, just twenty-four hours after she noted the onset of vaginal bleeding. The bleeding had stopped during the night, but a deep ache in the pelvic region persisted. She had just recovered two weeks prior from an acute upper respiratory infection. Examination, the first since the beginning of her pregnancy, showed a normal blood pressure of 100/60, temperature of 99 degrees, and pelvic findings of early pregnancy, including an enlarged uterus, and a cervix which was soft and bluish. Her last menstrual period was three months prior. Diagnosis was early pregnancy with threatened natural abortion.

"As treatment, the patient was instructed to stay at bedrest for the next three days, to use castor oil packs on the low abdomen one hour three times a day for one week, then three times a week for four weeks after that. Follow-up revealed disappearance of the ache in the pelvic region within the next three days and no recurrence of the bleeding throughout the pregnancy, which terminated normally at nine months."

McGarey was explicit in directing use of the packs:

"Prepare a soft flannel cloth which is two or three thicknesses when folded and which measures about eight inches in width and ten to twelve inches in length after it is folded. This is the size needed for abdominal application—other areas may need a different size pack, as would seem to be applicable. Pour some castor oil into a pan and soak the cloth in the oil. Then wring it out so that the cloth is wet but not drippy with the castor oil. Then apply the cloth to the area which needs treatment.

"Protection should be made against soiling the bed clothing by putting a plastic sheet underneath the body. Then a plastic covering should be applied over the soaked flannel cloth. On top of that place a heating pad and turn it up to 'medium' to begin with—then to 'high' if the body tolerates it. Then perhaps it will help if you wrap a towel around the entire area. The pack should remain in place between one and one and a half hours. You will be instructed regarding the frequency of use.

"The skin can be cleansed afterwards if desired by using water which is prepared as follows: to a quart of water, add two teaspoons baking soda. Use this to cleanse the abdomen. Keep the flannel pack in pan for future use. It need not be discarded after one application."

Although the medical fraternity, by and large, spurned Cayce in his lifetime, there were scattered expressions of interest from time to time. On one particularly noteworthy occasion, an elderly professor of anatomy had requested a Cayce reading after suffering a stroke which had forced him to give up teaching. His own physician, Dr. John Cannon, submitting his diagnosis to the sleeping Cayce, referred to a chronic mitral (heart valve) insufficiency, and an auricular fibrillation (cardiac disturbance) preceding a sudden left hemiplegia (paralysis of one lateral half of the body).

McGarey was intrigued by the liaison between an unconscious mind and a conscious professor of anatomy.

As might have been expected, the two diagnoses had little in common. Cayce did not even pick out a stroke. He did his own thing, referring to incoordination between the sympathetic and cerebrospinal nerve systems. "As we find," he said, "there are disturbances that prevent the body from its better physical functioning. These have to do primarily, we find, with that coordination between the sympathetic (or vegetative) nerve system and the cerebrospinal nerve system.

"While the effects produced are much like those from a leakage, hemorrhage, or the like, we find that these have *not* been caused by what is commonly called a stroke. While many of the organs are primarily involved, we find that the greater part of the distress arises from other sources than that ordinarily involved in such conditions."

Cayce proceeded:

"While the activities in the blood supply, the elements as related to the hormones of the blood force itself, indicate disturbances in activity, and the slowing of circulation through portions of the extremities of the body, these are not the effects as of the body or the circulation itself being involved.

"As we find then, more of the involvement is in the nervous systems, the energies of the body, the activities of the body having been such as to break down that proper coordination between the nervous systems; that is, the cerebrospinal, and the sympathetic (or vegetative) systems, as indicated.

"Because there have been those disturbances that weakened the centers or the ganglia along spinal areas, where the activities between the superficial and deeper circulation were involved, the effects produced are in the locomotories that were and are controlled by the energies from the central nervous system, the central blood supply, and the superficial blood supply.

"Thus we find these conditions existing through this body:

"The brain forces and their reflexes are active. These are near normal, save as they are disturbed by pressures that exist in the areas of the fifth and sixth dorsal (vertebrae), as through the sympathetic control, the activities in the locomotion to the left upper portion of the body. And there we have an inflammatory condition that causes pressures which prevent nerve impulse that flows with the blood supply through that portion of the arm, as to cause the lack of the ability of coordination usage of same."

The unconscious mind felt that the professor, even at his advanced age, could be helped:

"These, as we find, may be materially aided, if those elements are added to the system that are the basic effect of activity of nerve, muscle and impulses that go to supply sufficient activity in the vibrations of the body force itself.

"For all activity is of an electrical nature."

In his summation of a diagnosis made twenty-six years ago, in 1943, McGarey was obviously intrigued by the way Cayce had taken up the challenge. "Cayce indeed gave an anatomical-physiological monologue worthy of a professor of anatomy. His diagnoses seem to be a lack of proper assimilation of elements needed for nervous tissue regeneration; incoordination between the cerebrospinal and vegetative nervous systems; improper functioning and weakening of the sympathetic ganglia; and a vague glandular imbalance which affected the assimilation of foodstuffs. One might add to this a neuritis, if the inflammation he mentions is to be understood as involving sympathetic connections to the spinal nerves.

"Apparently, whether this has basis in fact or not, Cayce saw these conditions as being the underlying causes of what the professor's attending physician called mitral insufficiency and auricular fibrillation from rheumatic fever: anasarca (severe edema or swelling of dependent portions of the body due to accumulation of fluid in the intercellular spaces); left hemiplegia (or paralysis); and a neuralgia of the right shoulder and arm."

In the two diagnoses McGarey found there were certain similarities if one probed deeply enough:

"There seems to be a continuity here of (Cayce) concepts which persist in designing a physiology of the human body which has all the earmarks of being different in philosophy as well as function from that which is presently held as being valid. And yet it is only in subtle ways that there appears a divergence of ideas.

"To review Cayce's 'diagnosis' of this man's illness, we find that there is first mentioned that incoordination between the cerebrospinal and the vegetative nervous systems and this is the *primary* disturbance. Then Cayce describes an inflammation of the sympathetic ganglia which correspond to the fifth and sixth dorsal spinal nerves. His description leads one to believe that the inflammation perhaps involves not only the ganglia, but the ramicommunicantes—these on the left side of the spine in the thoracic cage (chest cavity). He indicates that this inflammatory process prevents the normal flow of impulses through the vegetative nerve supply to the blood vessels, and that which goes with the blood vessels to the entire left arm.

"Cayce implies that the inflammation in the fifth and sixth dorsal sympathetic area brings about a lack of sympathetic nerve impulse through the vasomotor system to the left arm, and that this lack produces in some strange way an inability to coordinate the use of the arm musculature."

As a traditionally schooled physician, McGarey was now on uncertain ground:

"This type of end result is not described—to my knowledge —in the medical textbooks, although it can be seen from what has been discussed in the past few paragraphs that the sympathetic disturbance which Cayce describes could have a basis in anatomic and physiologic fact. What is not understood is that such a disturbance could bring about any sort of incoordination between the autonomic and the cerebrospinal nervous system, or that it could bring about the inability to coordinate the muscles of an arm into coherent activity."

As McGarey had not described the outcome of the case, I wrote to Gladys Davis Turner, Cayce's closest associate and secretary, who had transcribed this very reading, to find how it had been received by the professor of anatomy—and what, if anything, had developed. Alas, the patient had apparently not accepted the diagnosis and corresponding treatment.

Nevertheless, a Connecticut doctor, studying the Cayce readings, expressed the view that one day Cayce would be considered a hundred years ahead of his time. For, with all of medicine—Galen, Hippocrates, and the modern researchers— there was so much still unknown of how body and mind worked separately and together. McGarey, with his thrusting mind, was at times excited by the sleeping prophet's precise delineation of how one part of the body affected the performance of another. This is why Cayce often recommended spinal adjustments even for mental illness, faintness, etc. All through Cayce there is a definite association between the cerebrospinal or voluntary nervous system and the autonomic or involuntary, controlling the subconscious functions of mind and body. "Cayce," McGarey pointed out, "indicated that these two systems meet intimately in the spinal cord or the sympathetic trunk ganglia, and that there is created there a coordination with the blood supply. He indicated that when an incoordination exists here, the blood vessels do not perform their varied duties well, thus bringing about certain disease conditions of the body."

This was amply illustrated in a Cayce reading for a forty-four-year-old woman with anemia:

"There have been those operative forces which have allowed or caused adhesions and lesions to form in areas where the cerebrospinal and sympathetic nervous systems and blood supply coordinate, in the brachial areas especially.

"The results have been and are incoordination and a form of anemia that will be hard to combat unless certain measures or precautions are taken. These conditions, as we find might be termed accidents, in that there were, in the healing of the body, conditions where nerve tissue or tendons became involved, and thus the circulation, especially in the upper extremities, is such that these have become useless, in a manner, in comparison to their normal activities.

"This is by pressure, and through the adhesions and lesions formed, there are those conditions producing the complications such that nerve and blood supply are not receiving their proper stimulation for the activity and circulation.

"Glands are involved in this. Thus, we have a progressive activity of incoordination, or poor circulation."

In the cases where Cayce used castor oil packs, McGarey noted that the most striking incoordination was described as existing between the autonomic and the cerebrospinal nervous systems, with singularly different effects in each instance. "Cayce," McGarey said, "indicated that lack of proper coordination at this level was deeply involved in the causation of diseases as widely diverse in their apparent etiology as multiple sclerosis, appendicitis, anemia, hemiplegia, and grand mal epilepsy."

Following along logically, as he thought, McGarey concluded that "this break in coordination must be found in the upper ganglia which supply sympathetics to the visual and auditory apparatus, as well as further down autonomically, where the organs of the body receive their nerve supply."

In one individual, a reading turned up a rather amazing complex of symptoms, which, according to Cayce, all come about as a direct result of this break in coordination. The symptoms: superficial circulatory disturbances, insomnia, arthritis, auditory disturbances, visual difficulties, probable psychoneuroses.

Long before traditional medicine considered a good share of illness psychogenic in origin, Cayce was saying in trance that frayed emotions were often the primary causation of this critical incoordination between the autonomic and the cerebrospinal nervous systems. "The field of psychosomatic medicine," McGarey relevantly observed, "has led our thinking in the present day more into the belief and understanding that emotions, attitudes and feelings are closely associated with disease processes, not only resultant from them but causative in many cases."

As a doctor of twenty-five years standing, trained at a conventional medical school, the University of Cincinnati, McGarey was all too aware of the problems connected with medical acceptance, even for research purposes, of a clairvoyant's physiological concepts. But he was hopeful. "Perhaps we will gradually accept more and more the fact that emotions cause physical changes through glandular outpourings of hormones and increased flow of energies especially over the sympathetic nervous system. In such an acceptance, the oneness of the body with the mind will be more completely seen and we will begin to associate our physical bodies more with the mind and the spirit within. Presently, however, this is too drastic a concept to tolerate. We (the medical profession) are not ready to look at an appendicitis, a kidney infection or a thyroid disease and admit that attitudes of mind in relation to our friends or family—an emotional flare-up with a father or a sister—could possibly have anything to do with causing this physical disease."

Then, with gentle irony:

"These, you see, are not yet today psychosomatic conditions. We do accept a stomach ulcer, among many other conditions, but it apparently must come just a bit at a time."

The cases Cayce had the most difficulty with involved a negative mental attitude. "This attitude is perhaps one of the most difficult to overcome," McGarey observed from his own clinical experience, "and at the same time causes perhaps more difficulty to the body through creating stresses and an easily upset nervous system."

He singled out the case of a fifty-one-year-old teacher, whose problem Cayce had obviously correctly diagnosed, in view of her own subsequent report. "Cayce," McGarey pointed out, "suggested a simple regime to overcome the asthenia (debility) from which the woman was suffering, but he apparently also was aware, in his unconscious state, of the woman's resistance to changing her mental attitudes—so his most important recommendation was almost an aside:

" 'Also, there has been, and exists in the present, incoordination between the nerve systems of the body. An overanxiety, a fear, has caused overtension in the nervous system, especially as related to the areas in the upper dorsal or through the brachial areas, and has caused a great shock to the body, so that the ability of the nerves to coordinate in replenishing energies through the circulation has caused this great weakness which exists in the body.

" 'These may be materially aided but it will require as much activity of the mental self as those administrations from any mechanical or medicinal nature.' "

As it developed, it was considerably easier to apply nostrums to the body than release resentments from mind and body. Seven years later the woman confirmed that Cayce had been right about her shock, described as an "emotional upset." And she was still upset whenever she thought about it, which was practically all the time. "The upset," she wrote, "was partly caused by a half-crazed principal with whom I was unfortunately working after a thyroidectomy when I was weak. He had suffered severe mental trouble, and in his mental weakness he had the idea I wanted his position and was more than unjust and cruel."

The thyroid operation occurred six years before the Cayce

reading. The teacher had also experienced appendicitis attacks, relieved, by her own testimony, by castor oil packs.

As with others who didn't report complete success, she followed the treatment only in part, and never changed her mental attitude.

What could be learned from Cayce? What, essentially, was the basic etiology—or causative process—behind a variety of illnesses which responded to a single therapy, castor oil packs?

Pressures on spinal nerves, even emotionally induced, as Cayce implied, apparently set up chain activity blocking or pinching off "impulses for proper function and tone of the arterial, venous and lymphatic systems." As McGarey reviewed the concept, "the incoordination then might be understood to derive from pressure on the anterior and posterior spinal nerves and the dorsal root ganglia," these being the centers of coordination referred to in this teacher's particular case.

How did castor oil packs affect this incoordination and remove the symptoms doctors call disease? In exploring this avenue, McGarey, having closely studied the Cayce readings on the packs, applied them empirically to the general practice of medicine. At random, he selected eighty-one cases representing dozens of different ailments which had not responded to conventional therapy. The dramatic results were confirmation, not only of Cayce's, but McGarey's judgment.

"Castor oil packs," he reported, "have taken me in my therapeutic efforts from the misery of a sprained ankle through the agonies of an inflamed perineum to the discomfort of a stiff neck."

But even more important than the fact that castor oil healed was the underlying Cayce concept of the coordinated whole, with dis-ease merely being symptomatic of dis-coordination. "At this point," McGarey observed, "we are confronted with the necessity of approaching an understanding—at a basic level—of the nervous system of mankind."

McGarey's own professional schooling was reflected in his search through Cayce for the key to man's well-being. He had five objectives:

"To stimulate interest in this therapeutic regime.

"To show the exceptionally wide latitude of use possible with the castor oil packs.

"To present and coordinate evidence that there is actual beneficial response in the human body to the application of these packs.

"To discuss theoretical considerations relative to the action of the packs on the body.

"To begin to explore the validity of a unique understanding of physiological functioning of the human body found in the Edgar Cayce readings."

In the course of this elaborate program, McGarey treated some 101 conditions in his 81 patients. In 74 instances, the patients responded in a manner rated "excellent." Oddly, the results were better—82 percent "excellent"—when the packs were all that were used, as against 61 percent "excellent" when they were used in conjunction with other therapy.

With castor oil packs there was little danger of overtreatment, the bane of so many patients. "It is fortunate indeed," the doctor observed, "that the human body takes even the least assistance at times and responds in a noble fashion. Even taking this assist of the unconscious vital forces of the body into consideration, however, the responses, especially in the group treated only with the packs, were highly gratifying."

In analyzing the Cayce castor oil readings, the doctor noted there were no cardiac conditions which were treated, no respiratory ailments, no basic neurological disorders (despite the importance of this area), and no true endocrine difficulties, except those directly associated with the ovary and its function as reflected in the many diseases of the female generative system that were listed.

The commonest area treated was within the abdominal and pelvic cavities, where the gastrointestinal and the genitourinary systems are situated.

Widely prevalent were muscular conditions, arthritic disturbances, circulatory problems involving hypertension, headache and tension syndromes, and trauma apparently of sufficient impact emotionally to produce the incoordination between the physical and nervous systems that Cayce—and McGarey—dwelt upon.

McGarey had his own ideas as to why the packs were especially effective in the abdominal area. "Cayce," he stressed, "talks of the importance of the assimilation of foodstuffs into our bodies and the elimination of body wastes, and there is reference to the castor oil packs being of benefit to both these systems. Thus, if there was anything to the readings, the stomach, intestines, and associated organs, and the kidneys, being the major areas of assimilation and elimination, should respond dramatically to the packs—and did."

McGarey treated 30 conditions which had their pathological site in the abdominal cavity. "Results obtained were 25 excellent, or 83 percent, 2 good, and 3 poor." Only 10 percent were clearly unresponsive.

Where the problem was specifically eliminatory, the results were even better. "Diseases of the large bowel produced the highest percentage of excellent responses, 92 percent," McGarey observed. These diseases "included such conditions as constipation, intestinal obstruction due to fecal impaction, colitis, diarrhea, hemorrhoids and rectal fissures."

The best results, curiously, were in bodily conditions traumatically induced and in postsurgical care of wounds. In twelve such cases, all responses were rated excellent. The conditions most resistant were basic hypertension and peptic ulcer.

Working in his Phoenix clinic, McGarey was understandably elated—and mystified—by the magical way in which hot castor oil soaked in flannel cloth and applied to the skin brought about a startling improvement in body function. "At times it caused me, even as I watched with unbelieving eyes, to ask myself, 'What happened? What really goes on within the body that restores a disturbed gravid pregnant uterus to normal; that cures a muscular spasm and dissipates a headache; that allows an inflamed gall bladder to regain its health; that heals an infected wound; that gets rid of a threatening appendicitis as if it were no more than a mild cough; that mobilizes a fecal impaction which hours earlier had threatened a life; that rids the body of a disturbance in the reproductive system that might have dislodged a pregnancy before the mother even knew she was carrying it? What happens when castor oil is applied, many times without any heat whatsoever, that can have such an effect? How is it absorbed? Why does it work? How does it work?' "

There were theories, but meanwhile, the treatment spoke for itself, making converts first of the patients. "Almost routinely," McGarey pointed out, "the individual who uses a pack for the first time will change from a hesitant user to a happily surprised enthusiast."

Every little ripple in the therapeutic ally was noted by McGarey. Five of his eighty-one cases were appendix problems, and the four whose response was excellent were children, nine, ten and eleven years old. The lone refractory case was a middle-aged woman, suggesting that "the young people were much more able to muster the forces of resistance to disease on stimulation."

All of the youngsters responded promptly. In one case a youngster had been given an antibiotic injection and a tranquilizing, antinausea suppository. But nausea, vomiting, lower abdominal cramping, and pain continued for three days, until the castor oil packs were applied to the abdominal area. The symptoms disappeared overnight. "These were gone," McGarey recorded, "when the boy was examined the next morning after using the packs all night. His abdominal tenderness was also absent and all findings were normal."

In a second case the improvement was equally dramatic. "The child noted onset of abdominal pain two days prior to his visit to my office. He vomited once and had some cramping pains in his belly. This eased up the next day somewhat, but recurred the following morning. There was no diarrhea, but some nausea. Examination showed a subnormal temperature of 97.8 degrees and well-localized tenderness over the right lower quadrant; a slightly inflamed pharynx was noted. The packs without heat were used three times a day for two days, when reexamination showed only minimal tenderness at the umbilicus (which subsequently cleared), and absence of the abdominal discomfort which the body had noted."

But the apparent appendicitis in a forty-six-year-old woman was another story. "There was nausea and lower abdominal pain which had its onset at 2:30 P. M. and was thought to be due to food ingestion. The castor oil packs were kept on for about twelve hours, brought no relief, and the patient was hospitalized. A complicating renal (kidney) infection was suspected but ruled out by I.V. pyelogram (pelvic X-ray). Surgery for the appendix was decided upon when the tenderness became more localized and diagnostic."

Despite this failure, attributable perhaps to the complicating kidney irritation—or possibly a lack of responsive lacteals—McGarey felt the successes advanced the concept that castor oil, absorbed through the skin, "stimulated the bodily function that removed the products of inflammation, as they existed in the appendix, from the appendix itself, leaving it freer to function normally."

Physician McGarey theorized that the lymphatics, stimulated by the packs, drained wastes from the individual cells much as the intestines remove wastes from the body as a unit. The efficiency with which the lymphatics operated was closely tied in, McGarey pointed out, to the parasympathetic or autonomic nervous system, charged with rebuilding and healing the body. "Thus we see the framework for a mechanism which could be effective in these four cases of appendicitis, and which would even explain why one did not respond. Castor oil, absorbed into the tissues, may in its vibratory activity (for all things are in essence vibratory in nature) act to stimulate that parasympathetic nerve supply which is anatomically located in the treated area, which then would stimulate the lymphatics to drain more adequately the tissues which are under duress."

The lone failure was as revealing, in a way, as the cures: "With such a mechanism in operation it can be readily seen that anyone who has gone downhill relative to resistance, endurance, response to injury or general body health, would not have a top-notch thymus-lymphatic system which is the basic regulator of health and disease. Such a person would have a slower response or perhaps little response at all to stimulation toward healing."

Elsewhere, McGarey had success with a stubborn gall bladder case and with severe irregularities in pregnancy. With the gall bladder patient, he was not sure that it wasn't just the heat —standard procedure for this disorder—and not necessarily the hot castor oil itself which had brought about a dramatic improvement overnight.

But with the pregnant women, there was little question what the ameliorating agency was. One patient was threatening to abort, while the other had a pelvic mass, and at the time did not know she was pregnant. "The packs, used conservatively—not all night long as in several other cases—produced clinical evidence of improved function of the generative organs and their associated structure. It became evident that through this medium of therapy, the body as a unit became more able to muster its defense mechanisms and reverse the conditions of ill health which were found to be present on initial examination."

Nobody poring over the Cayce files was long immune to the seer's philosophic reaction to life, illness and the pursuit of happiness. And the Phoenix physician was no exception. "This area of the body where woman becomes creative at least in the physical sense," he philosophized, "is also the area where cleansing of the body takes place, through excretion. The parasympathetic supply to both functions arises in the sacral nerves. So we wonder if these two functions—creativity and cleansing—don't have a closer association than we usually suspect."

The doctor-philosopher continued:

"Would it be unrealistic to propose that any striving of mankind, when it is done with true creativity, is cleansing to the consciousness of the individual? Or would it be more proper to state that any work or daily activity that a person might be faced with doing is done creatively in the truest sense if he feels a cleansing or a purification in his consciousness? Bodily functions running parallel with so-called mental or spiritual values —if these cannot be related to each other in the human body, then any philosophic, psychologic, religious or theological concept of the oneness of all things holds little validity."

McGarey—like Cayce—obviously believed in a Universal Oneness, the God-force from which Cayce's Universal Consciousness stemmed, with man at times the meaningful instrument of a Divine will of which at best he has but the briefest glimpse.

But the philosopher soon gave way to the practitioner. "To return to the gynecological conditions under consideration," McGarey stated, "we may be seeing here the acceleration of cleansing as it occurs in the body, added to the stimulation of the creative or generative organs through the mechanism of the improved functioning of the sacral parasympathetic and its ramifications throughout the lower portion of the body. For this one source of activity—the sacral parasympathetic—would, at least to some degree, control the rebuilding forces within these organs and structures, the general eliminative activity and health of the body, and the lymphatic activity as it pertains to drainage from cellular components within the area . . . acting here within the human body to bring about health and its more desirable state of the body."

Because of the packs' dramatic effect on the two pregnancies, McGarey postulated they might have a salutary effect on pregnancies generally. "One wonders," he said, "how many birth abnormalities and anomalies might be prevented through use of a series of packs during early pregnancy as a preventive routine. If the activity of the packs is such as to improve function as seems apparent, then it would follow rather naturally that less abnormal function would be found in the presence of more normal function." In other words, as the castor oil packs corrected one irregularity in the pelvic area, they created a better atmosphere for the healthy growth of the embryo.

With a delicate irony, McGarey speculated that possibly this was too logical for the so-called scientific mind, steeped in standard texts. "But then perhaps it is not advisable to be so direct in one's logic. But it would still seem reasonable that one could, through the use of castor oil packs, used preventively, bring healthier babies into the world."

Just as Dr. Ketchum had his Favorite Case—Cayce—Dr. McGarey had his favorite. He called it the Case of the Curly Hair, and Sherlock Holmes had no stranger case. A forty-two-year-old housewife, a registered nurse, had requested that McGarey check her blood pressure. She felt she was suffering from hypertension, and had a host of curious symptoms, the strangest being that her once curly hair had become straight and would not suds up when she shampooed. The symptoms had developed after she had started taking an oral contraceptive, but no medical doctor had related the two.

The case was so unusual that I combed through Dr. McGarey's records for a fuller report. The nurse had discovered that her blood pressure was elevated six months before she visited the McGarey clinic. But the history started sixteen months before when she began taking The Pill. After being on The Pill for two months, she had been emotionally upset by a daughter's quarrel with a boyfriend. She grew progressively more disturbed. "At four months on the medication," a report said, "she developed noticeable increased nervousness. At five months she experienced a twenty-one-hour uterine hemorrhage that was difficult to stop. At the six-month period, she noted cramps in both legs. At the nine-month mark, when her personal tension (from her daughter's romance) was at its height, she developed swelling of the left calf and the cramps in her legs became at times excruciating."

Now for the symptom that gave the case its name:

"Also, she noted when she washed her hair, for the first time in her life, she could not make her hair develop a suds. She changed shampoos three times to no effect, and the beauty parlor met with the same results—no sudsing. At this point it was noted that her blood pressure was elevated. Her legs continued to bother her severely, and the veins in her legs were distended until, after thirteen months on the medication, she stopped it of her own accord. Her gynecologist, according to her account, did not believe that the medication was causing her trouble.

"When she stopped the medication, her veins became normal and the cramps in her legs stopped bothering her. Her blood pressure remained elevated, however; she remained tense, and her hair retained the remarkable non-sudsing quality, and the texture of her hair was poorer and it could not curl as well as it did before all this was started."

McGarey's report continued:

"She then saw an internist (her second doctor) who examined her thoroughly and could find nothing wrong with her except the elevated blood pressure which he did not think was caused by tension or by the medication. It was within a few weeks after this that she came to our office. Examination revealed a blood pressure of 180/110 to 160/98, with no other abnormal findings.

"She did not tell me about the hair until later on. She was treated for three months with conventional medication for hypertension, and the blood pressure remained constant, not responding. Then about six months after she had stopped her medication, she complained of palpitation and tenseness again, and I was ready to administer the packs."

McGarey, primarily a traditionalist, had treated this patient as the other doctors had, with traditional therapy at first, turning to the packs only when orthodoxy didn't work.

His diagnosis was hypertension and oral contraceptive reaction, and therapy was continued with the hypertensive medication. The only other therapy was abdominal castor oil packs, applied three consecutive nights of each week for three weeks, one and a half hours each treatment. Each week, after the third pack, the patient took one ounce of olive oil orally for cleansing purposes.

The results were electrifying:

"The patient followed the instructions, and reported when she returned in three weeks that after one week's treatment with the packs, her hair sudsed like it hadn't in nearly ten months, and there was a marked improvement in its texture and its curling qualities. The hair was curly again."

Inexplicably, the packs were effective even in areas remote from the lymphatic centers. In one instance, when all else failed, a pack on the neck cured a pain in the neck. A music teacher had reported a headache of thirteen days duration. He used heat with his pack, applied to neck and upper back; within two days the pain had disappeared. Obviously, there was a relaxation of muscular spasm. "Other modes of therapy—including physiotherapy —might well have brought just as good results," McGarey conceded, "but this patient *had* already used many other means of treatment with poor results when this method was begun."

Where muscular spasm was the primary pathology, McGarey felt hot packs should be the treatment of choice—so effective were they. "The heat," he stressed, "was not the answer to the relaxation, else heat would bring by itself just as much response." It didn't. But it was questionable whether the pack without the heat would do as well. "The combination of castor oil and heat, in this situation," he decided, "together brought about the substantial therapeutic effect."

However, castor oil was effective without heat, as in the case of an injured finger, where a specific response was induced in tissues where organs were not involved. "Here," McGarey pointed out, "we find only skin, subcutaneous tissue, muscle, fascia, fat, interstitial tissue, blood vessels, nerves, lymphatics and bone. There were no organs, no glands, no tubular structures, no lymph center, and no ganglia or other nerve center."

The finger, that of a sixty-two-year-old man, healed in two days despite an infection running with pus. "Fingers which have been infected as his was," McGarey observed, "and which have developed a pustular reaction so severe as to cause a rather diffuse cellulitis, just simply do not clear up entirely in two days under the very best of therapeutic circumstances." But this finger did, and so did similarly infected hands, arms, and legs.

Since appendicitis and intestinal obstructions were conditions for which heat was specifically contraindicated, the benefits from the packs obviously came from the castor oil—and a positive attitude.

One of McGarey's favorite patients was an eighty-nine-year-old woman. She had an intestinal obstruction, which defied surgery because of her years. Her life was at stake, and McGarey had no choice but to use the packs as a last resort. "There had been a large bowel impaction with fecal material that produced actual intestinal obstruction to the degree that serious consequences were already being experienced. The large bowel was probably nearing a point of complete inactivity insofar as its proper duties of evacuation were concerned, and the small bowel was so at war with events as they were transpiring that reverse peristalsis was bringing fecal material up to the stomach to be expelled through persistent episodes of emesis (vomiting). Gas throughout the system producing serious distention completed the picture of an intestinal tract that had moved a long way from its original state of health which provided peristalsis and moisture sufficient to move the bowels regularly and without difficulty."

The organs and structures of elimination—both the large bowel from the midpoint of the transverse colon and the urinary system—receive their motor innervation, or nerve impulse, from the parasympathetic portion of the autonomic nervous system which has its source in the sacral nerves. "This eighty-nine-year-old patient spent a lot of her time sitting, and with little padding on her buttocks, undoubtedly produced many pressures on the sacral portion of her anatomy which could easily cause embarrassment to the sacral nerve supply. Reinforced by poor bowel habits and a diet that was not perfect, and enhanced by practically no exercise, the entire motor system of nerves to the large bowel undoubtedly became sluggish to the point of nearly complete inactivity."

Treatment swiftly followed diagnosis, for there was little time to squander:

"Packs were applied to the abdomen. Nausea ceased, emesis slowed down and stopped, peristalsis began in the large bowel, enough fluid was produced by the cells of the large bowel to soften the fecal mass, and the health of the cells throughout the intestinal cavity improved. After forty-eight hours, when an evacuant suppository was used, the intestine was in good enough health to respond normally and the contents were expelled. The edema (swelling) which had persisted then disappeared, undoubtedly due to the more efficient functioning of the other portion of the eliminating system, the kidneys."

Again, McGarey was not sure how the castor oil had worked. "Was the action here completely through the stimulation to the nervous supply," he pondered, "or was it another instance of cleansing of tissue cells so that, as nerve cells, as muscle cells, as intestinal endothelial (membrane-like) cells, they became more capable of performing the function to which they have been assigned by the body as a whole?"

Nevertheless, magically, it had worked. "The fact that she improved is indisputable, the fact that she made a remarkable change physiologically cannot be denied, and the fact that she had no other medication with which to do this than the castor oil applied locally was equally evident."

There was possibly another factor in the old woman's remarkable recovery. She had that most important attribute of all, according to Cayce, right thinking. She harbored no resentments, no grievances, held nothing in; there was no rankling lack of harmony to perpetuate bodily incoordination. Indeed, she was so cheerful that she won the doctor's admiration. "She even experienced pain with a joke and a smile," he said. "Her ability to keep all those taking care of her in good humor made the job easier for all concerned."

Like Cayce, McGarey felt a positive attitude was helpful, and a negative, harmful. "The part that this attitude of joy and happiness plays in the continuance of good health has not yet been adequately evaluated, but it has to be a major factor wherever it exists. Anger at the dinner table brings about indigestion, while a happy meal is a beneficial one. Humor, then, must help the gastrointestinal tract, perhaps far more than we know or realize. And, in similar manner, it may be that this little old lady with her happy disposition is alive only because of it."

Hemorrhoids responded similarly to room-temperature packs. A sixty-two-year-old man had hemorrhoids for three weeks before consulting McGarey; three days before his visit they became hard and started bleeding. "Examination revealed several large thrombosed (clotted) hemorrhoids, quite tender, and extruding from the anal orifice." The patient was directed to use packs for two hours, remove them for two hours, and repeat this pattern during the daytime hours for the next four days.

As with the old lady, the results were remarkable. "His bleeding stopped, the pain disappeared, and when he was examined at the end of the four-day period, only small hemorrhoidal tags remained—no thrombi or sign of such, and no residual tenderness."

The doctor had a tip for use of packs in any perineal (groin area) disturbance, hemorrhoids included. "A pack (without the heating pad) can be kept in place while the patient remains ambulatory by utilizing the same mechanism that keeps a diaper in place. The flannel, folded after being soaked in castor oil, is applied to the hemorrhoids directly. Then a protective plastic sheet is placed over that, and a pad made out of any sort of cloth, washcloth, towel or the like, applied over that and held up with a sanitary napkin belt. This provides excellent contact between the afflicted area and the castor oil, and promotes the accumulation of body heat at that point."

The packs apparently had a sedative effect, again emphasizing the close association between mind and body. "The peacefulness which several noticed," McGarey observed, "may point up a relationship between emotion and body." And this relationship was negatively apparent. A fifty-one-year-old woman, overwhelmed by a marital breakup, took on a veritable host of symptoms: depression, nervousness, numbness, anorexia, nausea, abdominal cramps, distention, mucus and diarrhea—a prime example of what Cayce meant by dis-ease.

Treatment with packs over a four-week period considerably restored the body, so that the patient could again function normally. However, the emotional problem was not solved, and the physical symptoms recurred. "Healing," McGarey philosophized, "may really be peace—a peace that comes to rest in the body, that is a reflection of the peace that passeth understanding. We see it come to the body much as peace is allowed to come to earth: a nation here and a nation there. When we find real peace in the earth, we may see a state of health having come to all bodies."

6

So Long, California?

"How come," slyly asked Los Angeles radio interrogator Joe Pyne, "that if Los Angeles is going into the sea, as Edgar Cayce said, that you are so calmly sitting here?"

I expected to be soon on my way East to New York (for which Cayce also predicted disaster), but in any case, the sage of Virginia Beach had not foreseen the holocaust shattering the island of Manhattan, California, Connecticut, Japan, and sundry other parts of the globe until the "latter portion" of a specified 1958 to 1998 breakup period—namely from 1978 on.

However, I replied, as Cayce had years before when questioned by a man concerned about a safe place for himself and his family to live:

"We shouldn't worry so much about where we live as how we live."

Pyne's reply, as I recall it, was a snort, as though only the destruction of Los Angeles on the spot would make a believer of him.

Actually, in reviewing the Cayce earth change predictions, many of which have already materialized, it becomes obvious to the Cayce-oriented observer that Americans have nothing to fear in the way of great coastal destruction until 1998 itself —the ultimate year, after which every other Cayce prediction will be necessarily anticlimactic.

Cayce's subconscious picked out the climactic chain of events on a sultry day in August, 1941, when he told a harried businessman who had been thinking of moving from New York to California: "Los Angeles, San Francisco, most of all these will be among those that will be destroyed before New York even."

Five years earlier, Cayce had been asked, "What great change or the beginning of what change, if any, is to take place in the earth in the year 2000 to 2001 A.D.?"

And he had replied:

"When there is a shifting of the poles [apparently the final decisive turn of the earth's axis which he said had been tilting since 1936]."

And so it would be off with the old and on with the new, in the interval between 1998 and 2000, with no clear idea of what that new would be like, except for the foreknowledge that the future stretches endlessly, despite a few possibly unpleasant interludes, its order already established, just as the movements of endless other planets have been ordained.

Still, many were filled with fear by the prophecies of doom and destruction, not believing as Cayce did—and Another—that life is an everlasting cycle.

And so the negative was accented. In the summer of 1968, when strong tremors shook the northern part of Japan, some news commentators expressed the view that with another jolt like it, northern Japan would crash into the sea, as Cayce had predicted in trance years before.

Alarmists, manufacturing a 1969 earthquake scare, were forever getting ahead of Cayce's own time clock, which gave New Yorkers and Californians three months to get ready.

The warning was well marked. "When Vesuvius starts to go," said a romantic young physicist from Los Angeles' neighboring Manhattan Beach, "that's when I'm going to clear out."

Cayce, as she pointed out, had keyed his climactic prediction of upheavals to telltale eruptions in Vesuvius and the West Indian island of Martinique. "If there are greater activities in the Vesuvius or Pelée," this girl quoted, wide-eyed, from a Cayce reading, "then the southern coast of California—and the areas between Salt Lake and the southern portions of Nevada —may expect, within the three months following same, an inundation by the earthquakes. But these are to be more in the southern than the northern hemisphere."

In other words, South America, whose west coast from Chile to Peru was earthquake-prone anyway, would be hit worse than even North America which would lose most of Los Angeles, San Francisco, and New York.

Since Cayce had also predicted flooding of the southeastern United States and the disappearance of northern Europe in the twinkling of an eye, I wondered what refuge point this girl had picked out for herself.

"Virginia Beach," she said. "That's where Cayce himself went because it was so safe."

There were other safety areas mentioned by Cayce: Ohio, Indiana, Illinois, southern and eastern Canada. But if a dream he had in 1936 was prophetic, there wouldn't be much choice if, and when, the upheavals occurred. In the only instance in which he manifested any prescience of flying saucers, Cayce saw himself reborn in A.D. 2100 in Nebraska, then the westernmost part of the country. With a group of savants as companions, he flew over the stricken nation in a cigar-shaped metal flying boat, traveling at tremendous supersonic speeds, finally settling on the ruins of a great city. Swarms of workmen were laboring to clear the rubble and rebuild a once formidable metropolis.

In the dream Cayce looked around in puzzlement. "What is this place?" he demanded.

A workman glanced up in surprise. "Why, New York City," he replied.

On waking, Cayce could not get the dream out of his mind, though not for five years did he forecast the geological changes entailing great destruction. As he sometimes did when consciously perplexed, he asked his secretary, Gladys Davis, to probe his unconscious mind on the significance of the dream. Replying, the sleeping Cayce declared that the Bible often meant exactly what it said, and he quoted from Scripture: "Though the heavens and the earth pass away, my word shall not pass away."

The girl from Manhattan Beach was less than reassured. "It's life on earth, not everlasting life, that I'm concerned about," she said rather tartly. She was barely twenty-five.

I wondered at her concern.

"So much of what Cayce predicted has already come true," she said. "He said that the forty-year breakup period would be ushered in with Mt. Etna erupting, and in 1959 the Sicilian volcano erupted for the first time in years. Then new land formed, as he said, in the Atlantic, off Iceland, and in the Pacific, off Ecuador; there were strange risings and sinkings in the Mediterranean after the devastating 1960 earthquake at Agadir, in Morocco, and now the latest destruction in that area in the terrible Iran quakes shows the momentum building up."

She cocked an eye at me.

"All of California," she said, "is a potential earthquake, and only a few months ago [in the spring of 1968] Professor Charles Richter, for whom the earthquake scale was named, warned people worried about earthquakes not to come to California to live."

Richter, viewing the Golden State's 2,500 miles of earth faults, acknowledged that no section of the state was immune, and two-thirds of the nation's leading geophysicists agreed that a major earthquake of the type that destroyed San Francisco in 1906 was long overdue.

Nevertheless, in certain circles, the very mention of a quake was taboo in California, and real estate interests successfully resisted earthquake zoning and put up housing projects right on the great San Andreas fault itself.

Greed and violence, Cayce said, would one day be reflected in the furious reaction of a long-suffering earth. And while it was hard to reconcile cause and effect in this connection, there was no doubt in Cayce's consciousness that the two were irretrievably interwoven, just as in Sodom and Gomorrah in Biblical times.

But even God had to work through the tools at hand. And the girl from Manhattan Beach was well aware that Cayce had attributed the predicted destruction to a tilt in the rotational axis of the earth. In a 1932 reading, Cayce said that the tilt, commencing in 1936, would first manifest itself in 1958, accelerate with time, as once before, 980,000 years ago when, some geologists think, the magnetic poles last reversed themselves.

There were already indications, the girl from Manhattan Beach said, that history might be repeating itself. There was definite evidence, some scientists felt, that the earth's magnetic field had already weakened to a point which would indicate a reversal of polarity. What is now north would become south, and south, north. What might happen in time, as the poles shift, was dramatically elaborated by Dr. Keith L. McDonald, a research physicist with the Environmental Sciences Services Administration of the U.S. Department of Commerce. Ice caps could melt, raising the sea level over coastal cities; valleys now lush and green could become deserts; and the barren wastes might become productive fields.

There were many theories about the dynamic changes the earth seemed heir to. Scientist McDonald, never having heard of Cayce, theorized that heat released from the inner core of the earth might be the cause of a weakening magnetic field, whereas Cayce obviously felt that the tilt might be causing the heat which in turn weakened the field serving as a shield against radiation bombardment from outer space.

Obviously, something was going on. Some land in England was inexorably sinking into the sea. Simultaneously, land masses in Scandinavia and Canada were steadily rising, making it possible for an eventual thaw to tumble down on more temperate regions below. The continents of Africa, Australia, and South America were moving, almost imperceptibly, in a northerly direction. A coastal area of California was sliding into the Pacific at the rate of two inches a year. The tempo of earthquakes was mounting in the Mediterranean and around the Ring of Fire, from Hawaii to the Aleutians, where North America's strongest quake had shifted the crust of the earth for hundreds of miles in 1964's unforgettable blast, foreshadowed by Cayce nearly twenty-five years before.

Certainly, it had all happened before. The Gulf of California, lying over a slumbering fault, had not always been a gulf, and the Arabian deserts, rich in oil, were once wooded, carbon-forming forests rich in foliage. As man measures history, we remember only a few thousand years. And yet, not having any certain knowledge of the recent past, we still close our minds to an Atlantis, when there could have been a dozen lost continents without our being the wiser. Fortunately, the younger generation, brought up in the Space Age, not steeped in stultifying tradition, has turned eagerly, pragmatically, to the study of Cayce and his marvels. Cayce's description of Atlantis was particularly entrancing. This continent, he said, first broke up into five great islands seventeen thousand years ago, and was finally wholly submerged, the victim of its own wickedness, in a catastrophic atomic explosion tied in with the great flood.

"In relation to the history of Atlantis as presented," Cayce had been asked, "at what period did the flood as recorded in the Bible in which Noah took part, occur?"

"In the second of the eruptions," Cayce replied, "or, as is seen, two thousand—two thousand and six [eight thousand years] —before the Prince of Peace, as time is counted now, or light years—day and night years."

Atlantis, for Cayce buffs and even for intrepid oceanographers, was now very much in the limelight. The girl from Manhattan Beach was properly excited by the Atlantean mystery and Cayce's prediction that the lost continent would show signs of rising again in 1968 or 1969. In the Bimini area, in the summer of 1968, scientists reported sighting an underground temple. In June of 1940, she recalled, Cayce had said, "And Poseidia will be among the first portions of Atlantis to rise again. Expect it in sixty-eight or sixty-nine. Not so far away."

Subsequently, Cayce was even more explicit, keying his prediction to the ominous turn of events toward the close of the century: "Yet, as time draws nigh when changes are to come about," he said, "there may be the opening of those three places where the records are one, to those that are the initiates in the knowledge of the One God. The temple [on Atlantis] will rise again." He added the forecast: "Also there will be the opening of the temple of records in Egypt; and those records that were put into the heart of the Atlantean land may also be found there. The records are one."

Dramatically, in September of 1968, a Miami archeologist, Dr. Manson Valentine, formerly at the universities of North Carolina and Yale, reported discovering an ancient underwater temple that could be part of the legendary lost continent. He was not quite sure, he said, because the temple was so near the surface that it would appear to be too recent to be part of a culture which had reputedly disappeared into the sea ten thousand years ago. "The structure is man-made," Valentine said. "It couldn't be a freak of nature. It is about one hundred and ten feet long and seventy-five feet wide. The top is about two feet above the ocean floor. It is rectangular, with the east end and southwest corner partitioned off. At the east end are three rooms."

Without closer examination of the structure, the Valentine search party, including oceanographer Dmitri Rebikoff, could not determine whether it is Atlantean, Mayan, or what. "The age of it is what is puzzling us," Valentine said. "I've found other temples with this pattern of structure, which has to do with metaphysical rituals." Actually, if Cayce was correct in placing Atlantis, and if the continental shelf in the Bahaman area is rising, there should be other exhibits in time. "The whole Bahaman area," Valentine said, "is a mass of strange geology. There are walls that have been discovered underwater near Bimini that we will investigate, and there are a number of other areas about fifty miles south of Bimini we'll look into."

Cayce had put the southeastern part of Atlantis right where Valentine may have found it, declaring that it broke up originally into five islands, the three largest being Poseidia, Aryan, and Og. In the breakup, he said, the natives of this presumably advanced culture dispersed to the Yucatan, forming the Mayan culture, and to the Mediterranean area, where they transformed Egypt from an agrarian to an industrial culture.

Historically, only Plato touched upon Atlantis. Quoting the elder statesman Solon, quoting the folklore of ancient Egyptian priests, he cited a successful repulse of these over-the-water invaders by the stalwart Athenians.

However, reading between the lines, it is obvious that the Athenians, if the Plato story is correct, merely turned back a group of stragglers, the main forces stretching out along the Mediterranean basin. The Cayce placement of Atlantis smack in the center of the Atlantic, with the Azores the easternmost part, had understandably puzzled the girl from Manhattan Beach.

"Not so long ago," she said, "I read in the New York *Times* that some scientists now accept Atlantis because they have found suggestive artifacts in the eastern Mediterranean."

The *Times* had not questioned the scientists' arbitrary decision to transfer a fascinating legend from one section of the world to another.

"I wonder," I now said, "why they called it Atlantis if it was in the Mediterranean and not the Atlantic."

The girl cocked her head quizzically. "These artifacts they found, couldn't they have been carried during the dispersal from the Atlantic to the Mediterranean?"

I looked at her with a smile. "I suppose they could have, but none of the great scientists apparently thought of that alternative."

"You know," she said, "if these scientists were to comb through the ruins of New York, Los Angeles, or San Francisco after the holocaust, they would probably think they had discovered England—that is, if England were also destroyed."

"How do you figure that?" I asked.

"Well," she said, "they would find things in English, remnants of English customs, English-style furniture, and it would never occur to them that these 'artifacts' had been borrowed from the original culture."

I finally saw her point.

"Would it have been possible," she asked, "for Cayce to have foreseen this recent discovery of the temple in Bahaman waters, without its being evidence of the existence of Atlantis?"

I didn't see what she was driving at.

"Well, as I understand ESP," she said, "he could have foreshadowed the discovery of the temple by Dr. Valentine, but time may yet show that this is not an authentic discovery, merely what Cayce had visualized as happening with Valentine."

"You must be a scientist," I said to the girl from Manhattan Beach.

"I hope not," she smiled. "I'd rather have an open mind."

My own introduction to Edgar Cayce had certainly required an open mind and was in keeping with almost everything else the Miracle Man of Virginia Beach had ever done.

Long before I had ever heard the name Cayce, the great clairvoyant had apparently foreshadowed my appearance as an investigator at the headquarters of the Association for Research and Enlightenment at Virginia Beach. I say apparently, for so it seemed, objective as I tried to be.

It was in the summer of 1961, as I was combing through the Cayce files in the ARE library, that Hugh Lynn Cayce, the son of the late psychic, approached me with a smile and said, "I have a surprise for you."

I had already been pleasantly surprised by the unexpectedly warm reception that ARE leaders, including Hugh Lynn, had given me, keeping the library open beyond its regular hours and having aides constantly at my elbow to lend any assistance I might require.

"And what may that surprise be?" I said, dissembling my slight annoyance at being drawn from my study.

The younger Cayce thumbed through a sheaf of old readings that the great seer had given in his miraculous healing of the ailing, and then, poker-faced, passed three separate files on to me.

"This man," he said, "is mentioned in all three."

I scanned the files perfunctorily. All went back to 1931, when I was in my teens and concerned with anything but the metaphysical, not even knowing what the term meant.

But as my eye now idly moved down the first file, it was struck by a familiar name—my own. I looked through the second file, and again my name—or a name like my own—was mentioned. In this year, 1931, there was a reference, in a March 3 reading, and again on June 1, to a person with a name phonetically my own, advising the Cayce group, the ARE, to contact this individual and make him welcome, as he would materially help the organization, given the chance.

I smiled now as I began to surmise why I had received so warm a reception at ARE headquarters, but I was not impressed. There were an awful lot of people with this name, and I certainly had no reason to believe that I fitted the description. It could have been anybody or nobody.

But there was still a third file, a third reading, and Hugh Lynn was pushing it under my nose. Politely, as I had done before, I began to thumb through this reading, and another name caught my eye—David E. Kahn. This was the man, this long-time friend of Edgar Cayce's and a trustee of the ARE, whom Cayce, I was now reading, had said should contact the man with a name like mine, presumably to interest him in the Cayce work.

With a start, I now recalled that I had inadvertently met Kahn, a successful New York businessman, five years before in the foyer of the Reilly Health Service in New York City's Rockefeller Center.

And Kahn, introduced by proprietor Harold J. Reilly, had been the first person to mention Edgar Cayce's name to me. As Hugh Lynn Cayce stood watching, not having the slightest idea what was rolling around in my mind, I searched my memory for every detail of this meeting.

As was my custom, I had dropped over to the health club in the late afternoon for my regular workout, and had seen Reilly, my friend and physical mentor, chatting with a prosperous-looking gray-haired man.

Reilly, in presenting me, had mentioned that I was doing a series of articles on extrasensory perception for the New York *Daily News.*

Kahn's face immediately lit up. "You got to get Cayce in there," he said.

"Casey who?" I said.

Kahn's teeth gritted together.

"Not Casey who," he said with exaggerated disgust, "but Edgar Cayce." He spelled the last name out for me. "The greatest psychic who ever lived."

There and then, he proceeded to tell me about the Sage of Virginia Beach, and his ability, incredibly, to correctly diagnose the ailments of people hundreds of miles away, whom he had never seen, and to prescribe cures for these ailments.

It seemed like so much balderdash at the time, but, without checking it out, I briefly recorded the claims made by Kahn in my newspaper article, stressing that these were only claims. This was in June, 1956, and here it was June, 1961, and I was now seriously exploring the wonders of Cayce, not only checking through the files, but consulting with people he had treated, therapists who had treated them, and living witnesses to the successful therapy.

But even so, what help could I—a reporter—be to the Cayce group, particularly in a material way, as was suggested by the dead Cayce?

At the time it certainly seemed unlikely. But, if prediction it was, it was one that, strangely, was to reach fruition, as had so many other Cayce predictions. For after *The Door to the Future,* published in March of 1963, in which Cayce was overshadowed by the living seer, Jeane Dixon, I wrote *Edgar Cayce—the Sleeping Prophet,* which, published in 1967, unexpectedly became a best seller, quadrupled membership in the ARE, and touched off a flood of Cayce books from which the ARE profited financially.

And so Cayce had been right about the man with my name.

Curiously, though I had never met the living Cayce, I felt a distinct empathy with him all through the course of doing my book.

Cayce appeared on the scene early in the proceedings. Before I had even signed a publisher's contract for the book, and having only just decided to do it, I received a telephone call at 1 A.M. from a New York City psychic incongruously named Bathsheba Askowith, with whom I had a passing acquaintance.

Without preliminary, she announced: "Edgar Cayce wanted me to tell you he was pleased that you would be doing this book about him."

Used to psychics and their strange methods of receiving information, I merely waited for her to continue.

"He will help you," she went on, "and he says the book will be very successful. He feels it should be called *The Sleeping Prophet,* as he doesn't want his name in the title."

"Thank you, Bathsheba," I said, not bothering to confirm that I was doing such a book. "And how will he help me?"

She replied in a matter-of-fact tone. "He will watch over you in the dark hours of the night, when you are working, and give you the understanding and wisdom you will require to properly present his work to the public."

I may never know, of course, whether the spirit of the dead Cayce returned to help, though there were times as I strove to appreciate the full significance of his work that I felt I could almost reach out and touch him. Sheer imagination? As one so closely involved, I would be the last to judge.

In accordance with the tidings from Madam Bathsheba, I suggested the title, *The Sleeping Prophet*. Even if not from Cayce, it seemed apt—for Cayce in slumber had made many momentous prophecies, and of these I was writing.

Without any action on my part (I had decided to sit on the titling sidelines), the publisher revised the title to *Edgar Cayce—The Sleeping Prophet*. When the book came out, in January of 1967, it moved slowly to the fore. Other publishers told me it was a mistake to have a proper name in a title, apparently agreeing with Madam Bathsheba. As the book slowly climbed in popularity, reaching for the top of the best-seller lists, thousands of reader's letters poured in. Almost without exception they referred to the book as *The Sleeping Prophet*.

Meanwhile, with the success of *The Sleeping Prophet,* there was a rash of Cayce paperbacks, new and old. Some, like *There Is a River,* were retitled with Cayce's name, to capitalize on the new vogue, and my paperback, with the Edgar Cayce name on it, almost got lost in the confusion. The advice through Bathsheba was giving evidence of being increasingly sound.

In the summer of 1968, the British publishers, without checking, blandly retitled my book. And what did they call it? *The Sleeping Prophet*. Edgar Cayce had apparently finally got his way.

I had regarded Madam Bathsheba's report with proper skepticism, despite the fact she had no way of consciously knowing I was undertaking such a book. And yet I had some evidence of her own psychic powers. She had sought once to warn Mayor Anton Cermak of Chicago of an attempt on his life, and he had been killed by a bullet intended for an even more distinguished figure, President-elect Franklin Delano Roosevelt. She had again been able, traveling through the subconscious, to tell a worried New York City couple what had befallen their daughter, and where—tragically preparing them for the worst.

Nevertheless, I could not accept Cayce's presence on the basis of Bathsheba's evidence. Yet, there was a precedent during the seer's life for his interest in developing books. Cayce, I recalled, had dealt with at least one book in its pre-publication phase and had even helped one become a best seller, appraising the material, suggesting the title, and naming the publisher.

The same David Kahn who had 'introduced" me to Cayce was the intermediary who brought the matter before Cayce, taking Edmund Starling, veteran chief of White House Secret Service, to Virginia Beach to find how he should go about writing the memoirs he had just received White House permission to put together. It was wartime, August 29, 1943, and the pair had traveled from Washington, D. C., by train.

Though busy with health and life readings, Cayce agreed to go into trance for an old friend to see what would come through. He had no way of knowing the problem beforehand, nor did he realize afterward what he had said until it was read back to him. But this is what he saw. Tom Sugrue, Cayce's biographer in *There Is a River,* would be ideal for the writing assignment. The book should stress human interest and shun partisan politics. It was to deal with seven Presidential administrations, never losing sight of the personal. "From the beginning with Theodore Roosevelt to the end in another Roosevelt," Cayce observed, "there are great human interest stories."

"Would it be better to open with the Wilson administration or the Coolidge?" Starling asked.

"The Coolidge," the sleeping Cayce replied, "and then begin at the beginning [the Theodore Roosevelt administration], with warnings to the nation."

While Starling had no reason to believe that Cayce was correct, he saw no harm in indulging his curiosity, since he had gone this far.

"How much should be said of the present-day visitors at the White House known to me?" he asked.

Cayce replied equably. "Enough to indicate the needs of the warnings, not to laud any particular President but principles. Nor belittle any, as it will not be the purpose, nor should it be sarcastic."

And then, without changing inflection, came his prediction:

"It will then be not merely a best seller, but for many years the ideal of many an American."

The living Cayce was asked to suggest a title.

He stressed that the phrase, "in the White House," should be featured. Eventually, remembering this injunction, the book was titled, *Starling of the White House.*

"Who," Starling asked, "would be the publisher to do the job?"

Without a moment's hesitation, Cayce replied, "Simon and Schuster."

There was a startled pause, and Starling asked, "What is the best approach to Simon and Schuster?"

Cayce's voice was almost bored.

"Just that it may be written. They will be waiting for it."

Now comes the amazing part of the Starling story, requiring all the documentation, which it fortunately has, for credibility.

After the psychic reading, the still dubious Starling went back to Washington by train to mull over what Cayce had said. Kahn, who had been trying to convince Starling that the great sage was never wrong, went on to New York City, where he lived in an uptown Manhattan mansion just off Park Avenue. He arrived late at night at Penn Station, in a steady drizzle. Because of wartime gasoline rationing, no car was there to pick him up, and a long line of people had queued up in the rain to wait for cabs. The aggressive Kahn grabbed the first cab that came down the station ramp, and climbed into it. As he triumphantly rode off, his attention was caught by a middle-aged figure standing forlornly on a curb, holding a bag. For some reason, unknown to him at the time, he called out to the stranger, asking if he could give him a lift uptown.

"I don't know why I picked on him," Kahn recalled later, "when there were so many others standing around."

The stranger quickly climbed into the cab.

Once settled, the two men introduced each other. "My name is Kahn," Cayce's friend said, "Dave Kahn."

"Mine is Schuster," said the other quietly. "Thanks for the lift."

Kahn, startled despite himself, regarded his passenger speculatively.

"You wouldn't by any chance be from the firm of Simon and Schuster—Mr. Lincoln Schuster?"

"I'm Max Schuster," the stranger said laconically.

Kahn beamed. "You may not know it, Mr. Schuster," he said with a rush of enthusiasm, "but you're going to publish a book about Starling of the White House. Tom Sugrue is going to write it, and what's more, it's going to be a best seller."

Publisher Schuster, considered one of the most astute men on Madison Avenue's Publishing Row, regarded the stranger with an amused smile. Politely, remembering that he was the beneficiary of a lift, he murmured that the firm of Simon and Schuster was always happy to have a best seller.

As they came to Schuster's destination, the two men shook hands and said good night.

"Remember what I told you," Kahn shouted after him, "Starling of the White House."

In time, the project was finished by Sugrue, in collaboration with Starling, and the manuscript was duly sent off to Simon and Schuster, as Cayce had suggested. They not only were ready for it, but published it and watched pridefully—and profitably—as it went right up the best-seller list and stayed there for months.

Later, as I found, Schuster confirmed the meeting with Kahn and the ensuing conversation in the cab.

"Just about this time," a reporter said, "you must have been shrinking to a far corner of the cab."

Schuster, accustomed to eccentric writers, wasn't at all nonplussed. "Frankly," he said, "he didn't seem like a crackpot, and I was rather convinced by what he told me."

"But weren't you surprised?" the reporter insisted.

Schuster smiled serenely. "In the publishing field we're used to surprises."

"What did Cayce, as you recall from Kahn, say about the prospects for the book?"

"Kahn quoted him as saying it was going to be a best seller." Schuster's natural caution as a publisher now asserted itself. Asked whether it had sold three hundred thousand copies as reported, he said guardedly, "At the last count we had sold copies [hardcover] in the six digits, and the book has become a legend in the publishing field."

He added almost complacently, "I wouldn't mind another just like it."

Since Cayce, clairvoyantly, had supported the reincarnation concept, speaking of the many lives he had lived before, presumably his spirit was in space somewhere, waiting to be reincarnated, as were millions of others. Therefore, it was not surprising, believing in Cayce, that many earthbound souls felt his ethereal presence from time to time. In one instance, the dead seer not only made his spiritual presence felt but ostensibly foreshadowed a world-shaking military event. Out of the blue, the Princess Grace of Monaco, formerly motion picture star Grace Kelly, tuned into Cayce during a séance and learned of the 1956 Allied attack on Suez two months before it occurred. The séance had deliberately invoked the departed Cayce. And it was with a thrill that the princess and two companions, one a visiting American actor, witnessed a remarkable response— Cayce's spirit dropping in on the royal palace after dinner.

"As it happened," the princess subsequently related, "we were three people sitting around a small table. I had just finished reading the biography of Edgar Cayce entitled *There Is a River*. I was very familiar with his life and work. It was for that reason that we tried to call him one night in August of 1956. The book was placed under the table as we began the séance. Two of us were very aware of a peculiar odor in the room. The séance began, and after a while we were led to believe that we had contacted Edgar Cayce. We asked many questions regarding the world situation and were given answers that amounted to the fact that there would be an armed dispute over Suez, with England and France taking part but without the participation of the United States. A few other minor questions were asked to which we were given answers that later developed to be true. The séance lasted about two hours. Mr. Cayce seemed reluctant to leave us, but we said we would try to contact him another time, which we did two nights later."

Two months later, the prediction materialized in the invasion of Egypt by Britain, France, and Israel in the final days of October. Rather startled by this development, the princess made no further effort to invoke the dead Cayce's subconscious. "I would like to say," she wrote me, "that in recent years I no longer participate in séances, as I feel very strongly that it is tampering with a world and with powers that we know little about, and thus can become very dangerous."

How dangerous, and to whom, the princess did not say. But there was little doubt in her mind, despite her new stance on spirits, that some apparition of the dead prophet had materialized on that remarkable night in Monaco.

I was constantly meeting people who would accept one branch of Cayce's work, the health readings, without crediting his belief in a continuous cycle of life. Yet it all came out of the same source, divine or not, without the slightest conscious knowledge. Cayce's remarkably complex formulas for some ailments seemed as miraculous as any reference to Atlantis or to a previous life cycle in Egypt or India. And though he discussed previous lives, he stressed that the only life that could be expressed was the present one. And so his remedies dovetailed neatly into a philosophy of helping others to fuller lives.

He was particularly interested in youth and its problems, whether mental, social, or physical.

He had not much to say about drugs, since drugs were not a pressing problem in his lifetime. But he did get into such sensitive areas as acne, an adolescent skin affliction, which could disfigure internally as well as externally.

Just as a Harvard doctor had assessed Cayce's handling of four "incurable" ailments, so had Doctor McGarey examined Cayce's physiology and etiology in equally inexplicable acne. Having suffered through this embarrassing, sometimes emotionally traumatic skin disturbance, I was aware that medical science knew neither its cause nor cure.

McGarey apparently shared a feeling for youth plagued with the problem. But his report strove only to summarize Cayce's observations with a fine objectivity:

"Acne was described as an inflammatory disease of the sebaceous glands (secreting fatty matter in the deeper layer of the skin), occurring most frequently on the face, back, and chest. The basic physiological malfunction occurring in the body that gave rise to acne was an imbalance of the eliminating systems of the body, although there were several mechanisms which could play a part in the production of this imbalance. When the eliminating organs became unbalanced, as it were—these being principally the liver and the kidney—then the superficial circulation carried a plethora (excess) of drosses and metabolic end products which should have been eliminated through the channels of the intestinal tract. This brought about in turn a clogging and a disturbance of the superficial capillary and small lymphatic vessels with subsequent inflammation occurring in the sebaceous glands of the skin.

"Some of the factors causing the elimination imbalance were incoordination between the deep and superficial circulation, improper diet during the period of menarche (beginning of menses), nervous tensions and suppressions of fears, and glandular reactions and the gradual building of difficulties related to the glands and circulation. Circulatory incoordination was frequently brought about by back injuries, even of a mild nature, which could bring about disturbance of those cerebrospinal centers located in the ganglia of the autonomic nervous system which had control over the coordination of the deep and the superficial circulation. The deep circulation went to the organs and functioning portions of the internal part of the body while the superficial circulation supplies the extremities and the peripheral body structure."

Almost any disorder reflected the body's complexity. "In one case an injury to the seventh, eighth and ninth dorsal area was the primary factor. Perspiration, induced by excitement, originated with the irritation in the dorsal centers. With this irritation any overexcitement made an extreme call for full circulation (rather than the normal), thus directing too much blood to the superficial circulation. The capillaries and small lymphatics became too full, as it were, producing the excessive perspiration. Inactive elimination brought impurities to the superficial circulation and thus produced odors which were described as being 'obnoxious.' This was described as happening in those places where the lymphatic circulation reached the surface of the body easily. A heavy meal under stress, in one particular case, put the food in the position of not having adequate blood supply to bring the digestive forces into full action. This brought the external blood in toward the central portions of the body and in this manner caused congestion, especially through those lacteals involved. This produced, in turn, a reflex which brought about a disturbed elimination with consequent constipation. A capillary uptake of the contents of the large bowel resulted, and in this manner a loading of the vascular (circulatory) system with substances which should have passed out through the intestines. *The skin attempted then to eliminate excessively* and this produced the inflammation as a gradual process of time and circumstance."

With all this, two things were lacking: an explanation of why acne usually begins with puberty, and why some youngsters are affected and not others.

In psoriasis, another incurable skin disorder, there is, the clairvoyant explained, a characteristic thinness of the intestinal wall through which wastes spilled over into the system.

In acne, too, there might be a thinning of the intestinal walls. This resolves one point, but aside from the single reference to the menstrual process, there is no indication of why acne coincides with development of the sexual function.

As elsewhere, Cayce stressed that the body had a latent capacity for normal functioning. "Thus," Cayce said, "we would administer those activities which would bring a normal reaction through these portions, stimulating them to an activity from the body itself, rather than the body becoming dependent upon supplies that are robbing portions of the system to produce activity in other portions."

Cayce's therapy, summed up by McGarey, is fivefold:

"1. A purification of the vibration of the body forces that would include a restoration to normal of the thin wall in the intestine. 2. A correction of the cerebrospinal centers and their vibrations, bringing about a coordination of the superficial and deep circulatory systems frequently disturbed in acne. 3. A cleansing of the glands of the elimination system, such as the liver, kidney, etc., a balance of these organs, and a correction of constipation and difficulties of the lower bowel. 4. A diet in accord with the needs of the circulatory and the elimination systems, and 5. Institution of local therapy to aid the skin."

Fivefold implementation was as follows:

1. To purify the body forces, the following mixture was prescribed, all of it to be used prior to further treatment (aside from diet and local therapy):

> Sulfur—one tablespoon
> Rochelle salts—one tablespoon
> Cream of tartar—one tablespoon
> These should be mixed thoroughly.

"Take a level teaspoon of this mixture each morning, either in water or dry, before any meal is taken."

2. To bring the cerebrospinal control centers—the autonomic and the sympathetic ganglia—to their proper condition, osteopathic therapy should be instituted after the salts have been used but given only following a shortwave diathermic treatment to the back for approximately fifteen minutes over the upper dorsal area. The combination of these two treatments should be used twice a week for seven weeks, should then be left off one week, and then another cycle should be started, again using the salts followed by the physiotherapy and manipulation just described. A third course could be utilized later.

3. A balancing of the glands of the emunctory system—the

eliminative organs—could be brought about after the original therapy with the salts has ended. Coca-Cola was suggested as a purifier for kidneys and bladder. This would be taken more as a medicine than a soft drink, with water (not carbonated). Various methods of relieving constipation should be utilized— powdered yeast or yeast cake, daily for ten days and then left off a week, was one such therapy.

4. Diet—no sugars, no ice cream, chocolates, pastries, pie, or candy; no white bread or starches. Fruit in season, except strawberries and fresh apples; bananas should not be taken. Lunch should be mainly fresh salads, alternated with vegetable soup. Fish, fowl, and lamb are preferred proteins. Occasional roast beef or beef juice when the individual needs building up.

5. Local therapy—cleanse the skin without puncturing the open pustular area with needles or pins. After a thorough cleansing, massage into the skin a combination of oils: camphorated oil two parts, witch hazel one part, Russian white oil one part. If a powder is needed, use Johnson & Johnson Baby Powder, preferably with stearate and balsam of tolu.

Atomidine, taken for five days, three to five drops a day, may sometimes be used for glandular balance.

Meanwhile, Cayce emphasized, the individual must think positively, his attitude optimistic and serene, laden with hope, the inner forces made aware of God's presence. "For all healing," Cayce said, "comes from the One Source. And whether there is the application of foods, exercise, medicine, or even the knife —it is to bring to the consciousness of the forces within the body that aid in reproducing awareness of Creative or God Forces."

The only Cayce recommendations that strike a familiar chord are dietary. Cayce's diet parallels that recommended by my doctor for my acne condition. The application of oils to an already oily skin seems contraindicated. But then so does much of the Cayce therapy that works when the orthodox does not.

I riffled through the Cayce file on acne. Here seemed a typical case, a youth the same age as myself—eighteen—when my own face had erupted painfully. The reading was in October, 1926, for a young man with painful skin eruptions on face and back. "Doctors think it is a stubborn case of acne."

The reading began, as nearly all Cayce health readings did

—the request for help was read, together with the name and address of the individual, and then, as Cayce stretched out on a couch and closed his eyes, his wife, Gertrude, presented the problem:

"You will go over this body carefully, examine it thoroughly, and tell me the conditions you find at the present time. You will diagnose the case thoroughly, giving the cause of existing conditions, also the treatment for the cure and relief of this body."

As he invariably did, Cayce paused a moment, as though some extrasensory extension of himself was off in space, and then said with a sigh of satisfaction, "Yes, we have the body here."

He saw signs of anemia in the blood supply, and an over-taxed elimination system which would cause more damage in time than acne. He reported an old back injury at the seat of a nerve irritation resulting in faulty circulation with resulting chronic constipation. He called for a series of osteopathic adjustments. Internally he prescribed:

"Fowler's Solution of Arsenic. Begin with one drop, taken once each day, preferably just before retiring. Take this one drop each day for five days, then on the sixth day increase to two drops. Take two drops a day for five days. Then increase to three drops, not more than the three drops once each day. After this increase to the four drops. After this for five days increase to five drops. Then leave off five days, see?" The routine was then repeated. "This course," Cayce said, "should cleanse the system, with those conditions as would be received through the correct adjustments of the nerve plexus in the body, and the change as will be wrought by this."

Questions and answers followed:

"How often should the adjustments [osteopathic treatments] be given?"

"Every other day, until at least ten to twelve, to thirteen, have been taken."

"What should the diet be?"

"That of the regular diet, as was seen. Much of fruit and of vegetables. Not too heavy of meats, see? And never any fried meats. No pork of any kind, or hog meat."

"What causes boils to appear on different parts of the body?"

Cayce apparently zeroed in. "The circulation disturbed, as has been given," he said. "Poor eliminations, or misdirected eliminations, produced by the nerve condition as exists in the system—these as received by a wrench, as was received in wrestling, and a fall—a bicycle fall."

As was often the case, the subject was heartened by Cayce's amazing reference to a circumstance he could barely recall himself. He launched into the Cayce regimen enthusiastically. Two months later, he reported that he had not yet obtained any benefits, but he was still optimistic. In six months he reported that the skin condition had cleared entirely.

Acne is no respecter of the sexes. A young woman of twenty-six had been plagued for years with bad skin. "I have skin trouble on my face which has been diagnosed as acne," she said. "If the reading suggests an X ray, please advise the doctor to whom I may go. Also will you please suggest a diet? There is a discoloration left on my face from the pimples. Can this be removed?"

The Cayce diagnosis was faulty elimination and circulation, and a weak nervous system lowering resistance and causing the person to tire easily. Cayce stressed patience and persistence in building resistance. He prescribed a mixture for the skin, along with a specific diet, and suggested another reading in a couple of months.

The mixture was rather complex:

> To six ounces of compound simple syrup, add
> Essence of wild cherry (or extract)—one-half ounce
> Tincture of stillingia, essence of—one-half ounce
> Essence of pokeroot—one-half ounce
> Essence of yellow dock root—one-half ounce
> Essence of burdock root—one-half ounce
> Ten percent solution, iodide of potassium—one ounce

"Shake solution together before the dose is taken. Take half a teaspoonful four times each day, before meals and before retiring—ten to fifteen to thirty minutes before the meals.

"Take this consistently for ten days to two weeks. Then stop for three days. Nothing. Then for five days take three to five drops each day of Atomidine. See?"

And for the diet:

"Mornings—citrus fruit juices; coddled egg (only the yolk taken), with brown bread or toast. Sometimes there may be taken stewed fruits, but not at the same meal when the citrus fruit juices are taken. A little very crisp bacon may at times be taken.

"Noon—preferably, or principally, green vegetables; that is, *fresh* vegetables as lettuce, celery, carrots, tomatoes, peppers, spinach, turnip greens, mustard, and the like. Occasionally such a salad may be alternated with broths from vegetables that are well cooked, but no quantities of fats should be taken; that is, not large quantities of gross fat cooked in such broths, see? And preferably when any of the salads are taken, or the green vegetables, that only the mayonnaise or the olive oil dressing be used. Not too much milk at any time, and when milk is taken use preferably the Bulgarian or the dried milk— which is preferable to the raw or animal milk. Or, goats' milk may be taken.

"Evenings—a well-balanced vegetable diet. Beware of sweets; that is, foods that have quantities of sugar in them— especially cane sugar. No ice creams. No strawberries in particular. Blackberries and those fruits in season may be taken. No green or fresh apples, or raw apples, but the baked or cooked apples may be taken in small quantities. No bananas. Any amount of grapes desired may be taken at any time. Bananas are taboo, as given, even in creams; as these should not be taken, though there may be taken ices or any of the cold drinks—just so they are not made with too large an amount of carbonated waters. There may also be taken in the evening meals the meats such as fish (but no shellfish), mutton, lamb or fowl; but no pork nor any large amount of beef—and *never* any FRIED foods of *any* kind!

"As a wash to bathe off the blotches or places on body, prepare same as follows:

"Dissolve 1/2 ounce bicarbonate of soda and 3 to 4 grains corrosive sublimate (mercury bichloride) in 1 pint of water.

"To be sure, be mindful that it is not gotten into the eye or in the mouth. But this may be used to sponge off once or twice a day. It is not necessary that this be used *every* day, as a wash or to purify the external forces; only when needed, but it may be applied with impunity twice each day—morning and evening.

"And when using the powder for face (as blotches on face), only use the pure talcum with stearate and balsam of tolu in same; that is, the balsam and stearate and *pure* talcum *as* the powder. None of these that have been highly scented with other ingredients.

"Of course, when the Atomidine has been taken for the five days, then rest three days and begin with the blood purifier again. And so on, as described.

"As given, in ten weeks we would give further instructions."

Three months later there was a second reading, since the condition, while improved, was not completely relieved. In trance, Cayce advocated continuation of the internal treatments and the facial wash, and recommended additional massage, to reduce disfiguring scars, with the following compound: Camphorated oil two parts, witch hazel one part, and Russian white oil one part.

The diet was changed to "more of the building foods."

"While not using too much fats, we would take the juice of beef, and Wyethe's Beef Iron and Wine (a blood tonic) will be helpful also . . . a teaspoonful in the evening just before retiring and in the morning before breakfast would be the better. Beef juices would be taken as medicinal properties, not just drunk. Two or three teaspoonfuls two or three times a day, and preferably taken between meals, made in the regular way, but no fats, no butter, and the same character of foods as we have indicated, but more building foods now. Two or three times a week a portion of the meals would include broiled liver, tripe, pigs' knuckles, blood puddings (if these can be taken by the body) would be helpful."

Other recommendations:

"We would also change now to a series of fifteen to sixteen (shortwave) diathermy treatments—about fifteen minutes— about three times a week.

"And we will find this will build, and the resistance will be overcome, and all of the bottom of these sores cleared up, and the system regenerated."

The subject had not used the balsam of tolu and stearate; she now asked where she might obtain some. Cayce gave a drug store in Louisville, Kentucky, on Market Street—Peter, Bauer Drug Company.

The woman approached the treatment with good spirits, and three months later, as shown in a check report, had her just reward. "The troublesome condition had practically been eradicated by following the treatments outlined in her reading, the greater portion of which, she felt sure, was due to her diet."

A year later, the condition was only a memory, and a friend relayed her gratitude to the ARE. "She is getting along very nicely and thinks Edgar Cayce some kind of a god or other supernatural being."

7

A Slight Case of Baldness

As I glanced up from breakfast, I noticed the round-faced man at the neighboring table studying me speculatively over his newspaper.

"Are you the one," he asked finally, "who wrote about Edgar Cayce, the Sleeping Prophet?"

I nodded, scanning the headlines of my own newspaper.

"Well," he said, "I didn't believe it myself at first, but I think you might be interested in the fact that your book is growing hair."

I put the newspaper aside with a sigh, and gave the man a second look. He had dropped into a seat next to mine now and was eyeing me solemnly.

As my gaze moved upward to his head, he brushed his hands through his own thinning locks. "It's not me," he said. "I wish it was, though I may try it myself since it works with him."

I settled down patiently as he introduced himself. His name was Herb Kerman, and he ran a restaurant, The Three Lions, across from the New York *Daily News* in the heart of Manhattan.

"I just want you to know," he said, "that I'm no kind of nut."

He hesitated, debating how to begin.

"This fellow," he said at last, "was almost completely bald

when I first saw him, and now he's got a head of hair I should have."

The man was Jack Lubow, a hair stylist, a fancy name for a barber. He had a small shop on Fifty-Ninth Street, just east of Second Avenue, only a block or two from where we were breakfasting. Because of his English origin, he was sometimes known as Manchester Jack.

"It's a funny thing," Kerman was saying, "I go in every two or three weeks for a haircut, and one day it struck me there was something different about him." He couldn't figure it out at first, and then it hit him. The bald-headed barber was no longer bald. He had hair. And there were certain other changes, including a new youthfulness, too, which he attributed at the time to the dark wavy locks of the man whose head once resembled a billiard ball.

"You're wearing a toupee," he had said accusingly.

Lubow only smiled.

Kerman looked more closely.

"No," he decided, "it must be transplants. That's what you're getting those damn hair transplants."

Still smiling, Manchester Jack shook his head. "Everybody's wondering but I'm not telling."

"Why not?" asked Kerman.

"You wouldn't believe it if I told you." He finished off his customer's haircut with a deft stroke of the shears. "And besides, it would look like I was trying to sell something."

By now of course Kerman could hardly restrain his curiosity. "You can't be growing hair," he said, "you just can't."

Manchester Jack smiled carelessly. "Have it your own way."

"Now come on," Kerman pleaded, "tell me how you did it."

Jack looked at him doubtfully. "You'd only laugh."

Kerman crossed his arms expressively. "Why should I laugh, when you're growing hair and I'm losing it?" He ruefully drew his hands through his fading strands.

Still eyeing him doubtfully, the barber at last relented. "But if you start laughing at any point," he warned, "I'll stop."

Kerman shook his head impatiently. "Go on already," he said.

And so Manchester Jack explained.

He hadn't believed in the power of clairvoyance himself,

Cayce's or anybody else's, but somebody had given his wife the book, a recent best seller, and he had thumbed through it idly. He read incredulously of Cayce's medical diagnoses and cures, not quite able to credit them even with testimonials from those who had been helped. And then, unbelievably, he came to a section where Cayce, responding to a man with a receding hairline, had recommended a vigorous scalp massage with crude petroleum. There had been other instructions, but Kerman could not now recall them.

He looked at me across the table.

"You must remember," he said almost accusingly, "you wrote the book."

I shrugged. "His remedies were so elaborate, I wouldn't recall any offhand."

He regarded me curiously.

"Aren't you excited that this should happen out of something you did?"

I had received hundreds of reports from readers who said they had been helped by the Cayce remedies on file in Virginia Beach, at the Cayce Foundation, and interspersed through my book.

I had received help myself, removing with castor oil not only the nodule on my ear but unsightly liver spots from my hands, by merely applying the oil morning and night for a few weeks.

But when I mentioned the help I got to friends they would only shrug and say, "It could have been suggestibility."

And now, hearing about Manchester Jack, I found that my own practical mind, which had rejected the skepticism of these friends, was in turn skeptical about the barber's experience.

Kerman looked at me in some bewilderment.

"Don't you believe your own book?"

"Each incident has to stand by itself," I said rather sententiously.

"Well, why don't you drop over and find out for yourself," Kerman said challengingly.

It was as if all his own reservations, based on his own credibility reference, were resolved by what appeared to be my own unwarranted misgivings.

"It's only around the corner," he said, "what can you lose?"

That afternoon, I thumbed through *Edgar Cayce—The*

Sleeping Prophet for the passage on baldness, and there found the few paragraphs which had apparently changed the aspect of a man who was only a name to me.

Cayce had said quite a deal about baldness, pointing out many different causes and, therefore, many different remedies. In this instance, the right man had presumably found the right remedy.

The sleeping Cayce had responded to a request from a twenty-six-year-old youth, concerned over the loss of his hair. "Is there any chance of restoring my hair?" he had asked. "I am the only one of six brothers who is going bald."

Presumably, the young man was making the point that there was no hereditary deficiency, which would offset the possibilities of relieving an externally influenced condition.

Not only was Cayce optimistic, saying the hair could be restored, but blamed the loss on a thyroid imbalance.

"As we find," he noted in this February, 1944, reading, "there is a lack of activity of the glands in the thyroid areas. This causes a weakness in the activities to nails and hair over the body."

The treatment followed:

"We would take small doses of Atomidine to purify the thyroid activity. Take one drop each morning for five days in succession. Then leave off for five days.

"During that period, give the scalp a thorough massage with crude oil, using the electrically driven vibrator with the suction applicator. This should be done very thoroughly, not hurriedly, and should require at least thirty to forty minutes for the massage with the crude oil and then the application of white Vaseline and then the electrically driven vibrator using the suction cup applicator.

"Then begin the first of the next week with the Atomidine, one drop each morning for five days. Then during the next five days (now the middle of the week) give another crude oil shampoo, following with the white Vaseline and the vibrator treatment."

"Leave these off then for two weeks. Then have another complete series, but between each two series allow two weeks to lapse.

"Doing these, we will find that in six or eight months it will begin to stimulate the activities for the growth of hair over the scalp and on the body."

At the same time, in keeping with his diagnosis of a thyroid condition, the clairvoyant recommended a dietary boost for the thyroid:

"Do use the diets that carry iodine in their natural forms. Use only kelp salt or deep-sea salt. Plenty of sea foods. These are preferable for the body. Not too much sweets. The egg yolk but not the white of egg should be taken."

Do all this, Cayce said, and the general health would improve, along with a reversal of the balding trend.

The following morning after breakfast, I sauntered over to the small barbershop on East Fifty-Ninth Street. The store was adjacent to the popular discothèque, the Ondine. Peering over shoulder-high curtains, I briefly scanned the one-chair store. As my gaze moved to the rear, a short man with a rosy face and a shock of black hair stepped out of the darkness. As he looked into the big mirror facing his empty barber chair, I strode into the place and introduced myself.

His reaction was one of undisguised pleasure as he eagerly pumped my hand.

"I recognized you from the picture on your book," he said.

"I understand," I said, "that you have been growing hair." With a grin, he brushed his hand through his hair.

"I couldn't do that six months ago. There was nothing to brush."

He was thirty-two then and had started losing his hair from twenty-one on; two years before he had been almost completely bald. He produced a snapshot of himself attached to his barbering license. It had been issued in 1966. I studied the snapshot closely. There was a fringe of hair around the temples, and that was all. Lubow was otherwise completely bald.

Lubow followed my gaze with a gratified smile.

"Amazing, isn't it?" he said. He was as pleased as a child with a new toy.

"You know," he added with a chuckle, "my father was over here from England a little while back, after not seeing me for years, and he decided to drop in at the shop. He stood outside on the walk, like you did, looking right at me and not recognizing me. I finally went out and said, 'C'mon in, Pop, it's your son Jack.' "

Jack's father couldn't get over the change, and neither could Jack's wife, Diane. "You know," Jack said with a blush, "a woman likes to run her fingers through a man's hair."

The book which changed Jack's hairline had been given to his wife by a friend, Victoria Blanchard, of the Association for Research and Enlightenment, a study group affiliated with the Cayce Foundation in Virginia Beach.

"She believed in Cayce," Jack said, "and was trying to get us interested in his spiritual message."

The book had passed from Diane to her husband, and he had leafed through it, fascinated, as he read on, by the apparent miracles wrought by the Sage of Virginia Beach.

Not saying anything to anybody, he had decided to experiment with the crude petroleum specified by Cayce, and with the Atomidine. "I didn't do a thing that wasn't in the book," Jack said, with his eternally grateful grin.

"What I would do is rub the crude petroleum into my scalp and use a vibrator for about forty-five minutes; then I'd shampoo it out, with a twenty percent solution of grain alcohol, using a little of the white Vaseline." This he did every day for five days, and then he rubbed full-strength Listerine on his forehead twice a month.

What did that do?

Lubow shook his head. "I suppose it may have stimulated the area, but I just did as Cayce said."

After five days of the crude petroleum rub, he had let off for another five days while taking internally each morning a drop of Atomidine in a tumbler of water." This he did for another five days, before returning to the petroleum rub.

"I never take the two together," he said.

"What is the Atomidine for?" I asked.

"It's a fast-acting type of iodine," he said, "and I suppose it affects the thyroid, and maybe that controls the hair growth."

He laughed. "I know one thing. In gaining some hair, I also lost twenty pounds, and that must be the Atomidine—it couldn't be anything else."

In a whisper, he confided, "Actually, toward the end, I've been taking three drops a day, instead of one drop."

My book came out in January of 1967. Jack had received it that summer and had been treating himself for nearly a year. He bent down now to give me a good view of what he had to show for it. At the top of his head there was still a slight bald spot the size of a half-dollar, and the hair in front was sparse.

"If you examine the scalp closely," Jack said, "you will notice that the hair is coming in naturally in nearly all areas."

He acknowledged that customers had accused him of resorting to the painful surgery involved in transplanting hair. "If you observe transplants closely," he said, "you will notice that at the scalp there are separations between the transplants. My hair, contrastingly, is all massed together at the scalp."

Like others who have observed so many bald millionaires over the years, I wondered why these privileged rich hadn't availed themselves of whatever was around to correct their baldness.

"Why wouldn't Bing Crosby or Frank Sinatra do everything possible to grow hair, instead of wearing toupees?" I asked.

Manchester Jack shrugged. "Because they don't know about Cayce," he said. "I'm in the business of cutting and styling hair, and I wouldn't have believed it until it happened."

When had he noticed the first signs of new hair on his scalp?

"About three weeks after the first treatment I started to see some slight fuzz in the front." Encouraged, he applied the crude petroleum, the Vaseline, and the Listerine with renewed vigor, at the same time continuing the Atomidine.

"I never was so excited about anything in my life," Jack enthused.

However, he had confided only in his wife, carefully avoiding discussions with his customers until his confession to Kerman.

Being of a curious nature, I inquired, "Have you interested any customers in the treatments?"

He shook his head. "How do I know it will work with them? If the hair follicles are dead, nothing will grow hair—like grass when the roots have died."

He looked up brightly. "In my case, the follicles were still alive, obviously."

There was another difficulty. He had some trouble in the beginning obtaining the ingredients prescribed by Cayce. He had finally got six bottles of Atomidine from the Ingram's Drug Store in Virginia Beach, and the crude petroleum, difficult to acquire at first, he was now getting from a drugstore at Third Avenue and Thirteenth Street in Manhattan.

"What really stopped me from talking about it," he said, "was that I didn't want people to think I was insulting their intelligence."

A customer was about to come in, and I had done all I could. Jack bade me a warm farewell. "If not for your book," he said, "I'd still be bald."

That afternoon, pondering Jack's experience, it occurred to me that Jack's case could be truly unique, but even so, it was worthy of attention. Thinking it might be helpful to get an objective appraisal, I called an editor friend and related the incident, beginning to end. He snickered, and knowing Herb Kerman, whose restaurant he patronized, he observed dryly, "He must be drinking his own stuff."

"Well, why not send a reporter over to check it?" I suggested.

"And what have you been taking?" he asked.

"You're not very open-minded," I pointed out.

He had the grace to apologize. "All right, I'll have a reporter look into it."

Three days later, I got my report.

Over the restaurant bar, the reporter, who considered himself quite the iconoclast, had confirmed Kerman's story, and then, still unconvinced, as was proper, had wandered over to the tiny barbershop to check with Manchester Jack. Jack, it developed, had shown him the same "before" picture I had seen, and justly proud of his achievement, had detailed the steps through which he had conquered baldness.

As the reporter maintained a stony disbelief, Manchester Jack offered to produce witnesses—his wife, Victoria Blanchard, customers besides Kerman, his lawyer, accountant, even his doctor.

But the reporter was not interested.

Everybody knew that nobody grew hair, otherwise Bing Crosby and Frank Sinatra would have grown it long before.

And so with this remarkable reportorial detachment, the reporter made his way back to his editor with a negative report. As a newspaperman myself for twenty-five years, I had seen many reporters successfully evade a news story. This reporter was by no means unusual.

As luck would have it, shortly after receiving this report from a snickering editor, I had a singular long-distance call. The caller expressed thanks for the relief from arthritis he had received through the Cayce book. He had received beneficial treatment, he said, from physiotherapist Harold J. Reilly of New York and Oak Ridge, New Jersey, who had treated scores of patients sent to him by Cayce during Cayce's lifetime. And he was apparently still treating people successfully with the Cayce therapy now that Cayce had gone on.

I accepted the call perfunctorily.

"I can't get excited over a little case of arthritis," I said lightly, "when I'm contemplating a bald-headed man growing hair."

The caller laughed. "You mean, with Cayce's formula for crude petroleum, don't you?"

I registered surprise.

"Well, I've tried that, too," he said over the long-distance line, "and I've grown some hair, too, not much yet, but enough to be noticeable." He was middle-aged.

As I hung up the phone, I was beginning to wonder whether I wasn't the butt of some ill-conceived hoax.

Why, if Cayce's method grew hair, were there so many bald people walking around hairless, when the facilities to gratify their vanity lay within their reach?

Later that day, still bemused, I was working out at a Manhattan gymnasium, alone except for Arthur Levitt, the distinguished comptroller of the State of New York, who was widely respected for his down-to-earth practicality in managing the complex finances of the Empire State.

The comptroller, though in his mid-sixties, had a healthy shock of graying hair and, because of his vigorous conditioning program, was in good shape for any age.

In the gym we frequently discussed the passing affairs of the day, and I knew that his official state chauffeur had purchased the Cayce book and regarded it almost as his Bible. It was the only book, the comptroller had told me, the chauffeur had ever bought.

"What do you think," I now asked Levitt, "of a man growing hair, where he had no hair before?"

I had expected a burst of laughter. Instead, Levitt remarked solemnly, "How did he do it, with crude petroleum?"

My jaw must have dropped.

Had the comptroller read my Cayce book?

He shook his head and smiled. "No, I let my chauffeur handle that reading."

"How did you know about crude petroleum?" I asked.

Levitt thought back over the years. "When I was a teen-ager, I suffered some sickness, and it left me completely bald. Naturally, my family took me to all kinds of doctors—and quacks —to see if they could restore my hair."

This was some fifty years ago, and Levitt had to search his memory.

"Finally, as I recall," he went on, "my parents saw an advertisement for something called Crudol in the newspapers—it is no longer on the market—and the ad said Crudol was guaranteed to grow hair. They didn't quite believe it, but there didn't seem any harm in trying."

And so Levitt had begun rubbing Crudol into his hair. It was black and gummy, essentially crude petroleum drawn off from the well before the refining process, and it gave him a sticky, unclean feeling. But he had applied it faithfully, and within a short time the first curly wisps of hair began to appear, followed by fuzz, and then a rapid growth. In a matter of weeks, Levitt had a lustrous new head of hair.

I gave him a sharp look, wondering whether he was jesting, though I had never known him to be anything but serious. He shrugged expressively. "What more can I tell you, except that it worked? It may have come back anyway, but obviously the substance, or the massage, or both together, stimulated the follicles enough to grow new hair."

"Have you used the crude petroleum since?" I asked, glancing at his still heavy shock of hair.

"What for?"

A reflective look crept into his eyes.

"You know, in connection with my own experience, I have

heard repeatedly over the years that riggers and roustabouts and other men working around oil wells seldom if ever go bald—apparently they are so exposed to crude oil that it seeps into their pores."

Of course, what helps one man does not necessarily help another. Dr. William A. McGarey, studying the Cayce health readings from a purely medical standpoint, expressly pointed out:

"No two individuals are the same, so generalizations are bound to be statistically less effective than the personal approach demonstrated in the Cayce readings."

In his analysis of Cayce's peculiar power to correctly diagnose the symptoms of people he had never seen, and to properly prescribe cures for ailments he otherwise knew nothing about, Dr. McGarey theorized that Cayce, knowing nothing about medicine, had a unique ability to peer into the body and mind, his subconscious traveling through the autonomic system and establishing a working rapport. "This finger would tell Cayce's subconscious that it hurt, and his subconscious would respond helpfully, by suggesting the proper oil that should be rubbed on it."

Without Cayce, therapists falling back on the Cayce readings for treatment could not be sure that what was effective in one case would be equally effective in another. "It is to be understood," McGarey pointed out, "that all the physical readings with but five or six exceptions were for individuals. Thus any routine of treatment that is instituted without full understanding of the disease process which is going on and the attendant physiological changes is subject to failure at least occasionally."

Many with hair problems had sought help from Cayce, and in a multitude of cases it seemed likely that treatment for diverse hair problems could be best examined for results comparable to those obtained by Jack Lubow.

Oddly enough, in reviewing Cayce's jousts with baldness, one of the first reports approximated the strange experience of Jack Lubow. One, Max Sidelman of New York City, adapting another's reading, had reported to the Association for Research and Enlightenment as far back as 1949 that he had grown new hair with crude oil massage.

"For about two years," he said, "I have been using the suggestion made for stimulating growth of hair. Results have been very favorable—by massaging scalp with crude oil, cleansing with twenty per cent alcohol, applying white Vaseline—have re-covered half the bald area with new hair. Recommend this system very highly. When I began these treatments, the bald area was six inches in diameter, with a few nice long hairs on the top of the head."

Sidelman was not quite as thorough as the New York City hair stylist, and for that reason, perhaps, the results were not so dramatic.

"I started by using it three times a week, then twice a week, now once a week."

His testimonial:

"I do not hesitate to recommend this to anyone who has lost or is losing his hair."

In a circulating file on baldness, which I pored over in Virginia Beach, I found the case of a young woman of twenty-one with a complaint of "very weak hair and a decided tendency to baldness."

Certainly, her problem, unusual in a woman of that age, would be essentially different from Jack's, and yet might correspond with that of other young women suffering similarly from uncommon loss of hair.

Even in discussing hair loss, the sleeping Cayce viewed the body as a distinct whole, seeing it as a sort of electrical apparatus which showed wear and tear at its vulnerable points when the flow of innervating electricity was interrupted at any point. Pressure on a nerve at one area could very well turn up in a weakened nerve or motor impulses affecting an apparently unrelated part of the body.

"As we find," in the case of the twenty-one-year-old girl, "there are conditions causing disturbances with this body. These are because of improper coordination of the activities of the inner and outer glandular forces as related to the thyroid. This allows for deficiencies in certain chemical forces, especially as related to the epidermis, or the activities in the toes and fingers and the hair. These are distressing disturbances to the body."

And now the cause:

"There is that," Cayce explained, "which has caused much

of the disturbance—a long-standing subluxation [lesion] existent in the third and fourth lumbar centers [of the lower back] which prevents the perfect circulation through the glands of the thyroid area. We would make corrections osteopathically in that specific area, coordinating the third cervical and the lumbar axis with the same."

Lubow, apparently, had had no critical osteopathic problem, as he had grown hair without a spinal adjustment. The cause of baldness in his case remains unknown.

Cayce again recommended Atomidine for improved thyroid activity. "We would also begin taking Atomidine internally as a purifier for the glands [unspecified] and to stimulate better thyroid activity. This may change the heart's regularity for the time, but if it is properly administered and the osteopathic corrections are made properly, we will find changes wrought in the activities in the epidermis and as related to the hair."

The lubricant varied dramatically.

"For the scalp we would prepare a close-fitting cap—oil cap —to be used once a week or left overnight, when the scalp would be massaged with pure hog lard. Not that which has been mixed with vegetable matter but the pure pork or hog lard. Massage this in at night. Sleep with it in the hair and scalp, using the cap as protection. In the morning have a thorough shampoo with olive oil shampoo, massaging the scalp afterward with white Vaseline cut with a little alcohol solution —just sufficient to cleanse same; about a drop of grain alcohol to an ounce of water, just enough to change the activity of same. [Or just enough to rinse most of the Vaseline out of the hair.]"

There was a special dietary supplement:

"Do eat more of sea foods, more carrots, and while certain times will have to be chosen for such, do eat onions and garlic."

Probably the most comprehensive Cayce treatment for hair loss came for a thirty-two-year-old woman, who felt herself a victim of hereditary susceptibility. "I am losing my hair at an alarming pace," she reported in April, 1944. "Apparently it [the condition] is inherited from my mother and several doctors told me there is nothing they can do to help me. Otherwise, I am well and have a baby six months old. A few years ago I took some electrical treatments to stimulate the scalp but I do not think that has actually helped my condition. Lately, since I have had my baby, I have lost some more hair."

In no Cayce reading was there more explicit recognition of the interrelation of the glandular, nervous, and circulatory systems in keeping body and mind free of what Cayce called dis-ease.

"As we find," he said, "general conditions in a manner are very good, yet there are disturbances that cause a great deal of anxiety to the body. These, however, are more in the purely physical . . . the activities in the reflexes in the sensory and sympathetic nervous system, and arise from the body attempting to improve in a selfish manner upon what nature had intended for the body to be. [The woman had been bleaching her hair.]

"There has been an upsetting of the glandular system by the activities in the body that destroy the effect of these glands, producing such elements in the thyroid glands especially; thus destroying the oils that were a portion of the activity in the sympathetic nervous system as related to the epidermis."

There it was, clairvoyantly at least, the connection between the thyroid and the body oils presumably enriching the hair roots.

Cayce saw manifestations of dis-ease beyond baldness. "These may later—unless corrections are made—cause splotches where there will be discolorations in the skin until these may become rather patches over portions of the body, especially the upper portions of the limbs, the hands and the arms. Yet, as we find, if there will be a change mentally—much change may come physically—the body needn't laugh at this for it will find that one day the conditions will be rather serious, unless there are measures taken to correct the mental, and not merely the physical or pathological conditions."

As usual, when confronted with bad mental attitudes, the sleeping Cayce was gently chiding: "For, as it has experienced, these [a positive attitude] have had little to do with changing of the activities in the gland force of the body."

Then came the prescribed treatment, so precise, so detailed, it seldom failed to excite wonder:

"We would first begin with the taking internally once a day for at least four days out of each week—and have it the same four days each week—one grain of Calcidine as prepared by the Abbott Company, Chicago. This take—say Mondays, Tuesdays, Wednesdays and Thursdays. Leave off until the next week and repeat for a period of at least six weeks.

"After this has clarified the respiratory and perspiratory system by the increasing of the activity through the respiratory and the lung and the throat area and the iodine has acted upon the system, begin by massaging the scalp about once every twelve days with pure hog lard—yes, this is an aversion to the body—these properties will be needed in the physical self. Massage this thoroughly into the scalp, then cleanse with soft tepid water and with Fitch's Dandruff Remover Shampoo. This will purify the scalp but let the grease that is rubbed into the scalp remain for at least twenty minutes before it is washed out. Then add a small quantity of white Vaseline, massaging thoroughly into the scalp.

"In the diet eat the soup from the peelings of Irish potatoes. Add more often the raw vegetables such as lettuce, celery, watercress, radishes, onions, mustard greens and all of those that may be prepared as salads and the like. Carrots will make better conditions in combination with these for the sparkle of the eye and for the general vision."

Cayce's advisory continued:

"Have the full evacuation of the alimentary canal at least once a day and do at least once a month purify the colon by the use of high enemas. These may be taken by self, provided the colon tube is used. Use about a half gallon of water, putting at least a heaping teaspoonful of salt and a heaping teaspoonful of soda in same, dissolved thoroughly. Have the water body temperature and have the thermometer at least ninety above.

"Do these, be very careful with the general eliminations."

A final injunction:

"Keep away from all of those things such as hard drinks, carbonated water or the like, and we [the editorial we] will gain better health and have better superficial circulation."

The young mother asked: "Did childbirth cause this condition to become worse?"

"It only aggravated, it is not the cause of the condition, but too much of drying out of the scalp, as has been indicated, to improve upon nature. Be natural—you'll be much more attractive."

Again a subtle rebuke that his subject was dyeing her hair, impairing the natural health of the scalp.

Other hair conditions were considered by Cayce, and treated accordingly.

"Why is there so much dandruff?" one man asked.

"Use Listerine and there won't be so much," Cayce replied.

"What causes the scalp to itch?" the man persisted.

"It is caused by irritation, which is produced by the accumulations [toxins] in the system. The digestion is bad, and the nerves are kept on edge. Use the Listerine twice a week on the hair."

The man was still not satisfied.

"What should the body now do to cause the growth in the front of the forehead?"

This question, obviously prompted by vanity, drew a sharp retort from the sleeping Cayce.

"You won't have much brains there and hair, too. This may be assisted, though, by using any vapor rub, or the use of Listerine will keep the hair in a healthy, normal condition."

To groom and thicken the hair, Cayce recommended massage with pure crude oil, cleaned out with a twenty percent solution of grain alcohol.

In some cases, Cayce recommended substances which might help one person but be inimical to another. In others, he advocated soaps for massaging one scalp, and avoidance of soaps for others.

Diet played a major role in his hair regimen. He recommended certain raw vegetables, the skin of the Irish potato, the skin of cooked apples and of apricots, on the ground that they stimulated the glandular activity promoting the growth of the hair and nails. But it was all on an individual basis. Consequently, on the ARE's circulating file for baldness, there was this cautionary note: "These extracts are not presented as prescription for treatment of diseases. Rather, they are selected simply to indicate what point of view was taken on the particular problem of the individual who sought psychic information at the time."

However, any individual could conceivably suit the reading

to his condition, as had Manchester Jack. I looked around for one suitable to myself. In middle age, I still had a good bristly head of hair, but was troubled periodically with dryness and dandruff. I was interested in a holding operation.

"Please tell me," an apparently applicable reading went, "what to do in order to put my hair in good condition and prevent falling out?"

Cayce:

"Use plain Ivory soap as a shampoo about once a week, following same with a massage of the scalp using a teaspoonful of olive oil in which there has been squeezed one drop of lemon juice. Doing this, we will make for a much better condition of the scalp and in a little while—a few weeks, not in the first application of course—we will see a variation in the hair."

Well, we would see. At least I wouldn't have to contend with unpleasantly gummy substances or thirty to forty-five minutes' massage.

I was quick to note the change, perhaps because I was looking for it. In two weeks loose dandruff had vanished, and my hair seemed more ruly and easier to brush. But, as Cayce had said, the result was not immediately startling and nobody commented. My experience certainly did not compare with Manchester Jack's. He was very much in my mind, and finally in August, 1968, some six months after our first meeting, I dropped by his shop again. Jack was looking at himself admiringly in the mirror, and no wonder. His dark hair was rich, luxuriant, and bushy on top, and below the temples he had sideburns any hippie would envy.

With a last dab at his hair, he turned with a bright smile.

"Imagine you walking through the door," he said.

I was too struck by his hair to think his remark odd.

"You have grown quite a bit more," I said.

"I've just been keeping up the treatments," he said with quiet pride.

He brushed his hand through his hair. It was thick and wavy.

"I never had hair like this before," he said, "not even when I had hair." He smiled. "My friends can't get over it and neither can I."

He had not varied the recipe an iota, except for gradually

increasing the Atomidine, having read that Cayce had stepped it up in a case similar to his own. It had obviously increased his thyroid activity, for he had lost more weight, and was now slimmer than at any time since being a boy.

It was now a year since he had started the Cayce treatments. Proudly he bent over, as he had once before, to show the crown of his head. The bare spot that had been the size of a silver half-dollar was now dime-size, and the surrounding hair was thick and strong.

"There's hair growing from the whole base of the scalp," he said. "I can hardly believe it."

He had continued rubbing Listerine on his forehead twice a month, as Cayce had suggested in still another reading, and he felt this had further stimulated hair growth, improving the superficial circulation of the scalp.

I mentioned that I might write about his case, provided he didn't mind.

He fairly beamed.

"Mind, why should I mind?"

Now he regarded me with a strangely quizzical smile.

"Besides, I don't have any choice."

In a glow of good feeling, Manchester Jack explained, "I went to a psychic a while ago and he told me"—he crossed his heart solemnly—"should I never move from where I stand—that a tall middle-aged man with some influence would come through the door in the next two weeks, and he said I must listen to him, for he would help me."

I wasn't sure how well I fit the description, but I still didn't see how I could help him.

Jack's smile broadened. "If you write about me, people may beat a path to my door."

Jack's success with Cayce had led him to a psychic reading, his first.

"Who was the psychic?" I asked.

"Leonard Montone," he replied, "he's a young fellow, and he gets your past lives, just as Cayce did."

Before I could inquire further about Montone, a dark young man wandered into the barber shop to be greeted heartily by Manchester Jack.

The man was accountant George Teichner. They had been

friendly for some time, and the accountant remembered Jack when he was bald.

"Tell him, George," Jack said eagerly, "didn't the psychic tell me somebody was coming in here?"

George smiled. "I wasn't there, but Jack told me about it a week ago."

He combed a hand through his hair, and looked at Jack admiringly. He was only thirty or so, but his hair was already thin in places.

"I think," he said with a sigh, "that I'm going to need some treatments."

Manchester Jack's was a remarkable experience. I had no way of knowing, of course, whether his friend or anyone else could be similarly helped. But, still, human systems having much in common, it seemed likely that others, with a similar loss of hair, could be similarly helped.

Skeptics, like the inexcusably incurious newspaper reporter, would doubtless insist that if hair could be grown, various millionaires and theatrical personalities would have managed to do so long ago. But how could anyone be helped without an effort? There was no questioning the barber's experience, and yet a professional observer, on the doorstep of a good story, had refused to push the latch and walk in. So how receptive would the average bald man be, not even knowing what happened to Jack Lubow?

Some day, perhaps, the Cayce material will be submitted to a comprehensive test. Until that day, it seems to be helpful to acquaint the public with his work, not claiming too much, but giving the therapy—if not the therapist—its due.

I found myself reflecting on the phenomenon of Edgar Cayce —spurned in his lifetime by critics who had never examined his work pragmatically and who still sneer without even exposing themselves to those bringing his work to a public more open than the media.

Even as I mused thus sourly, the phone rang. The caller was a man I had never heard of before, but the conversation was by now familiar. He had read *The Sleeping Prophet,* and had been helped by one of the Cayce treatments. The man was Mel Burka, general manager of radio station WTIP in Charleston, West Virginia. He had called to express thanks for help for his arthritic condition. And he had also found relief, as had his family, in one of Cayce's home remedies, taken from the Cayce Black Book, a loose-leaf compendium of Cayce treatments available through the ARE in Virginia Beach.

In the Black Book, under the heading "Coughs," Burka reported the formula for a syrup which had ended the seasonal bout of endless winter coughs in his family. He mixed eight ounces of the formula at a time, following a Cayce reading given thirty years before, and gave it to his children. Gratefully, he reported:

"I have three daughters, ages eleven, sixteen and nineteen, all of whom suffer miserably during the winter with hacking coughs brought about by the common cold and aggravated by medically diagnosed allergic conditions and sinusitis. In every instance, when each of my three daughters (at different times and dates throughout the past winter months) was besieged by coughing attacks, administration of the Cayce cough formula, as often as every hour, produced almost immediate relief from the coughing symptoms. Recovery from the individual attacks was noticeably shortened, relief from hacking coughs, without narcotics, was always immediate."

The children were helped by a reading which Cayce had originally given for a fifty-eight-year-old woman on March 10, 1938.

"As a cough medicine and expectorant," Cayce said, "and for a healing through the whole system, prepare: two ounces of strained, pure honey in two ounces of water and let come to a boil. Skim off the refuse, and then add one ounce of grain alcohol. To this as the carrier, then add—in the order named:

"One ounce—syrup of wild cherry bark
"One-half ounce—syrup of horehound
"One-half ounce—syrup of rhubarb
"One-half ounce—elixir of wild ginger."

Although these ingredients were hard to come by, Burka had managed to find them at a Virginia Beach drugstore, which had served Cayce regulars in his lifetime.

Cayce had issued directions for taking the cough medicine: "Shake solution well before dose is taken, which should be about a teaspoonful, and this may be taken as close together as every hour. It will allay the cough, heal those disturbing forces through the bronchi and larynx, and make for better conditions through the eliminations."

Another Cayce beneficiary, Mrs. Ann Milano of Yonkers, New York, had given the cough syrup formula to her local druggist, only to have him study it, and then return the recipe, saying the ingredients would be too costly to assemble. Eventually, the medicine was put together by the Kiehl Pharmacy on Third Avenue in New York City, and Mrs. Milano gave it to her eleven-year-old son, a chronic sufferer. An unsolicited testimonial follows:

"My son caught cold last July [a year before]. Coupled with a nasal drip, strep throat and infected sinuses, he developed a hacking cough. I gave him the medicine the doctor prescribed plus bed rest. It seemed to clear up for a while and then would start all over again. He also got an upset stomach from the drugs. This went all summer and into the fall. It was a vicious cycle." The Milanos finally consulted the Cayce Black Book. "We obtained the formula for the Cayce remedy and Atomidine for gargling, and it all cleared up."

There were hundreds of messages from people like the Burkas and the Milanos. I was convinced by now that Cayce was helping more people posthumously than he had in his lifetime. His was the concept that the cure for all our ills, if it could only be identified and applied as needed, lies somewhere in Nature. What was the miracle drug penicillin for endless years but a useless green mold?

But even convinced as I was of Cayce's wonders, through having checked out so many of them, I could still be surprised. At a picnic of an ARE group in New Jersey in September, 1968, I was introduced to Roland E. Horvath of Paramus, New Jersey, a founder of the American Health Education Foundation. Horvath, a robust forty-two, greeted me warmly. "I met Edgar Cayce through you," he said.

I mumbled a polite acknowledgment.

"It was no ordinary meeting," he said.

In 1965 he had developed plantar's warts on his right foot. Firmly imbedded there, they spread to his left hand, then the right. Besides being unsightly, they were painful, torn and bleeding through constant scuffing. Being a health addict, Horvath first tried organic foods and herbs to revitalize his immune system. But the warts only got bigger. Finally, toward the end of 1967, he went to a doctor and had them removed with an electric needle. A month later they were back, worse than ever. "They were now deep into my sole," he said, "covering half the foot." On his hands, too, they were larger than before.

In January of 1968, he acquired a copy of *The Sleeping Prophet.*

"And there," I interrupted, "you found something that got rid of your warts."

He smiled. "I was struck by something Cayce had said about a tunnel of light before launching into one of his readings."

I did not recall the precise reading.

"That night," Horvath went on, "after getting into bed, I concentrated on this tunnel of light; I felt a glowing warmth suffuse my body, including the area of the warts. I repeated this visualization the next night and the next, not directly connecting the tunnel of light with the conscious thought of healing my warts. My whole body was bathed in this new warmth, and I felt lighter and freer, as though great changes were taking place within me."

In five or six days, the warts were clearly diminishing—what doctors would term spontaneous remission. Each day, even as he watched, the warts became smaller, and in three weeks they had completely disappeared. The only sign was the scar left by the electric needle.

Accustomed as I was to Cayce testimonials, I still found it difficult to connect the Cayce therapy with the elimination of the warts.

"How do you explain it?" I asked.

Horvath shrugged. A Catholic, he believed in a motivated God, and impressed by documented reports of the sage's cures, he believed in an activated Cayce. Certainly, as Cayce had stressed, Horvath was in the mood to receive help.

As he finished his explanation, Horvath's solemn round face broke into a smile. "A miracle," he said, "is only that which we don't understand."

8

Over There!

Christ died to show that life was everlasting. That was the great message, beyond even that of everlasting love. He went to the cross, fulfilling the ancient prophecies when, as He said, He could have summoned the legions of the Lord to spare Him the death on earth visualized centuries before. The Twenty-second psalm sung by David provocatively begins, "My God, my God, why hast thou forsaken me?" and spells out His torment on the cross: "All they that see me laugh me to scorn: they shoot out the lip, they shake the head, saying, He trusted on the Lord that he would deliver him: let him deliver him, seeing that he delighted in him."

Mocked by scoffers, his ordeal continues: "My strength is dried up like a potsherd; and my tongue cleaveth to my jaws; and thou hast brought me into the dust of death.

"For dogs have compassed me: the assembly of the wicked have inclosed me: they pierced my hands and my feet."

And then the marvelously prophetic:

"They part my garments among them, and cast lots upon my vesture."

He is poured out like water, his bones are out of joint, his heart like wax, but is not the next psalm, the Twenty-third—the most celebrated—a revelation of His resurgence of hope as in a burst of light He calmly accepted His own message of glorified immortality:

"The Lord is my shepherd; I shall not want . . . He restoreth my soul. . . . Yea, though I walk through the valley of the shadow of death, I will fear no evil: for thou art with me; thy rod and thy staff they comfort me. Thou preparest a table before me in the presence of mine enemies. . . . Surely goodness and mercy shall follow me all the days of my life: and I will dwell in the house of the Lord forever."

To His apostles, Christ constantly said that what He did, they could do, and more, with faith in the Father. And so could others with the same faith.

To reincarnationists, who accept past and future lives, there is no mystery about Christ's life everlasting: "I tell you that Elijah has already come, and they failed to recognize him, and worked their will upon him. . . . Then the disciples understood that He meant John the Baptist."

Again, in the Gospel of Matthew:

"When He came to the territory of Caesarea Philippi, Jesus asked his disciples, Who do men say that the Son of Man is? They answered, Some say John the Baptist, others Elijah, others Jeremiah or one of the prophets."

Elsewhere, Jesus had said, "Before Abraham was, I am." And what of the man born blind because of his sins or the sins of his fathers? What sins does a newborn babe have, unless he carries them into this life from another?

As Edgar Cayce said about these dialogues, "If they weren't talking about reincarnation, what were they talking about?"

Christ was the Universal Man. He trod the earth as a spiritual manifestation of God's interest in man. That manifestation prevails not only in the eternality of Christ but in the marvels of contemporary psychics who strike a high spiritual note.

In my explorations into the psychic, I discovered that probing people from all walks of life ceaselessly sought to solve the riddle of their own link to the vast universal scheme. Why were they born? What could they accomplish? Was death the end or, as Christ suggested, a greater beginning?

The great Tolstoy, a seeker himself, said in a work still unpublished: "Life is unreality, death the awakening."

The pathologists questioning the immortality of the body were correct, even as they scoffed. For the body without spirit is a blob of flesh. It is the spirit, that unquenchable flame of energy, that is the essence of life, and since the spirit is surely an energy force, is it not, as Benjamin Franklin suggested, an indestructible combination that may return one day in a new suit of clothes?

"When I see nothing annihilated and not a drop of water wasted," said this apostle of thrift, "I cannot suspect the annihilation of souls, or believe that He will suffer the daily waste of millions of minds ready made that now exist, and put Himself to the continual trouble of making new ones."

Some can accept terrestrial psychic phenomena because they can be proved. Researching the health readings of Edgar Cayce was like fishing for herring in a barrel. The evidence is lacking only to those who will not see. For everyone Cayce read, there is a name, an address, a success, sometimes a failure. The testimonials are undeniable. A fifth-grade dropout, illiterate, uninformed, Cayce could correctly diagnose ailments of people he had never seen and prescribe a cure, sometimes suggesting the healer by name, or picking an obscure medicine off a drugstore shelf in some distant city, when it could be found nowhere else.

A Maude Robinson could advise a spinster, nearing three score and ten, that she would meet and marry a man within six months and live in a city three thousand miles away, and be right against all logic and common sense. A Helen Stalls or a Florence Psychic could anticipate the death of a President, even as a Peter Hurkos could single out a murderer he had never seen.

But is it possible, pursuing an evidential frame of reference, to test the immortality of the spirit?

Mediums are forever picking out the dead, but this can be explained as the dramatic subconscious of a gifted psychic tuning in to the universal mind.

But can one be sure? In 1964, in Concord, Massachusetts, I dropped in, unannounced, on spiritualist Kay O'Connor of Revere, Massachusetts. She had no idea who or what I was, but closing her kindly old eyes and staring into space, she suddenly asked: "Do you ever feel somebody looking comfortingly over your shoulder, a white-haired woman who was like a mother to you?"

"I think of my grandmother often," I said. "She brought me up."

Mrs. O'Connor responded with a smile. "She's so close you could almost reach out and touch her."

I had this feeling myself at times, but had ascribed it to sentimental imagery.

Mrs. O'Connor kept looking over my shoulder. "Would the name Sarah mean anything to you?"

"That was my grandmother's name."

She paused. "She wants you to know that in November things will clear up for you. You will always be protected."

It was now early June, and the tidings were most welcome to one with marital problems. By October I was divorced, and in November I was in a new home, looking hopefully ahead.

But that day in June, Kay O'Connor had still another message for me. An old friend, Walter Belmont, with whom I had shared many a laugh, had passed away recently, but I could see him as clearly, at times, as if he were at arm's length.

Out of nowhere, Kay O'Connor had asked: "Does the name Walter mean anything to you?"

I nodded, startled. "He was my friend."

"I see him laughing," she said, "as if joking with you."

I could see him as though it were yesterday.

"Don't feel sad about him," she said. "He is happy where he is, happier than before."

Walter, I knew, had not been happy toward the end, and the gay laughter had not been as frequent as formerly.

And what did it all signify? Could Mrs. O'Connor, not knowing it herself, be dredging up out of my subconscious two persons dear to me and always in my thoughts? Was this a dramatization of her own subconscious? Was her own sensitive receiving set tuned into my transmitter, so to speak?

It is a problem man has grappled with from the beginning of time. Is death the finality, the end-all, and if not, can we establish, with any assurance, evidence of a continuing life cycle?

Like Cayce, I felt that the only life we could express was the one we lived, but this didn't diminish my interest in the experiences of Bishop James Pike and others who professed a link to the dead.

Therefore, I was very much intrigued by a recent experience

in Washington that came about quite unexpectedly when a friend mentioned that her sister wanted to sit down and talk about something most unusual. "Please be patient with her," was her only injunction.

I had no idea what it was all about. The two sisters were from a politically prominent family—wealthy, social, steeped in tradition. My friend, a familiar of Presidents, cabinet members and senators, had never married. The other's happy marriage to a distinguished government figure had been cut short a few years before by a tragic accident. The two women, middle-aged now, were interested in the metaphysical, but, how deeply, I had no way of knowing. Both seemed intensely practical, knowing the value of a dollar, and they lived comfortably, even sumptuously, in the stately suburbs ringing the nation's capital. If there is an aristocracy in a democracy, they are part of it.

Eventually, we sat down in one of Washington's most fashionable cocktail lounges. We had a corner table, deliberately secluded, and the sister I shall call Martha quickly established the reason for the meeting. She had a message which she felt should be communicated for the hope it might bring others. But because of the prominence of the family, her name could not be used. The facts would speak for themselves.

"You have looked positively into reincarnation and the life hereafter," Martha said, "so I am sure you will understand what I am about to tell you."

Sister Lydia gave me an expressive glance, which Martha didn't appear to notice. She went right ahead with her story.

"You know, just before my husband was—killed—" she hesitated over the word, "he had just bought this business, and he had been counting on it to one day take care of us all. He left insurance and other things, but we had our children, and there was his previous wife and her children."

Strapped for cash, Martha had thought of selling the business some time after his death, but she had been offered only ten cents a share, hardly enough to make it worthwhile. She remembered, too, her husband's saying that one day the business would make them independent. Still, she had no business experience herself, and didn't know what to do with it. In this frame of mind—confused, concerned about her children's security and education, missing her husband dreadfully—she dropped in unexpectedly on a medium in New York City.

"My friends were going," she recalled, "and I decided at the last moment to go along with them. Nobody, including myself, knew I would be calling on her."

It was a surprise to the spiritualist, Margaret Shelford, who was expecting only two men, but she was used to surprises. The group sat silently a few minutes before the medium said anything. Finally, shading her eyes, she asked, "Who's —?"

Martha sat up electrified. "That's my husband's name."

Margaret Shelford looked up. "Well, he's here, and he has a message for you."

Apparently, the husband wanted his widow to be sure of his credentials. He mentioned that he had died of a broken neck, not publicized at the time of his death, and he expressed some concern for a book and a stamp album that had been his since his teens. Though he had been dead some time, Martha had never gone through his office where he said these things could be found. She made a note to do so the moment she got back to Washington.

At this point the medium, as if straining for voices, suddenly frowned and asked Martha: "Do you have two businesses?"

She nodded.

Through the medium, the husband had some business advice to give her. Indeed, he made several points. "There were ten different things my husband wanted me to do," Martha now recalled.

Lydia, hitherto silent, groaned painfully. "Martha, please."

Martha turned imperturbably to her sister.

"Well, doing what my husband said made me two million dollars."

I looked questioningly at Lydia.

She nodded, defeated.

Enjoying her small triumph, Martha glanced over to see how I was taking it.

"What were some of the things he—or the medium—told you?"

Martha smiled serenely. "The medium didn't know anything by herself. She didn't even know my husband's name before she said it, and she also got the names of his previous wife."

She grimaced. "Even her pet name, and the names of their children."

"Well, you knew them," I said.

She frowned. "What difference did that make?"

"The medium might have dredged them up out of your subconscious mind."

She thought a moment. "Well, she couldn't have dredged the business out of my mind because I didn't know what to do with it." A smile lighted her face. "And I didn't know where the book or album was, either." She had found them, as the medium had said, in her husband's old office.

I wondered how she had made the two million dollars.

As her sister toyed restlessly with her drink, Martha fairly beamed at the opportunity to give her dead husband credit for a financial coup.

"I don't know what I would have done without him," she said. "As it was, everything worked like a charm."

He told her not to fire anybody, and she hadn't. He advised her what old associates she should turn to in administering the business. And he told her when she should sell.

Martha had protested at the time. "We'll need the business for the children."

The answer had come back cold and clear from medium Shelford, "They'll never use it."

Certainly, they had shown no business aptitude.

In the end, proceeding as counseled, she sold out, and instead of the ten cents a share she was once tempted to take, she settled for ten dollars a share—one hundred times as much.

She looked up at me with a smile.

"My husband had given me instructions to take care of his former wife and his children by her. I was happy to do this, as it was not only his wish, but he had made it possible for me to make the money to do it with."

Aside from the business, he had certain records he felt the government would want, and she had found these where he had said they would be, and turned them over to the proper agency.

All in all, it had been a most rewarding experience, and not the least reward was the knowledge that her husband was still watching over his family.

She had seen Margaret Shelford once more, in Washington, and the husband had said he would not come through again. There was no longer the need.

Martha, not satisfied, had also consulted the famed medium Arthur Ford. Ford's message was notable for prophetic references to other matters.

His guide, Fletcher, presumably functioning from spirit, had a couple of political messages quite disconcerting at this time—March, 1968. He said that President Johnson would take himself out of the Presidential race, and there would be a political assassination during the campaign. It was hard to credit either prediction until Johnson's surprise renunciation and Senator Kennedy's shocking murder with victory apparently in sight.

When news of the séances got around, several members of this distinguished family were concerned that Martha was losing contact with reality. One of the most prominent, a nationally known politician, gently chided his cousin for steeping herself in nonsense.

"These mediums are all frauds," he insisted, not nearly as tolerant as sister Lydia.

Martha had reacted calmly, knowing how right the medium had been.

"True," she said conciliatorily, "she was wrong about one thing."

The politician trumpeted impatiently. "One thing—what was that?"

"She got a message from your mother's sister, and of course she isn't dead."

Her cousin turned pale. "But she is dead," he said in a startled voice. "We all thought it strange that your side of the family wasn't at the funeral."

There had been an inexplicable breakdown in communications within the family, and the death, hundreds of miles away, had passed unnoticed by Martha's family.

I thought about the Martha case long and deeply. Her husband had been not only a prominent government figure, but a banking authority. Certainly, he would have been able to run the business efficiently had he lived. It was not a question of his suddenly acquiring wisdom and know-how in spirit that he did not have before. He had died with the knowledge Martha later profited by so dramatically.

It was difficult to dismiss not only Martha's sincerity but the obvious reality that out of the séance, regardless of the source, had come the information that had helped her when she needed help so badly. If one believed in God, was it asking too much that God be a beneficent interventionist? It all depended, of course, on what God's purpose was at the particular time. I recalled another psychic miracle, Jesus at the well, telling the woman of Samaria that she had had five husbands after she had mendaciously denied having one. And this He told her, so that she would know who He was and who had sent Him.

Almost without exception, the great mediums—the Arthur Fords, the George Daisleys—felt they were instruments of a higher power which flowed through them. They did not presume to have the power themselves, and for this reason, perhaps, they comfortably annexed spirit guides which put the power outside of the human realm.

The more I thought about the Martha case, the more intrigued I became, and the more confused. In July of 1968 I decided to call on Margaret Shelford. She lived in the East Eighties, in a gracious apartment, and she immediately put me at ease with a cup of tea. She was an old woman, well over seventy, but she had a serene countenance and a hearty sense of humor. Even as we examined each other, she scrawled out a few verses of doggerel, making me welcome. She spoke generally about current affairs, and said matter-of-factly, considering the political conventions that were still in the offing, "Nixon, when elected, will adjust the wrongs. He is the man the country needs right now."

I wondered how she knew before his nomination that he would be elected.

She shrugged. "It comes through me that way, just as I saw President Kennedy going the way he did."

I mentioned that I had Martha's permission to discuss her case.

Margaret Shelford nodded thoughtfully. "I'm glad I was able to help her, or rather her husband was."

"It would be a lot more impressive," I said, "if I could use her name and that of her husband."

She pushed a scraggly hank of hair away from her eyes. "The last time her husband came through he said that the story should be written and his name used."

I laughed. "Well, he didn't tell her, so I guess they'll have to be anonymous."

Suddenly, I noticed her studying me curiously.

"Do you have a crick in your neck, the left side?"

I moved my neck gingerly. "The right side," I said.

"Better see an osteopath or chiropractor," she said. "He'll loosen you up."

The following day I dropped in on Edward Crozier, chiropractor extraordinary, sometimes known as the man with the seeing-eye hands.

"My right shoulder is bothering me," I said.

He pressed gingerly on the affected area. "It may be reflected there," he said, "but it's the left side that's out."

I wondered if Margaret Shelford was as good with spirits as with worldly aches and pains.

The following night, quite by chance, at a gathering in Manhattan, attractive blond divorcée Jane Jarvis Durgom happened to be discussing the psychic and mentioned Margaret Shelford.

"How well do you know her?" I asked.

She smiled. "She knew more about my divorce than my lawyer did. Or, for that matter, myself. When it seemed all set, with my husband in agreement, she told me, 'Be patient, you won't get your divorce for two years.' "

The divorcée looked up now with a tight smile. "And do you know she was right—my husband changed his mind at the last moment, and didn't change back for two years."

I have listened to many mediums, and some have been quite provocative. However, I could never understand why the spirit, apparently more omniscient in death than life, required an intermediary to get through to loved ones. In the celebrated case of Bishop James Pike and his son, James Jr., who had committed suicide recently, three mediums, beginning with sensitive Ena Twigg in London, had combined to bring the Episcopal churchman word from his tragically departed son. Those who have wondered sardonically why the spirits do not have something important to say for their trouble would have been confounded by the ghost of young Jim Pike. Before responsible church witnesses, out of the mouth of medium Twigg, the youth explained that he had not solved anything by taking his life. "I'm sorry I did this," he ostensibly said through Twigg. "I had problems, I wanted out. I have found there is no out. I wish I had carried on and worked out my problems in more familiar surroundings."

After a sixteen-day lull, which followed Jim Pike's death by shooting in February, 1966, the spirit was engaged in a remarkable burst of poltergeist activity. All this was witnessed by the senior Pike and two independent witnesses in the flat in Cambridge, England, which he had shared with his son. Without any discernible human agency, books were mysteriously moved; others left closed, were found open; snapshots tucked in the frame of a wall mirror were discovered hidden under clothing in a closet at the opposite end of the room; clusters of safety pins appeared where they had not been before, all open to the position of the hands of a clock at 8:19—the time, in England, which apparently corresponded to that of James Jr.'s death in New York.

There were sixty-five incidents in all, though only one, involving a moving mirror in the bedroom used by young Pike, was observed by the entire group—Pike and two aides—as it occurred.

Thoroughly mystified, the bishop recalled a suggestion by the Reverend Canon John S. Pearce-Higgins, vice-provost of Southwark Cathedral in London, that he, Pike, seriously explore the field of psychic communication. Pike now went back to Pearce-Higgins, who explained that frequently, when a person had died a violent death, the spirit was so stultified that it did not manifest itself for two weeks or so. Pike's own son had been dead sixteen days before the first phenomena revealed themselves.

On the canon's recommendation, Pike looked up Ena Twigg, who promptly brought in the spirit of his departed son. The ghost or spirit, or dramatic subconscious, gave a brief but provocative description of the hereafter. It was a nameless place with no time, no space, only a curious limbo of helpful souls. These souls had no physical substance, as we know it, but they could make things happen by willing them. Spiritual progress could be accomplished through increased knowledge and a willingness to improve.

Before the séance ended, the spirit, presumably of Jim, notified his father through Ena Twigg, "I'll be in touch August 1." It was now March.

Months after his son's death, on the evening of July 31, 1966, in his new quarters in Santa Barbara, California, Bishop Pike was startled to find a snapshot of the Holy Land, of Beersheba, inexplicably pasted to a page from a book on the Dead Sea Scrolls. The picture, taken by them in the Holy Land, had been of special interest to himself and his son. Puzzled, his eye turned to the calendar. It was the eve of August 1, and he suddenly recalled it as the date his son had advised he would be in touch. It was also the day Pike was to begin duties at the Santa Barbara Center for the Study of Democratic Institutions.

The next day, fateful August 1, Pike had an unexpected caller, John McConnell, a New Yorker touring the country with a prayer movement for peace. McConnell announced that he had just seen the Reverend George Daisley, an English-born spiritualist resident in Santa Barbara, and Daisley had said he was in touch with Pike's son.

Apparently chosen as a channel, he had been reading a local newspaper report about Pike's coming to the "Think Factory," when, he said, a voice spoke up, saying, "I am Jim Pike, the bishop's son."

Daisley looked up to see a tall, pale young man—"as clearly as if he stood before me in life."

The apparition came directly to the point. "I want you to help me communicate with my father."

The medium shook his head. "Your father must come to me first."

"He will," the apparition said, fading from view.

After McConnell left, the bishop telephoned Daisley and made an appointment.

There were six sittings with Daisley over an extended period. At the first session, the spirit apparently wanted to assure his father that the communication was valid. He now, through Daisley, told him about a small matter that only Pike—and an unseen witness—would have known about. "I was with you the other day," he said, "when you could not find a book in your library. If you recall, after you left the room and returned, you were startled to find a book on the floor by your bedside." There was a slight pause. "I want you to know I placed it there in your absence."

Very clearly now, the Bishop recalled searching for a volume of a history of civilization, which he had stuffed away in a carton, only to find it by his bed after he had given up looking for it.

The son now gave his real reason for "returning." It was not only to comfort his father and express his own disillusionment with his impulsive act, but to edify the mundane world about the other side. "I want to do all I can to bring forth the knowledge of life after death. I have a role to fulfill by becoming more effective in this type of communication."

The presumed spirit of young Pike continued to make itself felt. In September of 1967, one year later, before an understandably startled television audience in Toronto, Canada, medium Arthur Ford, with Bishop Pike at his elbow, publicly announced that the son was in contact with Fletcher, Ford's spirit guide. "Before he came over," Ford told Pike as the TV cameras ground away, "Jim was confused and mentally disturbed." But, as he had stressed before, he didn't want his family to feel guilty about his death. It had been a necessary step to find the truth.

Pike was ever the pragmatist. He felt this particular message could have resulted from the medium subconsciously anticipating what he, Pike, wanted to hear. However, his belief in the authenticity of the communication was supported by Ford's references to names and events which Ford had no way of consciously knowing, and some of which Pike himself didn't know about until later.

A Carol Rede came through. At first, Pike could not recall the name. Carol Rede identified herself as secretary to Bishop Horace Donegan in New York. She now reminded Pike of how protective she was of her superior when Pike, then dean of the Cathedral of St. John the Divine, and others tried to push in to see him.

With a jolt, Pike recalled that she had indeed been a formidable sentry. But Carol Rede, the last he had heard, was very much alive. Still, it did seem as if somebody was trying to tell the bishop something. Directly from Toronto he went to Seattle for an Episcopal conference, and ran smack into Bishop Donegan.

He could hardly wait to get his question out. "How's Carol Rede?" he asked.

Donegan's eyebrows went up, but he answered promptly. "She died about three or four years ago."

His son's message was getting to the bishop. "Life after death," he told a California congregation, "is not supernatural but natural." And then, closely paraphrasing Paul: "If there is no resurrection of the dead, then Christ is not risen. And if Christ is not risen then is our preaching vain, and your faith is also vain. For if Christ was resurrected, we are all resurrected."

With it all, I still wondered why the departed dead required mediums. There were all sorts of individual reports of visions, in dreams and otherwise, but they were by their very nature hardly objective. Nevertheless, it was difficult to explain away these experiences. For instance, radio personality Arthur Godfrey, an old iconoclast himself, was serving at sea on a destroyer when he awoke one night and saw his father at the foot of his cot. The apparition announced it had come to say good-bye. As the figure faded away, the startled Godfrey checked his watch. It was 2 A.M. The next day, a wireless arrived with its message—an announcement of his father's death. The time? 2 A.M.

Granting Godfrey's account, which he had no reason for manufacturing—and which was not intended for publication— there were obviously only two explanations: Had Godfrey received a telepathic message from his dying father, so strong it created an illusion of his presence? Or was the spirit of the dead, just then leaving the body, actually in communication with a son spiritually close?

Faith in spirit, as they know it, is so inherent in some mediums they cannot function without a spirit guide. Fletcher had been Arthur Ford's intermittent companion for fifty years; the Irish-born medium Eileen Garrett had an Indian guide, and one of the newer breed, Patricia Harmon of Billerica, a Boston suburb, felt that every act, thought, wish, and desire was recorded by an individual's own guides. Spirit and the guide were on a similar vibration, and the person aware of his guide could then tune in.

The poet Whittier said:

> A presence strange at once and known
> Walked with me as my guide;
> The skirts of some forgotten life
> Trailed noiselessly at my side.

Patricia Harmon's own awareness of the spirit world took place around the age of six or seven when her family moved into an old house which reportedly was haunted. "I never saw this entity," she recalled, "but I heard his footsteps and always knew when he entered the room." Her dog, keenly attune as some animals seem to be, also displayed awareness. "Whenever this soul entered a room," Pat Harmon recalled, "my pet dog had a terrible reaction. He would froth at the mouth and bark and tremble." The child would then address the entity, whose presence she also felt, and tell him to go away as he was scaring her dog. "I guess he understood, as he would leave and my dog would settle down." Eventually the dog became a problem and had to be disposed of. But even so, Pat knew when "it" arrived; she felt herself being watched.

She grew up with this sensitivity, but within her own family there were misgivings. Her own brother, John, was quietly skeptical, but spirit eventually convinced him.

"When John was first in the service," Pat recalled, "he was slated to return to the Azores where he had been stationed. I informed him that he was not going in that direction, but heading for California, which he immediately scoffed at." She was so sure that she called her sister Joyce near San Francisco and told her to get the guest room in order. Spirit scored a modest victory here.

Again, at Christmas, with John still in the service, Pat notified him that he would be getting home for Christmas. He replied that spirit was off, since the furlough list had been posted and his name was conspicuously absent. Instead, he was slated for an immediate mission. Pat replied that when he returned from his mission he would find his name added to the list. Score another for spirit, and a Yuletide reunion for the Harmons. Brother John not only requested readings now, but regarded his experience as a manifestation of God's presence, restoring his faith in the power of prayer, since he now felt somebody was out there listening.

In the same way, Pat made a believer of her boss in the office where she worked before becoming a full-fledged medium. "At the time I went to work for him in February, 1965," she said, "Bill had never been beyond New York and Massachusetts. However, I told him that the following August he would be heading for New Mexico and that the company would specifically ask for him. He refuted this and said that he was not the one to be considered; if such a request came up it would be for another man. Well, August arrived, and one morning he stood in front of my desk and informed me that he had received the call. He added that George, our supervisor, would never let him go and I replied that he would be on a plane before the afternoon. No sooner were the words out of my mouth when George walked in and said the company insisted on Bill and he would have to take the afternoon plane."

But something else happened before Bill became a believer. She read for Bill again, and spirit came through to warn about an automobile accident, even to specifying the day. "I begged him to delay his departure for at least an hour," Pat said, "but he would not listen."

The next morning she received a call that Bill had been involved in an accident. He had asked that three people be notified, and she was one. The accident was so severe he had to be pried out of the car. She visited him at the hospital, and he mentioned they were putting him in traction. She had a terrible reaction and begged him not to let them do this. "You would not listen before," she said, "but promise me this time you will."

Subsequent X rays revealed his neck was broken. "He could have been killed," Pat said, "if he had allowed himself to go into traction."

How much does suggestion figure in the enactment of events

that appear to be influenced by the spirit of the departed? Is this suggestibility part of the pattern intended to bring the desired event about? In my varied research, I had never heard a more curious story of a protective spirit than that of the Melander family of Flushing, Long Island. Before his death, the family patriarch, Jacob de Rytter Hiorth, a Norwegian ship captain, had often told his grandson, Everett Melander, that he would watch over him in spirit just as the captain's father before him had watched over him. The old ship captain, based in Brooklyn, was fond of elaborating on three instances in which his father had intervened to save him. Once, during the Depression, he had walked away from a freighter command in Brooklyn, to be berated by his wife who pointed out that jobs were few and far between. But his dead father had whispered a warning in his ear. Three weeks later the ship broke up at sea with a heavy loss of life. During World War II, the captain was in convoy when his father again whispered in his ear. He broke convoy, and though later court-martialed for his infraction, he was nevertheless justified when an enemy attack shortly thereafter scattered and destroyed a good part of the convoy. The last time his father appeared, the captain was skippering the yacht of millionaire sportsman Billy Leeds in the Caribbean. He changed course, contrary to his owner's instructions, but was vindicated soon thereafter when a hurricane swept across the original course, raising havoc with ships in its path. Summarily dismissed, he was as summarily reinstated.

Everett Melander, twenty-five, was in the Air Force, working in the base hospital ward in Trier, Germany, when his grandfather died in Washingtonville, Pennsylvania, on September 26, 1966. On this day, when, as usual, Everett was working on patients' charts, he began to shake so that he couldn't write. He started to hand out pills to patients but the pills jumped out of the cup. One chart, which seemed to put itself together, reflected a cardiac attack—but there were no heart cases in the ward.

Later, from his sister, Mrs. Lynn Chion of Huntington, Long Island, Everett learned that his grandfather had died at 9:30 A.M., at precisely the time—3:30 P.M. in his German zone —that all the unusual activity had been taking place. Everett, startled, remembered what his grandfather had said about watching over him in death. Indeed, it looked almost like an announcement.

The next six months were quiet. In March of 1967, still in Germany, Everett decided to take a holiday in Munich with his roommate Tony Smith of Cleveland, Ohio, and a buddy, Thomas Gannon of Akron, Ohio. Preparing for the six-hour journey, he was tuning up his Volkswagen, and lifted up the rear seat to check the battery. He could not believe his eyes. There, sitting right next to the battery, was a tiny snapshot. He picked the snap up and regarded it curiously. How could it have gotten there? He had checked his battery two weeks before, and there had been no picture. Somebody must have put it there since then. But who? He examined the picture closely. It was no larger than his thumbnail, and looked as if it had been scissored out of a larger picture. It was a head-and-face shot of a woman, totally unfamiliar to him. But on the reverse side, in old English script, was the name Tante Sylvia. With a jolt he recognized the handwriting as that of his grandfather. Tante Sylvia was Aunt Sylvia, and the picture, obviously aged, was clearly of the vintage of the 1880's or 1890's. Tante Sylvia, as he recalled, had never been out of Norway.

Totally bemused, Everett Melander showed the picture to roommate Tony Smith, describing his own bewilderment at finding it there. His grandfather might have left the picture as a sign. But how? Grandfather had not been in Germany since 1920, when he had stopped briefly at the port of Bremerhaven. The Volkswagen had never been out of Germany. Young Melander had bought the car in the country of its make in June 1966, a month after he got there.

Everett sent the picture back to his mother in Flushing, Long Island, and she sent it to her sister, Mrs. June Sutter, in Dayton, Ohio, with whom his grandfather had spent his last days. They had been on a trip when his grandfather had suffered a fatal heart attack. Mrs. Sutter recalled the picture. The last time she had seen it, it was in the grandfather's wallet.

The mystery had only deepened. But with the ebullience of youth, Melander put the incident out of his mind and cheerfully drove off with his friends for the holiday in Munich. Everett and Tony shared a Munich hotel room. They got in late, and that first night they lay down wearily to rest up for a festive day. But sleep was not to come easily. There was an uncanny noise as of something banging together. The sound came from the closet, and it was heard by both young men. It sounded as if hangers were knocking together. Frankly, they were just too frightened to move, as they knew there was nobody in the closet. Finally, the closet door swung open, and Tony, galvanized, leaped across Everett's bed to investigate. There was nothing there.

They snapped on the lights and looked at each other sheepishly. Everett shrugged and smiled wryly. "It must be the captain," he said.

On that note, they went back to bed and fell asleep.

Another six months passed without incident. Then in October, 1967, Melander, now a sergeant, bought a more expensive car, a Porsche, which he intended to take back to the States with him in January.

However, he was short two hundred dollars for the necessary insurance and shipping charges. There was nowhere he could turn for the money, since his enlisted friends were in a similar financial fix. So, one day, he said a silent prayer to grandfather. He could now use the help that had been promised him. That very day he ran into an acquaintance, Pat Blinn, who had been admiring Everett's used Porsche. "I never saw a car that had such good care," Blinn said.

Melander groaned. "Yeah, but it's brought me a lot of headaches." He then explained, without a thought of getting a loan from Blinn, who drove an old beat-up Volks himself and had less income as a subordinate two ranks below Everett.

Blinn gave him an appraising look. "How much do you need?"

"Two hundred dollars," Everett replied.

Blinn nodded abruptly, as if he had come to a decision. "I'll give you the money on one condition," he said.

Everett could hardly believe his ears.

Blinn smiled. "That you don't pay it back."

He explained. He came from a wealthy family and had always had anything he wanted. And never had he seen anybody who seemed as devoted to anything as Melander appeared to be to his Porsche. "I'll get my pleasure out of your pleasure," he said.

He wired back home for the money, and soon Everett had the two hundred dollars in cash. Grandfather, he knew, was watching over him.

Curiously, on his return to the States, after he was mustered out of service in March, 1968, Everett was drawn into a career that placed him close to the dead. He became a funeral director. He was not one to see the morbidity of his calling. After all, grandfather had shown that the spirit carried on after the body gave up the ghost.

9

Reincarnation

Why, if people lived before, don't they remember their past lives?

Skeptics usually ask this question, generally with a smile or a sneer, and in all likelihood wouldn't accept a positive answer if they received one.

The fact remains that countless people, regardless of the authenticity of their impressions, have reported distinct memories of previous lives, which express themselves in some way in this life.

Almost everybody, at one time or other, has had the feeling of having always known someone he has just met. What is love at first sight, the reincarnationists insist, but the stirring of an old love from a previous life cycle?

In aptitudes, too, in vaguely recalled skills, in affinities for certain cultures, many, reincarnationists say, are manifesting a recall of previous existences in which these qualities were developed through long usage. How else, they ask, could the prodigy Mozart turn out sonatas at the age of five? Or Josef Hoffman play the piano before he was three? What made a whole strange breed of Englishmen, Lawrence of Arabia and Gordon of Khartoum, so curiously obsessed with the Middle East? How did Heinrich Schliemann, German-born, bred a businessman, with almost celestial certainty know exactly where to find an ancient Troy, the location of which had baffled generations of archeologists.

How did an American doctor, on a battlefield at Anzio, suddenly recall a surgical method he had never been taught but which the sureness of his fingers proclaimed a skill carried over from a suddenly remembered experience in the Civil War, dreamed about for years?

How did clairvoyants and others, long dormant memories opened up via hypnotism, suddenly spout Homeric Greek, Latin, and Sanskrit of which they had no waking knowledge?

Countless Americans living today have experienced that baffling phenomenon, *déjà vu,* an often exasperating feeling of having been somewhere before, without quite knowing how or when. Still others, in the throes of this feeling, have anticipated buildings, roads, or landscapes just around the corner or over the hill in an area they had never known before.

Like Bridey Murphy, many under hypnosis have age-regressed to birth and beyond, and remember places and dates in a previous era, demonstrating either a clairvoyance they had never before manifested or a tangible recall of something that lay genetically latent. Is this the instinct which leads fledgling swallows to fly south, unguided, over the identical course of older swallows before them, and salmon to swim upstream, as their predecessors have done, and there spawn and die? Or is it more?

Perhaps because of man's stepped-up quest for spiritual direction, his desire to know more about himself and his purpose in the universal scheme of things, many people are seriously contemplating subjective experiences they would have been ashamed to acknowledge a few years ago.

General George S. Patton, Benjamin Franklin, Thoreau, Emerson, Mark Twain, Louisa May Alcott—great Americans all—have one unique thing in common. All believed in the concept of rebirth and had experiences, subjective and otherwise, to bolster their belief in a continuous life cycle. Thoreau felt he had once walked with Christ and that his friend Hawthorne, though not similarly aware of Jesus, had lived at that time. Mark Twain, dreaming, recalled the same teen-age girl of his youth in different life cycles in Missouri, London, Athens, and Hawaii—and this dream state was more vivid and real than anything in the waking life of Samuel Clemens. Many distinguished Greeks, among them Socrates whom he recognized by his peculiar nose, passed through Sam Clemens' dreams. Houses and market squares were totally familiar, and remembered as though he had spent a lifetime among them. "I noted the details of the furniture and the ornaments—a thing which I should not have been likely to do when awake—and they took sharp hold and remained in my memory; they are not really dim yet, and this was more than thirty years ago."

Louisa May Alcott, about as American as apple pie, spoke freely about a philosophy, until recently only widely contemplated in the esoteric East. "I seem to remember former states," said this author of *Little Women,* "and feel that in them I have learned some of the lessons that have never since been mine here, and in my next step I hope to leave behind many of the trials I have struggled to bear here and begin to find lightened as I go on."

Patton of course is the anomaly. How could this man of action, the greatest pursuit general of modern times, believe in anything so strange and kookey, so seemingly out of character? But, pragmatic as he was, it would have been difficult for Patton not to have believed. Not only did he have subconscious recollections of past lives as a ruthless conqueror, but he could recall battle arenas and military dispositions from the misty past.

In Southern France, during World War I, Patton was on a secret mission to a place he had never been before. Though it was night and the itinerary had been carefully kept from him, he had an uneasy feeling he had been over this ground before. As his staff car, piloted by a monosyllabic driver, approached the crest of a hill in the darkness, Patton observed: "This camp we're going to, isn't it just over the hill to the right?"

The driver shook his head. "No, sir, our camp is farther ahead. But there is an old Roman camp over there to the right."

It was exactly where Patton had suggested it would be, though it went back two thousand years or so, to the time when Patton had the remembered experience of leading the legions of Rome.

In Sicily, during World War II, the conquering hero was taken on a tour of the island by Signora Marconi, the curator of antiquities. In the middle of her discourse he casually corrected a description of a Carthaginian advance on the capital city of Syracuse.

The Signora's eyes widened. "Have you been here before?" she asked.

In Sicily for the first time in his life, Patton nevertheless replied carelessly, "I suppose so."

He knew!

In the clairvoyance of Edgar Cayce, with surprising evidential support at times, many have found a clear indication of a continuous life cycle. Not yet believing in reincarnation himself, Cayce, in 1923, began describing the past lives of people in response to requests for explanations of their role in this life. Many of these lives were placed in Egypt, India, Persia, and other exotic areas, including the legendary lost continent of Atlantis. But Cayce did more than merely chronicle a series of events, such as would have come out of any hypnotic regression. In drawing on a past experience, Cayce often pinpointed with remarkable accuracy what the individual would do in this life experience. Reading for a newborn baby, at the parents' request, Cayce cited two strong vocational hangovers from the past—medical and agricultural—and said the subject would be torn between the two in shaping his career. The life reading was carefully kept from the subject as he grew up, so as not to unduly influence him. At twenty, still unaware of the reading, the subject was nevertheless the only medical student in the history of a certain university who was growing his own vegetables outside his dormitory window.

In another reading, Cayce, contrary to scholarly opinion, spoke of a pre-Incan civilization in Peru, and only recently have certain archeological discoveries supported this view.

Like everybody else he read for, Cayce had past lives of his own. In the most recent, he had been an old frontier scout in the War of 1812. He remembered being on a raft, floating down a river with a band of howling Indians in pursuit. There was only a little food, and one of the younger men offered the older scout his share. However, the food problem was soon resolved when the Indians finally overtook the small party and massacred them.

The scene now shifts to the twentieth century and a prosaic barber shop in Virginia Beach, where the sedate-looking Cayce was calmly waiting to have his hair cut. As he riffled through a newspaper, a five-year-old boy casually climbed on his lap and put his arms around him. While Cayce, loving children, responded good-naturedly, the boy's father sternly rebuked the boy. "You mustn't bother that man," he said, "he isn't anybody you know."

The boy looked up with a quizzical expression. "But I do know him," the boy said, "we were hungry together at the river."

Skeptics routinely decry recollections of glamorous past experiences as wishful thinking by persons bored with present drab existences. But droves of the famous and successful, of sound body and mind, have recalled past experiences and quietly offered supporting evidence for their flashes of memory. They were not trying to impress anybody with their stories, nor did they much care how they were received. The experience, philosophically, had significance only for them. For most of her life, the well-known writer Adela Rogers St. Johns, a fine objective journalist, was as convinced of reincarnation as of anything she had ever had evidence of in gathering her news reports.

"I remember very well," she once said, "standing on the English shore with a company of soldiers awaiting the Spanish Armada as Queen Elizabeth traveled up and down on her horse encouraging the troops." She had a perfect recollection, in the waking state, of Elizabeth as a gallant figure in a special light armor that Adela Rogers St. Johns had never seen before. It was that unique. But years later, visiting London, she was intrigued to find a suit of armor just like it in a British museum. It had been worn by Elizabeth some four centuries before.

While deploring reincarnation because of the prospect of returning again to a world they find painfully tasteless, some people have remembered experiences coloring the intellectual fabric of their lives. While she apparently had memories of a past in many times and places, novelist Taylor Caldwell preferred any explanation to reincarnation. "I find the whole idea personally depressing," she once said, "for I shudder at the very thought of being born again into this world. Life to me, practically from infanthood, has been a monstrous, painful, agonizing affair, and the idea of repeating such an existence— even if better in a way—is horrifying to me. I think I'd prefer total oblivion. At least, in total oblivion, as in sleep, you are safe from the revolting mechanics of living and being a prey to 'outrageous fortune.' "

Psychic herself, English-born Taylor Caldwell gave public warning of both the John F. Kennedy and the Martin Luther King assassinations. She was possibly more sensitive than most. As a child in England, not even knowing what the word reincarnation meant, she had her first specific recall of an earlier existence dramatically suggesting previous life as the nineteenth-century English novelist George Eliot, a pseudonym for Mary Ann Evans. "When I was six," author Caldwell recalled, "I was visiting a large country house in England with my parents. Our hosts were friends of my father and mother and they had several children. I remember one very clearly, a girl named Alice, about fourteen. She showed me a book she had been reading, *Mill on the Floss,* and I took it in my hands and I said, 'This was my favorite book over all the others I had written.' The kids looked at me with their mouths open, and I heard myself telling them about the story plot, though of course at six I had not read it, and had never heard of it before. Then I came to myself with a shivering jolt, and put the book down. When years later, I did read the book, I knew every word of it, and where the author had some trouble, and where she had been stuck."

But Taylor Caldwell was not ready to accept a previous life as Mary Evans on this evidence. "Surely, no one is going to tell me that once I was Mary Evans. I couldn't bear it, it would prove reincarnation. Yet, long before I read *Mill on the Floss* or any other of Eliot's books, I had already won several school prizes for essays and short stories, and my teacher told me, 'You know, you write just like George Eliot.' It was then that I bought the *Mill on the Floss.*"

Like Mark Twain, Taylor Caldwell had a constant dream of another life experience, of being somebody else, that haunted her for years before it was finally bizarrely resolved. "I first had this dreadful dream," she told me, "when I was about three years old, and still living in England. I dreamt I was standing at a small, open casement window in a very high building like a tower, and I was looking with anguish down on a roof below the casement that was covered with dirty red tiles. [There were no such red tiles on roofs in England.] The sky was a cold, dull white, and the sea of roofs beyond was all crowded and jostling red tile, too, and seemingly spread for miles. In the distance I saw a narrow river and several ornate stone bridges crossing over it. I felt, not a child of three, but a mature woman, say about the middle twenties, looking about the same as I did when I was really in my middle twenties."

The dream continued:

"I was in a sort of icy stone cell, high over the city, with only a cot, a table and one chair in it, and there was a wooden door at the rear. I knew the door was bolted and that I was a prisoner in this city I knew well and in which I had lived and had been born. I knew that outside the locked door was a narrow and winding staircase of stone. Then I heard footsteps on the stone, and I knew who was approaching. I knew that in the company there were three men in strange costumes, and one was a man I knew very well. I knew his costume in that awful dream, and *now* I know it was the white habit and hood of a Dominican monk. All of them were familiar to me, and I knew why they were coming up the stairs—they were going to torture and kill me. I heard a key grating in the lock and turned to the window again in despair, and I knew the only way to escape those men was to throw myself out of the window. So, as the door opened I did just that: I threw myself down onto the sloping roof, very high over the teeming narrow street, with relief and even joy. Then, as I rolled down that cutting tilt of tiles all memory was blanked out, and I woke up screaming in my little trundle bed in England."

This dream kept recurring, frighteningly:

"I dreamt it over and over dozens of times, awakening with shudders and despair, and yet with relief that I had escaped my enemies. And, invariably, there was no change in the setting, and nothing to remember after I had almost completed my roll-out." But then occurred the experience that was to clarify the dream and at the same time indicate a previous existence, subconsciously at least, as vivid and real as anything she knew in this life.

With her husband, Marcus Reback, the celebrated author of *Dear and Glorious Physician* was on a visit to Italy for the first time. After touring the south of Italy and Rome, the two went on to Florence. "I longed," she recalled, "to see Florence and its elegant and intellectual people, and all its rumored beauty. We were to be the guests of Count and Countess de Moretti, of a very old family which had given numerous Popes to the Church and other dignitaries and statesmen. We arrived at Florence at six in the morning. It was still dark and a large thorny white star hung in the moonless sky. Nothing was moving. We went to the de Morettis and a servant showed us to our rooms. We hadn't slept on the train all night, coming from Naples, and so I decided to sleep now. Before drawing the heavy curtains over the big window in our bedroom, I looked down with interest at a very huge plaza, a round plaza with many streets streaming into it like the spokes of a wheel. In the center of the empty plaza stood a tall pillar surmounted by a medieval horseman. All at once a sensation of utter despondency, fear and foreboding came to me and I pulled the curtains across the window and went to bed."

She tossed and turned before finally falling off to dreamless slumber. "I awoke about two in the afternoon, and my first thought was that I hoped the plaza was filled now, and the streets, and so would look less gloomy and bleak. I did hear the sound of traffic and many voices, and I went to the window, pulled the draperies and looked outside."

She rubbed her eyes to make sure she wasn't dreaming. The plaza that she had looked out on with an inexplicable foreboding early that morning was no longer there. "Instead there was a big broad street outside, and many other streets radiating away from it, but no plaza except for a very small concrete island with a sort of modernistic monument on it." The writer was in a state of mild shock, and didn't even confide in her husband, for fear she would appear bereft of her senses. Silently, with her husband, she went downstairs to a late lunch with the de Morettis, a middle-aged couple who bespoke the culture and elegance of a departed era. The conversation lumbered at first because of language difficulties, but these were soon overcome. "Count de Moretti, though expert in French and German and Spanish, could not speak a word of English and, of course, I could not speak a word of Italian. The countess, however, was fluent in English and she acted as interpreter. Then, for some reason, I mentioned the plaza I had thought I had seen in the dark before dawn, and she smiled and told the count of it, and he got up and brought a large book to the table and turned several pages—and showed me the plaza just as I had seen it that morning!"

It was an old engraving, and as Taylor Caldwell studied it, her eyes widened with wonder. For there, as visualized through the upstairs window, was the prancing horseman high on the pillar, the gloomy shadowed streets, and the blank sides of the buildings. The period was obviously the Italian Renaissance.

As the writer stood musing, the count gave her a peculiar smile, but made no comment. Did he comprehend what was passing through her mind? Or was she imagining this, too? What had this fantasy to do with her, and how had the count so promptly turned to the book with the right engraving?

No answer offered itself, and gladly, as a distraction almost, she accepted the countess' invitation to tour Florence by car. But the day of surprises was not yet over. "She took us, among other places," Taylor Caldwell recalled, "to a spacious museum. I was much impressed by its gorgeous grounds, all green lawns and flowerbeds and fountains and statues, and stopped on the high stairs to admire it shining in the sun. Then we went through the museum, which was like all museums, and we'd seen dozens in our travels." She was anxious to get out in the sunlight again and stroll through the gardens she had admired so much before entering the musty halls. But once outside, again she couldn't believe her eyes. The gardens, like the plaza, had miraculously disappeared.

"There was nothing there but a very broad and busy street, full of buses and cars. The steps of the museum went right down to the teeming sidewalk, full of hurrying crowds. I must have stood there stupefied, for the countess looked at me strangely." Shaken by this second phantasmagoric experience, unsettling without being enlightening, the author continued the tour in a daze. But her eyes played her still another trick. "The countess took us to another concrete island, and then before my eyes the island disappeared and there was another small plaza, and crowds of people in strange costumes, and a whole company of white-robed Dominican monks. In the center of the little plaza a man, also robed in white, was burning to death on a pile of faggots in the bright sunshine, a small, plump man with a heroic face. Horrified, I said aloud, 'Savonarola.' " She had seen the crusading fifteenth-century monk burning at the stake for opposing the established hierarchy of the Church.

The countess regarded the writer curiously. "Yes," she said, "and that monument," pointing to a statue, "is there in his honor."

The scene, as before, shifted back to reality, and all the people that Taylor Caldwell had seen, including Fra Savonarola and the watching multitude, disappeared.

Very much taken aback, the writer drifted back to the car. Had she actually seen Savonarola and his tormentors? How was this image plucked out of the past connected with the other illusory scenes cutting across her vision? And suddenly now, back in the dark corners of her subconscious, memories were stirring of the dream that had marred her slumbers for years.

But the strange experience was far from over. The countess, on the way home, stopped to show her distinguished visitor the bridges over the Po—handsome stone bridges familiar to every sightseer to the fabled city of the Medicis. But nearer at hand, on one side of the stone bridge, the writer paused before a medieval bridge beautifully carved of white marble with embossed figures on it. She turned to the countess. "Now, there is something really lovely, that bridge."

Suddenly, like the plaza and the rest, the bridge blinked out. There was no bridge at that spot. And the countess, like the count earlier, was smiling at her oddly, though she made no comment.

Now thoroughly bewildered, the novelist returned to the house for dinner, and a lively repast it was, though the count still had to be talked to through his English-speaking wife. After dinner, Taylor Caldwell found herself alone with the count. "The countess, who had taken a fancy to my husband, had left the table to talk to him about my books, for she was a fan of mine. I was left with the count, who could not speak English, or so I had been told."

But the count unexpectedly became part of the strange illusion—if illusion it was. For he spoke now in apparently perfect English. "I have some very special wine, very old," he said, "which I hope you will join me in drinking, for this is an unusual occasion."

He brought the wine and poured it into two beautiful goblets with long stems. The writer paused uncertainly over her drink. "I felt a little foolish," she recalled, "assuming (though I had been told) that he could not speak English, and we had a very animated conversation. I told him of my experiences that day, and he smiled and nodded and said:

"You have been here before, long ago. I have known of these things all my life."

He brought out the engravings he had shown her earlier that day and opened at once to the beautiful gardens she had seen at the museum. "These," he said, "were the gardens of the Medicis."

He leafed through a few pages and came to the medieval bridge she had seen over the Po. He smiled tightly. "It was swept away and lost, at the time of Savonarola, in a flood."

At this point, the novelist was understandably staggered by all the strange developments that had suddenly confronted her, the least not being the count's lucid exposition in meticulous English.

She digested his information in a sort of daze, and looking at him quizzically, said, "Count, you speak wonderful, perfect English."

He smiled, shaking his head. "No, you speak perfect Italian, though in an archaic form."

Again, the writer could not credit her senses. "I called over to the countess and my husband, and said, 'Please tell me— have I been talking to the count in Italian and has he been talking to me in English?' "

The countess and her husband both laughed, and Marcus, a practical down-to-earth type, rejoined, "You have been talking in English and he in Italian, but you seemed to understand each other perfectly."

The writer realized by now, of course, that she was going through some strange recall tied in with the dream plaguing her from childhood. And she had a feeling that the count, with his own special wisdom, could help straighten her out.

"I looked at the count, and he gave me that mysterious smile again. My husband and the countess went back to their talk, and then I told the count of that awful dream I had been having since I was a child. He listened very seriously and intently, nodding his head."

Then he offered his explanation:

"You lived in Florence at the time of Savonarola, and you must have been one of his followers, and that was why you were condemned to death."

He showed her another engraving of medieval Florence, with the same sort of tall, narrow building in which, in her dream, she had been a prisoner. It was all very familiar to her, and very terrifying; even the jostling red tiles were there.

One positive thing came out of the experience. She never dreamed that dream again. It had apparently fulfilled itself in her Florentine journey into the past. "I never had that dream again," she said. "And I shall never go back to the brooding city in Italy in which the count said I had lived at one time. I couldn't get away fast enough. We cut our visit short, something my husband did not understand until I told him the story. But the count seemed to understand. It was no strange secret to him."

Taylor Caldwell's experience was highly unusual, not to say unique. Undoubtedly, her psychic sensitivity effected the remarkable raising of the curtain of time over centuries gone by. Edgar Cayce went to sleep and regressed in time deliberately; but the writer's flashbacks often came involuntarily, triggered by the uneasy stirrings of her own subconscious. However, as a child, unexposed to a recognizable world which touched off this subconscious, the principal channel into the remembered past was her dreams. There, she knew many people, including the English poet Swinburne, who was contemporary with George Eliot. But she had never heard of Swinburne when she had her first intimate recall of the poet and of one of his poems, which she remembers as a memento of that dreamlike encounter. "When I was a child of seven," she recalled, "I had not heard of Swinburne yet, but I had a dream of a bearded man's study, in the gloomy and heavy English fashion, and a man stood there and he was quoting a poem to me, and then he said, 'I will write that poem, and it will be called "The Lost Garden."'

"He then repeated a stanza, and I woke up. But I remembered the stanza. Years later, I discovered Swinburne and found he had, indeed, written 'The Lost Garden,' but that stanza was not in it though it was of the same meter!"

From her childhood dream, she recalled that "missing" stanza:

> Where the northernmost tip of the westerly mountain
> Hangs falcon-like over the heart of the bay,
> Past seven sad leagues and a last lonely fountain,
> A mile from tomorrow the dead garden lay.

Nobody can say for sure whether Swinburne had written these four lines and discarded them. But Taylor Caldwell is as certain of it as she is of anything she has written herself. And so she analyzed the stanza. "It was not the 'lost' garden, you will notice, but the 'dead garden.' " But she is confident she remembered correctly. "That stanza has haunted me all my life—from the time I was seven, when I did not know what a 'league' was, or a 'falcon,' either."

Her own favorite poem was Swinburne's "Garden of Prosperine." It reflected her own view that "the thought of eternal death is like a balm—and the dearest hope."

How had the bearded man in the gloomy study said it?

> I am tired of hope and laughter
> Of men who sow to reap,
> Of what may come hereafter,
> Of men who live and weep.
> I am weary of days and hours,
> Blown buds of barren flowers,
> Desires and dreams and powers,
> And everything but sleep.

There have been few like Taylor Caldwell, through whom the subconscious has flowed so deeply; few who have remembered anything, without some external prod. Drugs—LSD, ether, or nitrous oxide—and hypnotism seem to open up the subconscious; hypnotism invariably wrenches such truth from the subject as can be known. Supermemory, clairvoyant impressions, and dreams are associated with the subconscious; deductive reasoning with the conscious. But the subconscious, as a master hypnotist explained, frequently seeps its impressions to the conscious, without awareness of the specific events forming these impressions.

"Most of us," hypnotist Joseph Lampl said by way of illustration, "have conscious impressions of people. We may like or dislike a certain person without remembering exactly why. In other words, the incident that formed our impression is forgotten, but the impression remains."

Because of his widely acknowledged skill, I was to take Lampl to Canada to age-regress under hypnosis a seventeen-year-old Ontario girl who had supposedly lived before, and whose experiences were described in *The Search for the Girl with the Blue Eyes*. I had watched many regressions before. The first one I saw was in Concord, Massachusetts, at the home of Yoga teacher Marcia Moore, who, traveling in India, could describe market areas in some cities before she turned a corner bringing them to view. My Concord introduction was by Boston psychologist Dr. Kenneth Lyons, who got interested in hypnotic regression to disprove the Bridey Murphy story and wound up accepting it instead. Lyons, with professional detachment, had hypnotized Marcia's fifteen-year-old daughter, Loulie, taking her back to her fourth birthday, when she remembered a birthday party, and then to the first thing she could remember. She saw bright lights and confusion, many people moving about, and her mother close by. Incredibly, she was describing her own birth scene—Marcia recalled the dazzling lights of the nursery to confirm the remembered experience.

Taken back further, Loulie picked out a life as Matilda Argente in Italy. In the year 1764, as sixteen-year-old Matilda, she had been on holiday in France with her French-born parents. She rattled off a few words in French, but then she had studied French in the Concord schools.

It was not terribly impressive, and not subject to verification, as the name Argente—the only tangible clue—could have come from anywhere.

In Canada, three years later, with hypnotist Joseph Lampl, now living in Hollywood, California, I explored the subconscious personality of blue-eyed Joanne MacIver of Orillia, Ontario. I was impressed by the reality with which this seventeen-year-old high school girl relived the life of a Susan Ganier Marrow, who had presumably lived and died a hundred years before in a neighboring Canadian county.

Inadvertently hypnotized by her father, Joanne had become the teen-age Susan Ganier, wandering about on her father's farm, hiding in an apple orchard, covertly watching her brother smooching with his girlfriend.

She had had several past lives, but this Canadian life seemed the easiest to check. As Susan Ganier, later Marrow, born in 1832 and living until 1903, she had lived in the recognizable past. Hypnotized by expert regressionist Lampl, erstwhile founder of the Academy of Applied Mental Sciences of New York, she accurately discussed prices of sugar and saddles and other sundries a century ago. She had little idiosyncrasies of speech reminiscent of her French-Canadian background in the earlier subconscious life, and she spoke with a different lilt to her voice. Her face even changed under hypnosis, her eyes slanting unbelievably and her cheeks becoming pinched. It was almost as if she were assuming the appearance of another personality.

Birth and death records, which might have established a Susan Ganier, were not available for that time in that part of Canada. Still, Joanne—or Susan—recalled the names of several neighbors correctly. She described Susan's marriage to a young farmer, Thomas Marrow, his untimely death in a farm accident, and her bleak widowhood in an abandoned shanty. Unlike the previous existences recalled by so many others, hers was neither romantic, glamorous or important. While her memory was faulty, even subconsciously, it was little different from the average memory. As hypnotist Lampl pointed out, the person in regression is no more alert subconsciously than he has been consciously, in a previous experience.

The most provocative testimony to the Susan Ganier recall came after Joanne—regressed as Susan—described her own funeral, not only the ceremony but the precise site. Susan, she said, was buried back of a church in a sequestered thirty-five-square-mile area now the site of an Armed Forces Tank Range. The Canadian military took over the site in World War II, before Joanne MacIver was born. Civilians could not get on the site without permission, arranged through the commanding officer, Major John Malone.

Major Malone, our guide, and Joanne soon had a difference over the grave site. The major, pointing out that the Canadian military had agreed to maintain all graves when it moved settlers off the land, said there was no cemetery behind the church where Joanne said it was. As a matter of fact, bringing out official maps showing the early sites, he said there had never even been a church where Joanne had placed it. Nevertheless, in the precise area which her subconscious had picked out, Joanne now found the church site under the rubble of time and tanks, and the old abandoned graveyard with fragments of old gravestones, behind which the church had obviously stood.

However, reincarnation is more than recalled experience. Presupposing an interested God, it presumably marks the progress of the individual, building up a sort of credit and debit ledger by which he applies the lessons of one life, if only subconsciously remembered, to his next. Joanne, for instance, has been an indifferent mother in lives prior to the Susan Ganier experience, and thus, in her Canadian life, she had been denied the boon of motherhood. Observing her karmic pattern—her destiny cycle from one life to another—hypnotist Lampl and I predicted that if there were anything to reincarnation, Joanne should marry young, at eighteen or so, to a husband somewhat older, thirty or thirty-two—about the age of Tommy Marrow when he died—and that she would break out of the frontier country where she had now spent two successive lives. At eighteen, as predicted, Joanne fell in love at first sight with a geologist, who was thirty, and she was promptly whisked out of the North Country to Vancouver and then Toronto, where she is happily married today.

If true of one, reincarnation is obviously universal, hardly affecting one person and not another, though the cycles and the number of lives presumably varies with what the individual does with his opportunities. "The only life you can express," clairvoyant Edgar Cayce said, "is the life you live now."

Though some are better hypnotic subjects than others, hypnotist Lampl, in regressing scores over the years, had never regressed anybody not able to recall an earlier life.

"Either it is all a subconscious fantasy, a trick of the mind," he observed, "or everybody, not just a privileged few, had earlier existences."

If the truth can be examined and checked in this life, why

would the subconscious suddenly stray from the truth when it plunges from known reality into a vast unknown not susceptible to similar verification?

One never knows what a regression will bring out. And while skeptics are always ready to find some tangible memory source in this life—a forgotten story or experience, a buried picture or film—the fact remains that an often singular chain of events— such as Taylor Caldwell's without hypnosis—comes clean and neat from a subconscious never exposed to such images on a conscious level. As he had Joanne MacIver, Lampl regressed a young Hollywood actress, curious about herself without any wishful belief about reincarnation. It was remarkable how truthful she was under hypnosis, without ever having cultivated that reputation in her wakeful hours. Casually, at a typically swarming Hollywood cocktail party, she had mentioned being born in London (justifying an apparent English accent) and that she was twenty-three years old. But under hypnotic trance, deftly taken back in time, she said she was born not in England but San Francisco, and in the year 1943, making her twenty-five and not twenty-three.

Her subconscious, yielding the truth in this life, then cut through time to Wales a hundred years before, when she was secretly a witch, living in a small town some fifty miles south of Cardiff, and burning down the houses of people on whom she had chosen to cast a spell. Actually, the young actress was very witchlike in this life, and one wondered whether she was not fantasizing this past (or was this her karmic heritage?) except that in trance she had not fantasized before, delving realistically into childhood relationships, the convent school she had attended, and the parents she quietly resented.

In her British life as Melinda Morgan, she had originally lived in London with her parents, and had moved to Wales when she married. Her name became Evers then, her husband being an Englishman. She had some trouble recalling the name of the village, but this is not unusual in first regressions, and Lampl was hopeful of gradually extracting specific details. In view of her arsonist tendencies, it was intriguing that she casually mentioned her father's home had burned to the ground when she was still a child living there.

This was certainly a field to explore. But after this revealing regression, in which she described her collusion with other witches to set fire to a church, the young actress awakened troubled from the hypnotic trance. She didn't quite know why, since Lampl had given the posthypnotic suggestion that she forget everything she had said, but she still gave evidence of having suffered a terrible ordeal. Fretfully, she pounded the pillow on which her head had rested, and said, "I can't do it, it's stirring something up horrible inside of me."

We would now never know whether the subconscious personality that was Melinda Morgan Evers had burned her parents' home and was plagued by guilt. To avoid any subconscious conflicts, which might confuse her identity, the regression was discontinued and someone else substituted who had similarly volunteered for regression because of an interest which grew out of a vaguely recalled life in Germany two hundred or more years ago. Strangely enough, twenty-five-year-old Joan Waldron of Redondo Beach, California, a physicist and program computer, had twice traveled to Germany without experiencing any sense of familiarity. The impression she had of a German life was misty, almost like a musical fugue which could be translated into neither words nor pictures. She felt a German link at times, without knowing of any ancestors in that land. As she was led into regression by hypnotist Lampl, the possibility was there, of course, that her conscious mind would suggest a German life to her subconscious—or so it seemed to me.

Joan was by no means an easy subject—one of the most difficult, indeed, that the expert hypnotist had to contend with. First, she had trouble going under. Being so analytical a personality, she became both observer and observed as Lampl took her back to college days at Ohio University and then to her girlhood in New Rochelle, New York. In striking contrast to her own meticulous speech and thought patterns, her precise mathematical turn, Joan faltered in regression over dates and the arithmetical passage of time in this life; she was hard pressed to recall her different ages as time rolled back, though it was only a simple matter of subtraction.

Not until the third regression, with Joe Lampl patiently repeating his questions, did Miss Waldron finally get back to a previous life. It almost seemed, Lampl felt, as if she were subconsciously blocking something she did not want to face again. And then finally, in a low hesitant voice, she began to describe a bearded man at a desk in a long study, working feverishly over manuscripts and drawings. The time was 1728, more than two hundred years ago, the place was—Germany, and the man's name was George. She stumbled over the last name, which began with *Sch,* but she could not quite make it. And yet this man, subconsciously, was as close to her as any personality could be. It was she, Joan Waldron, who had presumably, in her earlier life, been a man, but was now a woman for some karmic purpose that was not readily apparent. Joan was as pretty and shapely a young woman as one would find anywhere, and yet in her meticulous directness there was a definite masculine aspect, which in no way detracted from her essential feminine appeal. It was just a recognizable quality. In reincarnation, a change of sex is by no means unusual, and clairvoyant Edgar Cayce suggested it was a karmic way of working out problems carried over from the earlier life experience.

However, in this prior subconscious experience, Joan—or George—appeared to have no role problems, at least none that brimmed to the surface under hypnosis. George was reasonably happily married to a girl named Anna, Anna Hoffman. Very reluctantly, as if pulling teeth, Joan-George disclosed that Anna's father, a farmer, was the wealthiest landowner in the area. As a matter of fact, the farm on which they lived was Anna's dowry, and without this farm, it soon became obvious, George could not have afforded the leisure time to work on his manuscripts. Joan was a little hazy about the locale of the farm, but she finally worked it out. It was in a triangle formed by Hamburg in the north, Hanover in the south, and Berlin to the east. George seldom moved off the property, and when he did, he traveled by horse and carriage no farther than Hamburg to discuss his work with people there. She was vague about names that George knew, just as she was vague about George's own last name, but she did manage, falteringly at times, to convey a picture of farm life at that time in a German principality. Occasionally, they found entertainment at nearby inns, or rather the men did. (One of these was run by an Obermeyer.) The women stayed home and sewed and cleaned, or pitched in with the help. There were eight hired hands to help work the farm, which took an hour to walk around—so it was perhaps a mile square, a goodly size for a farm. They grew grain and feed and assorted root crops like cabbages.

As Joe Lampl strained to evoke detail sufficiently precise to merit investigation, I remembered that a wise old philosopher had suggested that reincarnated people—if there were such—did not come back to satisfy the curiosity of reporters but to take advantage of the lessons learned in the past. It was hard, of course, without knowing more about Joan, to know whether there was any karmic pattern in which the past had laid a significant groundwork for this life. In other words, had anything been carried over? Certainly, the change in sex was interesting, but what did it mean?

There seemed some sort of bridge between the two personalities in the nature of their work. The George personality worked with technical books dealing with mathematics and chemistry and formulas. "One of the basic books," Joan recalled under hypnosis, "described what happened when you mixed one compound with another."

George seemed obsessed with his work, and the impression grew that the marriage was one of convenience.

"What," asked Joe, "is the prevailing attitude toward women?"

"Very much of a business relationship," Joan-George replied.

She constantly referred to her own regressed personality of George in the third person as if subconsciously trying not to identify too closely with him.

There was no real togetherness in this presumably German household. "No real sense of harmony in working as one," Joan said slowly. "They were friends and felt warmth, but each had their own particular function."

"What do you think of this arrangement?" Joe asked.

She shook her head negatively and then, reflecting a curious overlapping of lives despite the regression, said with a flat voice, "I have thought on that. But as a woman now I don't like that attitude toward me."

She had slid from George to Joan, and then back again, still remaining true to the prototype of each personality.

As I thought about this, I wondered with a start if this was how it worked. Did the spill-over from the previous existence, if there was one, seep into the conscious mind and influence its thought patterns? Here was Joan, an unusually attractive girl, at a highly marriageable age, and still unmarried. As George-Joan, she was obviously skeptical about marriage because of perfunctory German attitudes toward women two centuries ago—and as plain Joan Waldron she had obviously avoided the marital situation, though she had felt close at times to several young men, including a college classmate to whom she had been pinned before breaking off the engagement.

I was to discuss this with her later. Her reasons for remaining single had not yet crystallized. She was still young and could marry today, tomorrow, or the next day. It just did not seem that important. I wondered what she thought of her regression and the information that had been almost painfully extracted. She did not know what to make of it. But the vague stirrings of a life in Germany were still there.

Was she blocking? She would be the last to know, of course. I had found it strange that while she couldn't quite bring off her own last name in the German experience, she had responded with alacrity when asked to describe the study in which George had labored over his manuscripts.

"One part of the room is higher than the other, and there is a fireplace which furnishes the heat. There is a big table on the right, facing the wall, and that wall has a small window near a bookcase. To the right, as one sits at the desk, the floor goes down, and there is a door back of that."

Had she as Joan ever known a room like this?

She shook her head. "I really don't know where that came from," she said.

After several hypnosis sessions, she had recollections of a farm in Hanover and of books piled up on the desk through which she rummaged constantly all day in an effort to conclude the work. It was finished in five years, but she could not remember what had happened to it. But then she had had only a few sessions. Bridey Murphy had been hypnotized fifty times; it is not an easy process to dredge up from the subconscious all the dormant secrets that nature apparently intended to be dormant.

Was she the better for her subconscious experience? Not really, for there was no influx of fresh understanding or appreciation of life. She was no more than amused by the transition in sex, not uncommon in reincarnation regressions. But did it help in her understanding of herself? Only, of course, if she accepted the experience as gospel.

She was not aware of any masculine attributes in herself, though many people had commented on the contrast between her clipped speech and manner and her soft femininity of feature and form.

"Do you think," I asked with a smile, "that you could possibly have been a man in an earlier life?"

She frowned. "I don't know," she said, concentrating seriously, "but I do know that as a kid I was the biggest tomboy on the block."

10

The Psychics Do Their Thing

There was a birthday party at the Beverly Hills home of actor John Conte. An unscheduled guest, Peter Hurkos, had arrived with movie star Glenn Ford, and soon occupied the center of the stage. Everybody, of course, wanted a reading from the celebrated psychic who had been credited with solving crimes baffling the police of two continents. Hurkos was not reluctant to perform. He turned first to the host, Conte, held an article of his—a watch—for a moment, closed his eyes as though concentrating, and then spoke rapidly as if a scene were unfolding before his eyes:

"It was during the war, you were in uniform, walking across a gangplank to a ship going to the European military theater, and then at the last minute there was an order changing it all and sending you off to the Pacific theater instead."

All eyes in the room traveled to Conte. He was standing bemused, but having been exposed to the marvels of the psychic before, he gave no indication of surprise.

"Well?" somebody said.

Conte nodded. "I had forgotten; it happened so long ago, but that was exactly it."

Hurkos' interest shifted to a middle-aged woman whom I had met earlier that day—real estate operator Thelma Orloff, the wife of Arthur Orloff, a Hollywood writer who had volubly expressed the opinion that the psychic was all nonsense.

For a moment Hurkos fondled the personal article Mrs. Orloff had given him, apparently trying for the vibration that would tune him into the Universal Subconscious.

"Ah," he said, finally, "I see an older woman close to you; she is in the hospital with a broken hip, and you are very concerned about her."

Thelma Orloff transfixed her husband with a look. "My mother," she said, "broke her hip and is in traction."

Hurkos again closed his eyes. "She didn't fall down a step, or anything like that," he said, "but I see her stumbling over a level surface, and falling like that."

Thelma Orloff nodded. "Exactly," she said. Her mother had been walking along in the house when she tripped and fell.

"Recovery will be slow," Hurkos went on, "don't expect too much."

He returned the personal article to Mrs. Orloff and looked around the room, his gaze stopping at my dinner companion of the evening, a young lady whom I knew but briefly.

The psychometrist held out his hand and she put a small compact in it.

I watched her curiously. Her young, unlined face, with its dreamy-eyed aspect, betrayed no sign of emotion or interest. It was as though she were the observer as well as the observed.

I had thought her the typical starlet, twenty-one or so, unmarried, ambitious for a career, and with thoughts only for that career.

Hurkos thought differently.

"You were married at a very young age," he said, "and are now divorced."

With surprise, I saw her nodding.

"You had two children, very young," he said. "The boy is now ten."

The young woman was regarding him quizzically. "I do have a son that age, but he is my only child."

Hurkos frowned in rapt concentration. "There were two children," he stressed, "but you had a miscarriage and lost one." He brushed a hand wearily across his eyes, as if what he saw was almost too much for him.

"You and your husband were in the kitchen," he said, "and you were having a furious quarrel. You were already pregnant with your second child, and this was just one of a long series of arguments, but worse than the others. At the height of the argument, you became hysterical and rushed outside in the rain, running, running, you didn't know where, just to get away. After a few hours in the storm, exhausted, you felt the first twinges of pain and returned to the house. It was now light. The pain increased, it became a dull throb, and that day you suffered a miscarriage, losing your child."

My eyes turned to my companion. Her face had turned deadly pale, her jaw hung slack, and her blue eyes had widened with wonder.

I regarded her questioningly. "You look too young for all that," I remarked rather vapidly.

She shook her head in bewilderment. "Nobody knew the details of that night," she said, "nobody—it's incredible."

Lost in her own thoughts, she was a poor dinner partner for the rest of the evening. Occasionally, I caught her looking at Hurkos across the table, and then she would quietly retreat into her shell. I did manage to learn that she was twenty-seven not twenty-one, as I had thought, and she had her first child at seventeen. Hurkos had not erred on a single impression.

The next day I continued to examine the marvels of the Dutch psychic machine. I heard him speak under hypnosis in a thick guttural Russian, a language he had no knowledge of consciously, warning of a Russian takeover in Castro's Cuba —a takeover not yet publicly acknowledged.

Hurkos looked equally into past, present, and future. Though a hulking man, he was very sensitively attuned and could be thrown off stride by rude interruptions, a confusion of thoughts in others, or horrible impressions of tragedy that sometimes flowed through him as he picked up an object or looked at somebody. He was a rare combination of ego and humility, bitterly defensive about his gift, resentful at being used or abused by people who were not properly appreciative, and yet strangely humble about himself as a man who didn't quite understand his own power.

In the Jackson murders in Virginia, where he had tuned into two suspects, one eventually brought to trial, he constantly amazed investigators with his psychic revelations, not only about the murder but about the police themselves. Inspector Jack

Hall, who gave Hurkos credit for turning up the right man, was even more impressed by the things Hurkos told him about himself that no outsiders knew. He was told about his bad back and how he had got it, about a son who had died of leukemia, and the date of his death, and that his wife, then verging on middle age, would have another child, a girl, in a year. Hurkos even gave the date—June 24, 1961. "We had a girl," Hall said, "born the very day he predicted."

When he first met Hall, Hurkos told the detective that Hall's wife was sitting impatiently in a doctor's office, and he was right. On another occasion, riding along the highway, he turned and said to Hall, who was driving, "Your wife is in a car a few hundred yards ahead of us." He had never seen the wife, nor the car, but as Hall picked up speed and overtook the car which was out of sight at the time, he saw his car with his wife in it. Hall's commentary was significant. "It's enough to make you believe in the Almighty God."

Yet Hurkos did not claim to be infallible. He felt he was doing well if he was 80 percent accurate. He was proud of his successes in solving crimes in his native Holland, in England, and in the United States, and of his record of not accepting payment for services on behalf of the police.

Hurkos apparently became psychic through a fluke—a fall on his head. Previously, he had been a Dutch house painter, hardly knowing what the word psychic meant, but after the fall, which landed him in a hospital, he developed a sixth sense which told him things about people they didn't know themselves. Long before he was brought to this country by the psychic researcher Dr. Andrija Puharich and department store magnate Henry Belk, he had been billed throughout the Lowlands as the Man with the Radar Brain. Hurkos, more than any other psychic, was like a psychic machine. In a crime, such as the Boston Strangler murders, he could pick up a hundred remarkable clues without being able to weave them into a satisfactory solution. And yet the man he picked out, and the one eventually saddled with the crimes, pretty much answered the same description, even to a pointed nose and a scar on the right side of the face.

In Holland, after World War II, Hurkos earned a local reputation for locating missing people or describing their deaths.

All he needed was one of their personal articles, and his psychometric gift did the rest. When a small girl disappeared from home, the people of a neighboring village sent for him and took up a collection to pay his expenses. He told them she had been strangled, but he couldn't find the body or the killer. There were too many distracting images. Later, her body turned up, strangled.

There was no evidence that Hurkos was spiritually motivated or that motivation of any sort had anything to do with the genesis of his gift. To some, he was an obvious gland case, a fluke created by an accident. They took no account of the fact that others had similar accidents without being similarly affected.

In this country, Belk used Hurkos as a store detective extraordinary to pinpoint employees' defections and embezzlements. Some felt this a misuse of a divine gift, but Belk contended he was only testing the psychic's potentialities and limitations. Yet Belk, unfairly perhaps, soon became disenchanted with Hurkos. A family tragedy helped sour him. Distraught at the disappearance of his ten-year-old daughter from the Belk home in North Carolina, Belk phoned Hurkos in Miami to ask what had happened to the child. Hurkos said he would have to concentrate.

Five minutes later he phoned back to Belk in Charlotte, and told him gravely: "I don't know how to tell you this, but her body is in the river near your house. She's drowned."

Hurkos said she would be found near a certain clump of bushes at the edge of the river. And there Belk found the huddled body of his dead child. He was inconsolable. In his grief, he turned momentarily against the man who had just proved himself anew. "If he could see ahead," the father said bitterly, "why couldn't he have told me what was going to happen to my child in time to save her?"

In Miami, Hurkos was credited with solving a double murder even before police knew the two crimes were connected. In October, 1958, Navy Commander John T. Stewart, retired, was fatally shot in his Key Largo home. A few hours later, in an apparently unrelated crime, cabdriver Edward Sentor was shot to death in his cab in downtown Miami. Police Lieutenant Tom Lipe, head of the Miami homicide squad, having heard of

Hurkos' strange powers, asked the Dutch psychic machine to sit in the cab and tell what impressions he got, if any. Hurkos, tuning in on the unknown killer, ascribed not only one but two slayings to him. Moreover, he not only described the killer but went into his past and even named him. "Hurkos," Lipe reported, "said the fugitive had also killed a man in the Keys, and had been in trouble before. He said he was tall and thin, with a tattoo on his right arm, walked with the ambling gait of a sailor, but could move like lightning when he had to." The killer was well known in Havana and Detroit, and he was called Smitty.

With the Detroit clue, Miami police checked with Michigan authorities. A merchant seaman, who had shipped to Cuba and served time in Michigan, seemed to answer Hurkos' description. His name was Charles Smith. A rogues' gallery portrait of Smitty, from Michigan, was identified by a Miami waitress as that of the man who boasted one night of killing two men. She thought at the time that he was bragging. A month later, Smith was arrested in New Orleans, brought back to Miami, convicted of murder, and sentenced to life imprisonment. Hurkos, with all his frailties, had done it again.

On the strength of these achievements, Hurkos was brought into the Boston Strangler investigation by the attorney general of the Commonwealth of Massachusetts, the present United States Senator Edward Brooke. Brooke's deputy, John Bottomly, having read my account of Hurkos' police work, phoned from Boston to ask if I could produce the psychic. He pointed out that routine police work had been unsuccessful, and nothing was to be lost as long as there was no publicity political adversaries could exploit.

Through Dr. Puharich, to whom I relayed the Massachusetts' request, secret arrangements were made to bring Hurkos from the West Coast. As Gerold Frank revealed in his best seller, *The Boston Strangler,* Hurkos confounded Boston police with his radarlike glimpses of their own suspicions, but his mind seemed to roam kaleidoscopically all over the criminal lot. As was true in the Jackson murder case in Virginia, he often seemed confused between police suspects and the actual perpetrator. Yet, as Gerold Frank was to tell me later, his description of the killer did tally with that of the man who subsequently confessed the crimes.

Hurkos was by no means the only psychic detective. Others were fellow Dutchman Gerard Croiset, the late Florence Psychic of Edgewater, New Jersey, and Anne Gehman of Cassadaga, Florida. There were still others, not as well known, their achievements not as well documented. As with Hurkos, the newspapers were full of Anne Gehman and her "miracles." A recent accomplishment was the location of a missing woman whom she correctly revealed to have been murdered. Anne, as pretty as she was psychic, was consulted by friends of Mrs. Robert Ritter of Leesburg, Florida, secretary of Lake County Public Defender Robert E. Pierce, after she had been missing for twenty-four hours. Alternately holding Mrs. Ritter's cigaret case, a cigaret lighter and a lipstick, Anne said the secretary had been the victim of foul play. She drew a map, showing the fork in the road where, a few miles away, the abandoned car would be found. The car was found on Treasure Island Road, forking off Florida State Road 44, on the right instead of the left fork which had been visualized. However, it was the same distance from the fork, and after trying one road, the police tried the other, and there found the car. Apparently, right and left were confused by the position from which the map was examined. The car was found in a wooded scene, some forty to fifty yards off the highway, just as Anne had foreseen. The wooded scene was exactly as she had depicted it. She had also reported where the body would be found and said Mrs. Ritter had been abducted as a reprisal measure, and was still alive but severely wounded. She said the secretary had been dragged from the car, stabbed, and then tortured. This was stated on a Tuesday, April 23, 1968.

On the following day, again consulted by the woman's friends, Anne said Mrs. Ritter was no longer alive. The body was found on Saturday, the 27th, and it became apparent that Anne had been tragically correct. Police said that the victim had been stabbed, then fatally shot. She had obviously been tortured—the hair on her body had been forcibly pulled out and some parts of her body cruelly mutilated. The time of death was set at twenty-four hours after her abduction. The

Orlando newspapers serving that Central Florida area were disposed to give Anne her share of credit: "This [time of death] adds more weight to the prediction of Cassadaga medium Anne Gehman who told friends of the woman on the first day she was reported missing that Mrs. Ritter was still alive, but hurt and in pain. Miss Gehman told the friends they should contact authorities before dark. The next day, Miss Gehman said she felt Mrs. Ritter was dead."

When last seen alive, Mrs. Ritter was getting into her car with a woman, who did the driving. Shortly after the body was found, this woman, Mrs. Marie Dean Arrington, a Negro of Leesburg, was charged with the murder and held for trial. Police said two children of Mrs. Arrington's had been represented by Mrs. Ritter's employer, Public Defender Pierce, in recent court cases.

Pierce thought it possible his secretary had been the victim of reprisal. Anne Gehman had said, "It all started with a threatening phone call."

Like most psychic detectives, Anne was a psychometrist, and by holding an object, she could tune into the owner's past, present, and future. After the Leesburg incident, police from other communities quietly consulted the girl from Cassadaga, by way of Petoskey, Michigan. In one instance, they already had the body and knew the girl had been murdered. They were looking for clues to the murderer, and the only objects they could produce for Anne were a watch and ring found on the body. But as Anne touched the two objects, strong impressions immediately surged through her subconscious. She felt that the murdered girl was pregnant, and she empathically experienced the sensation of two bullets entering her body. She saw the killer driving a truck and could even make out the emblem on the truck.

An autopsy confirmed that the girl was pregnant, and a missing persons alarm led to her identification. Her boyfriend drove a truck for the highway department. He was picked up by the police.

Despite her success as a psychic sleuth, Anne prides herself chiefly on providing spiritual guidance through the spirits she believes in. "I really don't like playing detective," she said once, "but feel I can be more helpful giving spiritual guidance."

Before becoming a spiritualist, Anne had taken nurses' training in Jacksonville, Florida. For this reason, perhaps, she often seems to concentrate on a subject's physical condition, at times with X-ray vision. The Orlando *Sentinel* reported one especially successful example of Cayce-like diagnosis:

"A Daytona Beach woman, being read by Anne, was surprised when informed that she had a large mass in her body and was advised to see her doctor. The woman took the advice although she had been experiencing no discomfort. She was X-rayed and found to have a massive tumor which required surgery. The woman's physician was amazed at the medium's ability and contacted her. They now have a close association, the physician sometimes sending patients to her."

In locating missing persons, the newspaper reported, Anne was similarly effective: "A distraught mother, questioning Anne as to the whereabouts of her missing daughter, was directed to the town and address where she could be found. 'And she needs you desperately,' Miss Gehman added. The mother took a bus to the out-of-state town mentioned. Her daughter was at the address given. She was alone with a tiny baby, deserted by her husband."

Anne gets personal satisfaction out of directly helping people. A young man from St. Petersburg, Florida, having suffered a severe heart attack, had come to the spiritualist community of Cassadaga to learn about life after death and to prepare to meet his Maker. "He had been told," Anne said, "that he could only live about six months." She had often worked subconsciously in trying to heal people and felt he could be helped in this way. "I worked with him," she recalled, "and taught him to direct the healing into himself." The cure, she claimed, was wonderfully prompt and effective. "One month later his doctor told him there was no trace of the damage to his heart."

Though usually tuned out when not concentrating, Anne has had spontaneous impressions about various people, including herself. One impression was especially interesting as it dovetailed with the prediction I had casually made during our meeting at Cassadaga. As a matter of fact, it occurred shortly after I had suggested she wouldn't marry the man she had been planning to. The phone rang in her modest home, and as she answered it, she felt an electric tingle. She knew at that moment, undeniably, that this man she would marry. He had phoned to inquire about spiritualism, and he visited her shortly thereafter. The romance developed quickly, and Robert Robeson is now her husband, giving her the inner support she requires for her often wearing work.

Nobody has profited more from her visions than Anne herself. The daughter of a spiritualist family, she wavered in her belief in God when she left home and tried to make her own way. She was living alone in DeLand, Florida, not far from Cassadaga, and was depressed and discouraged. Her mood was so black that she even contemplated suicide. But in the nadir of her despair, a vision of a lady in white came to her one night. "If you will follow me," the vision said, "I will lead you to a new life." The next morning, as though driving itself, her car took her to Cassadaga and the doorstep of medium Wilbur Hull.

Her meeting with Hull seemed ordained, and as mystical as anything Anne was to do subsequently. She circled the little town of two hundred inhabitants, then drove slowly through its handful of quaint streets, glancing at the shingles of the various mediums in residence. Each time she made a complete circuit of the town, her car stalled in front of the same house, that of Wilbur Hull. Finally, she got out of the car and climbed his stairs. He met her at the front door. "I don't know who you are," he said, "but I was expecting you."

Hull told the young girl that his spirit control, Rose, a medium who had died in 1945, had appeared to her in a vision to lead her to Cassadaga. She became a student of Hull's, studying the philosophy of spiritualism, meditating, communing with God, and in 1960 she became the youngest medium ever certified by the National Spiritualist Association of Churches.

She found herself completely at home in this winter headquarters for America's spiritualists, with its picturesque streets and even more picturesque inhabitants. There, she rubbed shoulders and thought waves with other mediums in residence, and communed with the spirits who, she feels, guide not only her but the multitudes who seek her out. By the very definition of spiritualism, there is no death, only a transition, and this is Anne's message of hope for the troubled and downcast.

Whatever the origin of her psychic force, it has been deadly accurate at times. In July, 1968, before the conventions had even nominated the Presidential candidates, Anne had chosen former Vice President Richard Nixon to beat Vice President Hubert Humphrey. In a prediction, reported from Freeville, Georgia, where she was attending a spiritualist assembly, she pinpointed: "Nixon will defeat Humphrey in a close race in November."

Many listened closely, remembering that she had predicted President Kennedy's election in a narrow race and his subsequent assassination. And they were not disappointed, for she foresaw every aspect of the election correctly, including the sectional run of former Governor George Wallace and the ineffectuality of Minnesota's Senator Eugene McCarthy. "It is definitely a Republican year," she said. "People are fed up with the Johnson regime and all its programs. More people are leaning toward conservatism."

Wallace's strength she confined to the Southeast and the South through Texas. "He will not have enough strength to throw the election into the House of Representatives."

As for McCarthy's impact on the Presidential race: "He will have little effect in spite of his support by young people."

Before the convention, she accurately foresaw Governor Ronald Reagan of California weakening his national image with a belated push for the Presidential nomination. However, she anticipated a comeback and said that, in 1972, Reagan would yet be President or Vice President. She saw him in the White House, but apparently was unable to distinguish the type of tenancy.

As for Massachusetts Senator Edward Kennedy, the youngest of the Kennedy brothers, she saw him gradually fading from the political limelight, despite an early thrust for power.

Anne Gehman was reassuringly consistent. In the April 21, 1968, issue of the Orlando *Sentinel* magazine, she first publicly picked Nixon to win over Humphrey that November, and made still another prediction, months before the unheralded event: "Jackie Kennedy will remarry soon."

She sometimes saw the right result, despite faulty reasoning. On March 29, two days before President Johnson unexpectedly took himself out of the November election, she saw him withdrawing as a candidate in the fall, but from illness not choice.

She took his announcement good-naturedly and ridiculed skeptics who said Johnson did not really mean what he said. "We will never see him entering politics again," she stressed.

In Holland, where the Dutch government supported a psychic research center, sensitive Gerard Croiset was better known even than Hurkos. Croiset's extrasensory perception was checked at the University of Utrecht's Parapsychology Institute by its director, Dr. W. H. C. Tenhaeff, who first encouraged psychics to use their talents to help the police. Croiset, like Hurkos and Anne Gehman, tuned in to people by merely holding something that had belonged to them, or that they had touched. Near Wierden, Holland, in a lonely lane, a man had leaped out of the darkness to attack an attractive blond girl. He struck her several times before, resisting furiously, she wrenched the assault hammer from him. Croiset didn't even see the girl, who was under sedation in the hospital. Instead, he squeezed the handle of the hammer a few times. Then, as the police listened skeptically, he gave a detailed description of the assailant: "He is tall and dark, about thirty, with a deformed ear." He added that the hammer belonged to another, an older man living in a small frame cottage, whom the fugitive frequently visited.

Since this was one of Croiset's first cases, the police did little searching for somebody answering this description. However, months later, they picked up a twenty-nine-year-old man on another morals charge. He was tall and dark—with a disfigured left ear. Questioned about the earlier attack, he finally broke down and admitted he had assaulted the girl with a hammer he had borrowed from a friend living in a small cottage.

Croiset excelled in missing persons' cases. Once he was consulted by phone about a four-year-old child, fifty miles away, who had disappeared twenty-four hours before. He said the body would be found in three days in a canal near Eindhoven—and three days later the body was fished out of the Eindhoven Canal.

Even in laboratory experiments, dear to parapsychologists, Croiset performed remarkably. Ten days before a conference he was taken into the meeting room and asked to describe the persons who would occupy the chairs. Over one chair, he could only shake his head and repeat, "I see nothing." As Tenhaeff pointed to a neighboring chair, Croiset's face brightened. "I see a woman," he said, "her face scarred in a recent auto accident."

Thirty persons were expected at the conference; only twenty-nine showed up. The empty chair was the one for which Croiset could get nothing. And the lady with the scarred face? She was more intrigued by Croiset than by the conference agenda when she learned he had picked out her chair. "How," she asked the psychic, "did you know about my road crash in Italy two months ago?"

Croiset, like other sensitives, was not always effective. At a demonstration during a visit to New York, he strove to duplicate his feat with the chairs. Only in a few instances did he get any characteristic description of the individuals who sat in the chairs arranged for the experiment. His lack of success didn't bother him, and he seemed to relish figuring out how he went off scent.

Obviously, the psychic function is not always dependable, and psychics like Croiset are the first to accent their own failings. Croiset, a simple, unsophisticated man, felt that his gift was intended for good, and perhaps a nonutilitarian experiment does not motivate a subconscious response. Edgar Cayce, near the end of his career, spurned a request by parapsychologist Joseph Rhine of Duke University that he describe the contents of a filing case in a certain room at Columbia University. Cayce's retort applies to Croiset and all other psychics asked to submit to tests: "Unless such experiences create such in the lives of individuals that interest or apply themselves in the study of such lives, then it is indeed of little thought, nor has it any place in man's experience."

But like Cayce, Croiset, when properly motivated, could perform apparent miracles that made the chair experiment seem a game to amuse dabblers in the psychic. How much more significant was the appeal by a University of Kansas professor concerned about the disappearance of his twenty-four-year-old daughter. After the girl had been missing for six weeks without a clue, Dr. Walter Sandelius, former Rhodes scholar and professor of political science, put through a call to Dr. Tenhaeff in Holland.

"Can Croiset help me?" he asked. "My daughter disappeared from a Topeka hospital weeks ago and nobody has seen her since."

Croiset, put on the phone, closed his eyes and concentrated on a scene forty-five hundred miles away. "I can see her running over a broad lawn," he said, "and crossing a viaduct."

The father confirmed the topography.

Croiset then picked out the girl riding the highway in a truck and a large car, and arriving some distance away at a city on water, with many small boats on its surface. One scene after another crowded through his mind. "Do not worry," he told the father, "she is alive and well, and you will have definite news in six days."

Precisely six days later, as Sandelius was preparing another call to Tenhaeff, his daughter turned up at the house. After explaining her disappearance, she related what had happened to her. After fleeing the hospital—across a broad lawn—she had taken to the open highway, hitching one ride in a truck, another in a large sports car. At the very time her father had been talking to Croiset, she was in Corpus Christi, Texas, a city verging on water, with many small boats.

Yet another psychic, Sandelius reported at the time, had told him that his daughter would return home, unharmed, before Christmas. On December 17 she strolled into the house.

In psychic police work, there has been no more remarkable sensitive than the late Florence Sternfels, better known as Florence Psychic. Under this pseudonym she was listed for years in the New York City telephone directory because of her service to telephone company officials in locating missing papers of some importance. On numerous occasions I sat in Florence Psychic's small living room, while, merely touching billets of paper, she traveled into a subject's home, visualized the inside of the refrigerator, and described the furnishings in living room, bedroom, and bathroom. Then, having finished her tour, as she called it, she would look up brightly to see how correct she had been. The incredulous look of householders invariably revealed how close she was to the mark.

As a psychometrist, Florence specialized in locating missing people and objects, and in crimes of larceny and passion.

Many police departments called on her when orthodox measures appeared to have failed. In some cases, too, as I was to observe firsthand, the families of victims turned hopefully to her. Despite an aging body and a bad heart, Florence Psychic had an irrepressible optimism which stood her and her clients in good stead.

Once, holding the paper billet of a young man who had been looking around the room as if half ashamed to be there, Florence said with a twinkle in her eye: "This man is in the dry cleaning business, and he is here to find out how his employees are stealing from him." She looked over to where the man was sitting sheepishly, not really expecting anything. "They are robbing your warehouses," she said, "and it's an inside job and you know it. So what are you doing here?"

The man looked as if a bomb had hit him. "Incredible," he said, "incredible."

After the meeting, in which Florence had read briefly for a dozen people, the youthful dry cleaner—for that he was—moved up to Florence's chair for more details about the Great Dry Cleaning Robbery.

But Florence was not to be managed. "You know who did it," she said, with an offhand gesture, "you just don't want to face up to it."

The man smiled embarrassedly, and catching my eye, said, "I can't believe it. They told me she was good, but I didn't expect anything like this—in fact, I didn't expect anything."

"Can you tell who did it?" I asked.

He looked mysterious. "I thought I did, now I'm sure. But it was somebody I trusted, and—she's right—I didn't want to face it."

Unfortunately, the damage had usually been done before Florence was summoned. After the disappearance of millionaire brewer Adolph Coors III several years ago, the Colorado man's brother, William, brought Adolph's picture and belt buckle to Florence's home. She touched the objects and then sighed heavily, as a dark vision crossed her subconscious. She saw a pool of blood on a bridge and Adolph lying dead nearby. As she handled the buckle, she suddenly groaned, "My head feels like two bullets went into it."

Three months later, toward the middle of September, 1960, the body was found in the area suggested by the psychic. Coors had been fatally shot, the autopsy revealing two bullet wounds.

Florence's radarlike vision was often beyond belief. When eighty-year-old Phoebe DuBois of Kinnelon, New Jersey, vanished after a walk, Florence not only drew a graphic picture of the elderly woman's last hike but described how she had stumbled in the woods, fallen down, and succumbed to exposure.

Kinnelon Police Chief Gifford Whitmore listened in understandable disbelief, and when Florence mentioned in passing that Mrs. DuBois had been tightly holding ten dollars at the time, he had the uneasy feeling that he was ridiculously wasting his time. Fortunately, he suppressed his misgivings, and there, as the sketch had shown, lay the body of the woman who had disappeared two weeks before. The ten dollars was there.

Florence's strength and vitality were not up to the demands imposed on her. But she tried to help whomever she could when that help was needed. She had suffered a heart attack, and was in a New Jersey hospital, as I recall, when the unsolved murder of twenty-two-year-old Janice Wylie, niece of author Philip Wylie, was in the newspapers. The police had many clues, but all faded down blind alleys. There didn't seem to be anything to lose by turning to a psychic. Eddie Mahar, then city editor of the New York *Journal* wondered aloud whether Florence Psychic could conceivably throw any light on the slaying by handling an article belonging to the dead girl. This was willingly provided by the grieving father, writer Max Wylie, ready to try anything to bring his daughter's killer to justice.

I hesitated to call on an ailing Florence, but the gallant old lady did not hesitate for a moment. "Come over to the hospital anytime," she said, "and I'll do what I can." She apologized for not being up to par. "If I stop for breath once in a while, you'll have to forgive me."

An appointment was arranged, and we—Eddie Mahar, Max Wylie, and myself—proceeded to the hospital. Florence greeted us warmly and then fell back in her bed, spent by the effort. We stood around her bed as Max Wylie turned an object over to her. She squeezed it, then closed her eyes and sighed heavily.

She did not react as quickly as usual. The impressions seemed to trickle instead of flow through her. And when they came, she spoke haltingly, almost uncertainly. "I see a dark-skinned youngish man," she said. He had gotten into the girl's Manhattan apartment on a ruse, she said, after prowling the neighborhood. He knew neither Janice nor her roommate, also a victim. Both girls, she said, had been brutally surprised by the intruder.

Wylie listened stoically to the recital of his daughter's slaying. I can remember secretly admiring his inner fortitude at the time. Then, Florence, by some dint of will, mustered her resources for intensive concentration. She motioned Wylie closer, for something intended only for his ear. She whispered inaudibly, then sank back exhausted. At this point a nurse came in, and we had to leave. Florence gave us a brave smile. "I wish I could have been more help," she said, "but I am so tired."

We thanked her and left. Both Eddie Mahar and I were curious about what she had told Wylie, and he satisfied our curiosity as well as he could.

Frowning, he said, "She mentioned a couple of intimate things that only the police would have known about—they were never published or otherwise made known."

Sometime thereafter, a suspect was picked up and charged with the murder. I had the feeling that he was not the right man, for he did not fit Florence's description. Subsequently, the charges were dismissed.

Not long after, in 1965, the woman who had helped so many people went to her reward. I felt a sense of loss but had the comforting feeling that this blithe spirit could never be quenched. As though it were yesterday, I remember the sly smile on her wonderfully expressive face when a Boston reporter was teasing her about Peter Hurkos being brought into the Boston Strangler case before her.

"That may be true," the old lady returned, "but I see Mr. Hurkos in trouble very soon himself—arrested, as a matter of fact."

In a week or so, I picked up a newspaper and read that Hurkos, fresh from Boston, had been arrested by the FBI in New York and charged with impersonating a federal agent. On inspection, it didn't seem like much of an offense, but Florence had caught the vibrations. In the end, that was all the testimonial she ever wanted—recognition of a remarkable gift she never quite understood herself.

11

Do the Stars Ordain?

Astrology took a considerable stride forward in recent years with the newly revised version of the New Testament which transforms the Three Wise Men into three astrologers, though it does not add that they were looking not only for the Star of Bethlehem but for the peculiar constellation which traditionally heralded the coming of Christ.

It took on a further aura of respectability when the State Department permitted its officers in the Southeastern Asia service to study astrology, if not for the art itself, then to ingratiate themselves with officials in a world which accepts astrology more readily than it does medicine or law.

Even more intriguingly, several astrological forecasts, released before the act, pinpointed the John F. Kennedy assassination with a fastidiousness that revived the Biblical concept that the stars ordain. Eighteen months before Kennedy was struck down, Huter's *Astrological Calendar,* published in Germany, carried the highly prophetic warning: "The horoscope of the United States President shows health defects and the danger that a fanatic is preparing for his assassination." In addition, astrologer Leslie McIntyre, even more specific than David Williams, warned in the November, 1963, issue of *American Astrology,* on the stands in October: "In the past such configurations have coincided with personal danger to our head of state, all the more so in this case in view of the grievous attack by Saturn on Kennedy's natal trio of Mars, Mercury and Jupiter, along with Uranus square (opposed to) his sun. November is obviously fraught with perils of several varieties."

Aside from Williams, America's astrologers were not as fatalistic as their European comrades, and for excellent reason: The Europeans, from the remoteness of several thousand miles, could regard a Presidential assassination with practiced detachment. More significantly, European and Asian astrologers function on the premise that the stars compel—reflecting their belief in a fixed future—while American astrologers, in keeping with Protestant determinism, hold that the stars impel. In other words, knowing what the stars portended, Kennedy might conceivably have altered his destiny; heeding any one astrological warning, he might have canceled the Dallas trip and been spared. This, of course, discounts the fact that Kennedy proceeded in a way dictated by his personality and circumstances over which he had little control.

As a notable exception, the most distinguished of American astrologers, Evangeline Adams, held that astrology, with its eighth house of death, is obviously calculated to foresee the terminal point as well as the various midpoints of life—for certainly there is only one aspect as basic as birth and that is death. And still American astrologers, acquiescing to convention, have shrunk from dealing openly with this problem and yet have predicted births, marriages, business successes and reverses, journeys, even election results, all from the angles of the various planets in relation to the hour of birth.

Just as the moon affects the tides, so the planetary aspects appear to influence more than mere man. The late science editor John J. O'Neill, converted to astrology while trying to disprove it, astounded skeptical newspaper colleagues years ago by successfully pinpointing a major earthquake in the Puget Sound area three months before it occurred. Similarly, astrologer Carroll Duncan, in a prophetic 1968 issue of *Horoscope* magazine, clearly foretold the earthquakes which were to devastate Iran during the final days of August, 1968. "Saturn," he said, "rests on the zenith in Iran . . . making that part of the world vulnerable to quakes when Saturn receives the parallel of Jupiter." To the average layman it sounded like so much nonsense. Yet, citing additionally unfavorable planetary aspects between Mars and Neptune on the 30th of August, 1968,

Duncan also fixed the precise date of the quakes—and it was all in *Horoscope* magazine, for anyone to read, well ahead of time.

Perhaps as a reflection of the Space Age, the current interest in astrology has become almost a religion among some disenchanted youngsters rebelling from sham and hypocrisy and seeking in astrology a key to the natural universe. To others, astrology offers a blueprint by which some hopefully guide their lives. Presumably, it anticipates trends and cycles, affecting individuals and groups, indicating the best time to get involved in social and business relationships and any other activity, down to taking a trip. Similarly, astrology offers a blueprint or road map on the broadest issues, such as adolescent unrest around the world. "Neptune's current passage through Scorpio," reported astrologer David Williams, "accentuates the moral irresponsibility of the present younger generation." But, it is hoped, Neptune, leaving the passionate sign of Scorpio in 1970, would, in entering spiritualistic Sagittarius, betoken a great resurgence of interest in religion.

Nobody is more optimistic about man's future, generally, than the astrologers. With the advent in this century of the Aquarian Age after the era of Pisces the Fish—the sign of early Christianity—the earth stood on the brink of many changes. Aquarius, the eleventh sign of the zodiac, is the sign of the humanitarian (Franklin D. Roosevelt, Edison, Lincoln) and accordingly signals the broad upward sweep of humanity. Its effect, astrologers say, will be reflected, materially, in man's conquest of space and, spiritually, in the restless quest of the young for some meaningful purpose—hence the hippie interest in primitive Christianity and astrology.

Nobody can say for sure how astrology works. However, as convert John O'Neill once pointed out, the solar system, comprising the planets, the sun, and the moon, has a noticeable effect on the affairs of human beings. The only mystery arises from our own lack of insight. "If anything we do not see produces an effect," O'Neill once observed, "we are very much inclined to think of that effect as having something mysterious connected with it."

There have been many theories of astrology. Supported by the studies of such savants as the late Professor Ellsworth

Huntington of Yale, Consolidated Edison's David Williams has theorized that with his first breath the newborn infant is indelibly stamped by billions of cosmic rays. Influenced by the angles of the planets at the moment of birth, these presumably form the individual's magnetic field, which reacts predictably to the predictable shifting of the planets. "In other words," scientifically oriented Williams pointed out, "the individual is a microcosm of that greater macrocosm, the planetary system, and as the planets vary in aspect so does he."

Huntington himself elaborated on man's reaction to the constantly changing electrical atmosphere. "Studies such as those begun by Adrian and continued by Burr indicate that the human body has its own definite electrical field. If that is the case, variations in the external electrical field must inevitably influence the internal human field. It is likewise obvious that if the electrical field of the sun or of the solar system as a whole undergoes variations, there must be corresponding disturbances in the field of the earth. Thus, there is a logical connection between solar activity, the earth's atmosphere, man's psychological reactions, prices on the stock market and the ups and downs of business."

In his *This World and That,* physician Laurence J. Bendit stressed that the correlation between the individual and his planetary aspects at birth is mathematical, but the delineation varies with the skill of the interpreter. "Astrology is worked out on a basis of pure mathematics in connection with the positions of the planets at the time of birth," Bendit stated. "Here we are faced either with the fact that the extraordinarily accurate readings of astrological maps, without the astrologer ever having seen the person, are purely psychic or intuitive, or else a mystery which gets deep into the question of the relationship of man with the seemingly objective world, whether as shown in the heaven or in the more mundane sphere of everyday contacts."

One of the most striking examples of an astrologer's insight into these mathematical correlations came about in a dramatic manner in a New York City courtroom, with Evangeline Adams on trial on a fortune-telling charge. While the judge considered her skeptically, Miss Adams appeared in court with a mass of reference books and charts dating back to Babylonian days, to establish her defense that astrology was a mathematical science, not an occult art, or worse, a shameless fraud. She was in the middle of her defense, explaining how she could judge people's personalities and advise them about problems, when the prosecutor reached over and handed her a slip of paper bearing an unknown name, and asked her to tell what she could about this person. Crisply, Miss Adams pointed out that she was not a psychic and to get the information required, she would need the person's hour and minute of birth and the place of birth. There was a whispered consultation between magistrate and prosecutor, and the prosecutor scrawled the desired information on the slip of paper.

He then sat back, with a sly smile, as Miss Adams drew out an ephemeris, the astrologer's Bible, from which she could hastily compute the position of the planets on that particular birthday. The judge followed her with rising interest as, having finished her computations, she stood before the bench and began to describe the individual's personality, attitudes, disposition, and aptitudes. Almost involuntarily, as she proceeded, the judge kept nodding his head, especially as she picked out specific events in the person's background. And then, boldly, she passed on to an anticipated course of events, forecasting the individual's future—the very action for which she was on trial.

But the judge only smiled benignly. "Miss Adams," he said, "you have showed a better knowledge of that individual than I have—and he's my son."

The charge was dismissed, and in the dismissal the legality of astrology was tacitly upheld in the nation's largest city.

Many explanations of astrology have been put forward. These include the theory that different skills, emotions, and events are the reflection of observed planetary changes in the different signs or houses of the twelve-sign zodiac. In the face of evidence that planetary aspects do affect meteorological changes and business cycles, some students of astrology, including the great humanist Jung, see no relationship between the planets in motion millions of miles away, and the affairs of man. At most, they see only meaningful coincidence—the planetary positions reflecting a synchronicity of events at a particular time. As Sydney Omarr, the celebrated Los Angeles astrologer saw it, the stars didn't make anybody act in a particular way but merely indicated how a person was likely to act at a particular time. "When it is noon in Los Angeles," Omarr observed, "it is possible to say that more people are likely to be going out to lunch. Yet the fact that it is noon doesn't cause people to rush out to restaurants. The relationship between the two is meaningful but non-causal."

Synchronicity, favored by Jung, obviously has its flaws, for celestial bodies, particularly the sun and the moon, do manifestly have effects on man and his affairs, without having as much importance as the planets themselves—Mars, Jupiter, Mercury, Neptune, Saturn, Venus, Pluto, Uranus.

Just as the moon affects the tides, so it seems to affect human behavior and health. As a former police reporter, I was familiar with the waves of passionate crimes recurring with the full moon—a finding with some statistical support. Experiments at the University of Pennsylvania School of Medicine indicated that birds as well as people were affected by the phases of the moon. The electrical output of living organisms shows definite rhythms, marked by mood changes in people and increased activity in birds, corresponding to these phases. There were predictable behavior variations with both the full and new moons.

Many a doctor has learned to look at the moon before looking at his patient. The late Dr. Eldon Tice of Los Angeles Methodist Hospital learned that more babies were born during a 48-hour full moon phase than at any other time of the month, and regulated his maternity staff accordingly. Dr. Edson J. Andrews, in Tallahassee, Florida, discovered that the full moon was associated with excessive bleeding among his patients, and he would not operate at this time unless it was an emergency. In the lunar records of more than a thousand tonsillectomies, the number of heavy bleeders and the moon phase formed almost identical curves on his charts. To make sure he was not a bit loony himself, Dr. Andrews checked his records with an Orlando, Florida, colleague who was preoccupied with a similar study. The Orlando physician's findings were strikingly similar. "The astounding preponderance of hemorrhage at full moon and the relative absence at the new moon were plainly evident," Dr. Andrews reported to his medical society. But combing through medical literature, he could find nothing to support a causative moon cycle. However, he did stumble on an old custom dealing with farmers' disinclinations to have their livestock castrated during a full moon lest they bleed to death.

Having got into astrology through studying the correspondence of sun spot activity with rising and falling prices, David Williams went on to plot business cycles months and years ahead, even to predicting bull and bear markets on the stock exchange. For years, as cable purchasing manager of New York's giant utility, Con Ed, he spent millions buying his precious underground cable via the stars without his superiors ever knowing why Con Ed was doing its biggest buying when the market was depressed. In studying commodity prices over the years, Williams sensed a rhythmical rise and fall in the national economy, coinciding with the planetary aspects producing sun spot activity. And so he was introduced to astrology—the so-called science of planetary effects on the minds and moods of men, as opposed to astronomy, which merely studied the planets in relation to themselves. Reaching back two hundred years, Williams discovered financial and political stress every twenty years or so, marked by conjunctions of Jupiter and Saturn, and of Saturn and Uranus. Williams formed this conclusion:

"Business panics are dependent on mass psychology. But since we now know about human magnetic fields, we know that everybody's magnetic field is being disturbed in the same way, leading to booms and depressions, wars and peace."

With only two exceptions from 1762 on, after the depression following the end of the French-Indian War, the Jupiter-Saturn conjunction has coincided with financial and political crises. The exceptions occurred in 1881 and 1901, and were attributed to compensatingly favorable aspects known as trines, the best angular aspect in astrology—120 degrees.

Williams' stock market predictions, recorded in the *Wall Street Journal*, and his own carefully compiled records, reveal him as having been approximately 85 percent correct on business forecasts. His appraisal in *This Week* magazine, October, 1968, included a prediction of the Richard Nixon Presidential victory and a warning about the business slump beginning in March, 1969. By comparing natal charts, Williams

had picked every Presidential winner since Harry Truman's startling victory over Thomas Dewey in 1948. He had Eisenhower
over Stevenson, Johnson over Goldwater, and he saw Nixon's
victory as an almost mathematical certainty. He examined not
only the aspects of the two candidates at birth, but the movements of the eight planets and two lights (moon and sun) in
relation to their charts on Election Day, November 5, 1968.

Cutting through technical language, at times as complex
as any mathematical equation, Williams found that of roughly
a dozen astrological aspects (relationships of the planets in
the two charts) Nixon had four more favorable aspects than
his Democratic opponent.

Ironically, a comparison of the US chart (natal July 4,
1776) with the Humphrey and Nixon charts, indicated that
Humphrey's was perhaps more favorably aspected for the
country. However, as with John Kennedy, Williams saw destiny
having the final say. "The times (mirrored by the stars) bring
forth the man," Williams observed. "Just as Kennedy was
destined to be the President who would die in office, in fulfillment of the Jupiter-Saturn conjunction, so was Nixon destined
to be President during the recession of 1969, which was indicated by the unfavorable Jupiter-Uranus aspect (conjunction)
of April 4, 1969."

Astrologically, Nixon's election appeared to confirm the
market slump just as Kennedy's portended his own assassination.
"That Nixon would fit the astrological pattern better than
Humphrey was indicated by the fact that Nixon's natal
planets made only four favorable angles to the planets in the
US natal chart, whereas Humphrey had six favorable angles."
The predicted 1969 recession called for a national leader
whose planetary aspects would be unfavorable at that time.

As it gains new converts in the Space Age, astrology also
picks up new critics, who ask how two people, prince and pau-
per, for instance, born precisely in the same moment at the
same place, can lead such completely different lives.

Isidor Oblo, the Manhattan astrologer, had a ready answer:
"Two people being born simultaneously under the same aspects
didn't signify that both would be millionaires, or both paupers.
It meant only that their careers would parallel one another,
and when something good or bad was happening to one, it

would also be happening to the other. Should one be a lawyer, the other a gangster, both may have good or bad fortune simultaneously. When the lawyer was getting a judicial appointment, the gangster might be getting a reprieve or a pardon, and when the lawyer failed in court, the gangster's drop in luck might send him to jail."

In Southeast Asia, where few big decisions are made without consulting the stars, the fortunes of the Vietnamese often seem subject to astrological dispositions. Thieu and Vice President Nguyen Cao Ky are known to have followed astrology. Ky's future was remarkably pinpointed from childhood by astrology. "One relative of the vice president said recently," the New York *Times* reported in 1968, "that the Ky family could hardly believe an astrologer years ago who had predicted that young Ky, then a high school student in Hanoi, would move higher than anybody else and would reach one of the top positions in the country."

Because of a remarkable forecast, astrologer Evangeline Adams, fresh from Massachusetts, was hurtled to fame within twenty-four hours after her arrival in New York City. Shortly after she had checked into the Windsor Hotel on fashionable Fifth Avenue, Miss Adams drew up a chart for hotel owner Warren F. Leland. In it, she saw a "danger so imminent that it seemed the man in front of me was being pushed into the very depths of disaster."

Leland, a heavy investor, immediately thought of a stock market crash. But the market was closed the next day, a legal holiday. The following afternoon the disaster made itself known. The Windsor Hotel burned to the ground and many were trapped inside by the flames. The dead included Leland's wife and daughter. Miss Adams barely escaped. Her fortune was made, however, when the distraught Leland told newspaper reporters about the forecast.

Astrology is not always specific, but it does seem to catch situations. In 1922, for instance, astrologer Marc Edmund Jones predicted that in the fall of 1942, when the planet Neptune entered the sign of Libra, an event would occur that would drastically change the course of history. In the fall of 1942 the first controlled nuclear chain reaction took place in Chicago, and the Atomic Age began. In April, 1955, after studying Premier Georgi Malenkov's horoscope, astrologer Carl Payne Tobey of Tucson, Arizona, predicted that on July 10, 1953, an event of major importance would take place in the Kremlin. On that day the Russian government announced the overthrow of the powerful chief of the secret police, Lavrenti Beria, who was arrested and later liquidated. On December 20, 1957, astrologer Willi Bischoff announced: "Pope Pius XII is under unfavorable aspects. A maximum disturbance which gives rise to grave misgivings occurs in full power on October 10, 1958." On October 9 of that year, the Pope died.

Some unusually useful predictions have been made under pressure. The Hungarian astrologer, Louis de Wohl, reportedly performed some invaluable services for the British War Office during World War II. One day in the summer of 1942, a British officer gave him the birth dates of two men without divulging their names or any information about them. Both were born in Scorpio (October 22 to November 21), ruled by Mars—the planet of war. But oddly, according to de Wohl's charts, the older man was entering the peak of his career and would climb steadily, while the younger was on a downtrend. "The older of the two will triumph," he reported. "His chart is on the rise and success will follow him from now on." The older man was General Bernard Montgomery, Britain's victorious Monty; the younger was Field Marshal Erwin Rommel, whose declining fortunes were to end in suicide.

The detractors of astrology have constantly cited the fact that Hitler had recourse to astrologers. However, astrologers have indignantly rejoined that Hitler got rid of his astrologers when, as in the invasion of Russia, they did not agree with his vaunted intuition.

Because of a tarnished image, created perhaps by exaggerated claims of charlatans, practical astrology frequently passes by other names—astrodiagnosis, astrophysics, astrogeomagnetics, cyclical forecasts, etc.—but it generally adds up to the same thing: the inexplicable effect of the planets on man.

Many astute businessmen, following in the star steps of tycoons J. P. Morgan, Vanderbilt, and James J. Hill, who seldom made a move without Evangeline Adams, preferred astrologers' advice to their brokers'. And many physicians have consulted astrologers or used astrology themselves. The most unexpected consulted astrologers Oblo and Doris Doane of Los Angeles, as they would a specialist. And in Washington, D.C., the late Ernest Grant advised Dr. F. Regis Riesenman of a patient's suicidal background in time for the doctor—previously unaware of it—to forestall a recurrence.

Astrologer Oblo has helped a dozen physicians to pick out physical and emotional weaknesses—and strengths. Looking at my chart, he observed that as an afflicted Taurean my throat was a weak point, since natal Taurus governs the throat or neck, just as Pisces rules the feet, and Gemini the lungs. I had always ascribed this chronic weakness to a botched tonsillectomy as a child.

Thereafter, I noted that an inordinate number of throat sufferers are Taureans—obviously under bad aspect.

I was in Oblo's stargazing chamber when he received a phone call from a noted specialist. They discussed a patient as if it were a normal medical consultation, though the patient himself never realized how he had been diagnosed. As he put down the phone, Oblo commented dryly, "I once told this doctor he had kidney stones, and that if he didn't have them removed soon, he would unexpectedly collapse. He fell to the floor one day while operating on somebody else. It was his kidney stones."

Some doctors, aware that before the Renaissance most physicians were also astrologers—like the one and only Nostradamus—have used astrology as a shortcut to understanding their patients. Since a large percentage of physical ailments admittedly have a psychogenic origin, knowing the patient becomes of primary importance. One prominent internist, a Cornell graduate, used his patients' natal sun and moon signs and ascendant—the position of the sun in the eastern horizon at birth—as a means of getting quickly acclimated. "This often provided more psychological insight in two minutes than two months of tests," he insisted.

He is by no means unique. Many psychiatrists have picked up enough astrology to broaden their basis for understanding. And some lawyers, too, have turned to astrology. One attorney made horoscopes of his divorce clients and found that the best marriage risks were two zodiac signs apart—Taurus and Cancer, for instance, at a sextile, or sixty-degree angle, in the 360-degree horoscope. The attorney's report jibed with a study by psychoanalyst-humanist Dr. Carl Gustave Jung, who gathered the horoscopes of 483 couples in establishing an apparent correlation between planetary signs and marital success.

Astrology also deals with the impersonal. Called astrophysics, it has played a role in predicting the weather for a highly practical RCA Communications Inc. RCA's astrophysicist, John H. Nelson, for years anticipated magnetic storms by charting the positions of the planets and the sun, thus permitting RCA to reroute radio-wireless messages without delay. Just as these electrical storms threw off communications, so, too, did they influence everyday occurrences in often predictable fashion. On August 17, 1959, when 500,000 people in New York City were deprived of electric service by the failure of Con Edison's underground cables, astrologer Williams recalled that Nelson had predicted a severe magnetic storm for that very day. As a large part of the city wrestled with a power blackout, Williams checked with RCA's radio propagation analyst—another euphemism for Nelson—and was informed that shortwave radio communications were also out throughout the Northeastern area. Reflecting that these geomagnetic disturbances had been predicted almost a month before, Williams wondered whether in some way they had affected the cables which were his particular province.

He took his suspicions to Con Ed engineers, who, instead of sneering, asked Williams if he could predict the next disturbance on the basis of planetary movements. The cable manager picked out the weekend of August 29-30, 1959. On August 30 there were twelve cable failures, three times the normal number. But the public was not inconvenienced as before, because it was a Sunday and thousands of offices and plants were closed.

Williams studied the cable failures for the preceding five years and found a definite correlation with geomagnetic activity in the ionosphere. Following these studies he went to England and discussed cable failures with British engineers, returning home with a proposal for a less vulnerable underground cable protected with a wrapping of polyethylene over lead. Initially, the reinforced cables added 10 percent to already high cable costs, but the following five years brought a compensating reduction in power breakdowns over Con Ed's 8,375 miles of underground cable.

Williams gave astrology full credit for this revolutionary industrial change. Nelson, however, declined to call his work astrology—a term from which the conventional shrink. Unlike some stargazers, he made the sun, not the earth, the center of his charts, and he was concerned exclusively with the ionosphere rather than with people. Nevertheless, his remarkably accurate forecasts of radio blackouts over the North Atlantic obviously affected human behavior, as shortwave messages were transmitted over an alternate southerly route by a relay station in Tangiers especially designed for this purpose.

Nelson himself reported that the best radio reception occurred when any two slow planets (Saturn, Uranus, Jupiter, Neptune, Pluto) were at a trine, 120 degrees apart. The worst occurred when fast-moving Mars, Venus, Mercury and Earth were in "critical relationship" near the points of a Saturn-Jupiter configuration or near other slow planets. Or when two or more planets were at right angles to each other, or in line on the same side of the sun, or in line with the sun between them.

How Nelson, the radio propagation analyst, determined the time and place of the critical storms seemed to me to be quite celestially complicated. But an RCA Communications publicity representative was not nearly as baffled by the method, though he had less exposure to Nelson's work. "Why," he expostulated, "it sounds like astrology to me."

While some astrologers have concerned themselves with broad economic cycles, others have specialized in individual stock situations—like Wall Street specialists. Astrologer Peggy (P.H.) Reynolds put her clients in the aviation and electronic stock boom in 1965-66, and was backing stock exchange winners Xerox and Syntex long before the ordinary customer's man. She also did well with obscure issues. One day, on the American Exchange, she singled out New York, Honduras and Rosario, plotted its natal chart from incorporation date on November 17, 1880, and called it an instant winner. The stock promptly went up six points in five trading days on a down market. "A beneficent planet was in power," was her explanation.

Once she advised a client to stay out of a department store merger. The reasons were obvious to her. "The sun was adverse to Jupiter for one company," she said, "and an adverse Jupiter is not good for money matters. Also, in this planetary disposition, there would be a tendency for vexing legal affairs and involvement in matters that weren't aboveboard." Months later, she saw her position vindicated. One of the merging companies turned up with huge shortages.

On another occasion, a syndicate was considering the purchase of a corner piece of a Los Angeles country club. Peggy advised against it, since the buyer's Neptune was clearly afflicted, and Neptune, as anybody should know, rules fumes and noxious gases. "You wouldn't want anything like that, would you?" Peggy asked her client. He gulped and went home to think it over. Subsequently, he was laughed out of his misgivings by associates, and bought the property, anyway, launching a costly subdivision program. Just as the first homes were completed, a sulfur plant, previously abandoned, started up again in the neighboring section and drove home owners off. "He should have known about Neptune," Peggy observed judiciously.

Even a superficial interest in astrology develops curiosity not only about the personality significance of one's own sign but the signs to which it is best aspected. Young people at cocktail parties, drawn to someone of the opposite sex at sight, often inquire about the birth sign—Aries, Taurus, Gemini, Cancer, etc.—and only then about a name, address, or telephone number.

A brilliant young Manhattan architect, Robert Bruce Cousins, analyzing the twelve signs, conceived the idea of homes especially designed to suit the personalities of a particular sign —from Aries the Ram, the sign of spring and innovation, to Pisces the Fish.

"Headwork," he noted, "was the salient factor of Aries, Aries people (March 21 to April 20) being keen, creative, highly adaptive, as well as headstrong, impetuous, generous. They enjoyed music and entertainment, luxury and beauty, and were idealistic yet extravagant. As the first sign of the Zodiac, reflecting a pioneering instinct, their tastes were simple but daring."

Taurus (April 21 to May 20) is an earth sign, and the Taurus house should reflect this earthiness, as well as the integration of personality true of so many Taureans. Taurus wants his home, work, friends, and life style to reflect the unity within himself. "The determined Taurean seeks the best, and yet simplicity satisfies more than ostentatious display." The architect strove for a certain "feel." And so on, down the line: Geminis (May 21 to June 21) are creative, volatile, often fickle and changeable. They can be encouraged but never driven, as they require a feeling of freedom at all times. Cancer (June 22 to July 22) is a homemaker. The women make good mothers, handy with food and finances. The Cancer man seeks security, yet desires change. Leo (July 23 to August 22) people are magnetic, theatrical, and impulsive. Leo is a showman with a capacity for entertaining; a bully at times and subject to love affairs, not strong on detail. Virgo (August 23 to September 22) is analytical, frequently caustic, orderly, meticulous, ready for service and sacrifice. Libra (September 23 to October 22) is evenly balanced, with a love of beauty and justice, hence the balanced scales as the symbol. The Scorpio (October 23 to November 21) sign is usually associated with sex, and Scorpios are considered creative, with a deep sexual nature, loyal to friends, energetic, resourceful, and often overbearing because of an overweening desire for power. They are the revolutionaries; they refuse to be ignored. Sagittarians (November 22 to December 21) are ardent, talented, but often without tenacity. In love with love, and partial to the sea, travel, and the field of communications, they give the impression of flamboyance, while actually being quite conservative underneath. They are relatively openminded, ironic, adept at explaining, good teachers. Capricorns (December 22 to January 19) are tenacious—they never give up. President Nixon is a prime example. They are considered cold—this may be true of their thought processes but not of their essential nature. They are earthy, practical, worldly wise, often seeking insight through trying to understand the universe around them. Aquarians (January 20 to February 19) are open-minded but fanciful, generous, warm, restless, ever interested in new projects, but paradoxically inconsiderate of others' desires because of an overriding feeling of knowing best. They are idealistic in many ways, but with a fine regard for their own contributions—tyrant material. Pisces the Fish (February 20 to March 20) is generally a sensitive, unassuming sign. Pisceans often acquire knowledge but do not use it; a notable exception, George Washington, reflected the more admirable Piscean qualities of unselfishness, calmness, sacrifice, determination, and deep devotion to friends and causes.

Toting up all these attributes, architect Cousins had to consider houses for husbands and wives of perhaps strongly conflicting signs. "If they are sufficiently conflicting," he decided, "the marriage obviously won't last, and that will take care of the housing problem."

Natal signs can be surprisingly revealing at times. After attending an astrology class for novices at Santa Monica, California, I could frequently determine the birth sign of a person, with confounding accuracy. Beginning with a Gemini girl and concluding with a Leo man, I picked out seven in a row correctly. Lunching with editor John Denson, formerly my chief at *Newsweek* magazine, I happened to mention a reportorial interest in astrology. Denson laughed derisively, and turning to an associate, said, "It'll be witchcraft next."

Knowing Denson to be an impulsive type with a theatrical manner, I did not take offense. However, I did mention that I had successively identified the birth signs of several people, all virtually strangers.

Denson regarded me with exaggerated disbelief. "He really believes this nonsense," he said in a loud, bullying voice. "All right," he added, giving me a magnetic eye, "what sign am I?"

Only one sign seemed indicated by his character—magnetic, theatrical, impulsive, the showman with a capacity for entertaining, bullying at times.

"You are an obvious Leo."

Denson's jaw dropped, and his Sanka stopped enroute to his lips. "How did you do that?" he demanded.

There are misses, of course, but enough hits to make one wonder. That same day I called on my lawyer, the distinguished Frank Gordon. As I sat outside an open door, waiting for him to finish on the telephone, I reflected on a relationship which had become one of easy informality in a surprisingly short time. Only with Taureans had I ever known such instant rapport, and my three closest male friends were all Taureans. As my thoughts traveled along these lines, I marked Gordon's square jaw, his heavy neck and shoulders. He looked like Taurus the Bull.

At that moment, Gordon's secretary stopped by.

"Tell me," I said, "is Mr. Gordon a Taurus?"

She looked at me strangely. "Why do you say that?"

"I just have a feeling that he is the same sign as myself."

She smiled, still eying me curiously. "As a matter of fact, he is a Taurus."

She paused a moment. "What is your birthday?"

"April 26."

Her hand flew to her mouth. "You're kidding?"

I laughed, instantly comprehending. We had the same birth date.

As Gordon got off the phone, his secretary advised him of the coincidence—and that, of course, was all it was to this logically oriented disciple of Blackstone.

"You had one out of twelve chances," he said.

"How about seven in a row, what of the odds there?"

He shrugged, and the subject was closed. Gordon, like the rest of the conventional establishment, could not accept anything which could not be logically evaluated.

In my astrology class, conducted by a youthful Carol Peel, I listened to discussions, not only of birth signs and natal horoscopes, but of progressions reflecting the shifting impact of the moving planets on a changing life process. To show how all this worked in intimate human affairs, instructor Peel picked out two people who practically lived, loved, married and divorced in a goldfish bowl—Frank Sinatra and Mia Farrow. On a blackboard, with occasional chalk marks, the astrology teacher made the contrasting charts as clear as the stars themselves on a cloudless night.

First, the precise birth times and places: Sinatra a Sagittarius, born December 12, 1915, at 3:03 A.M., in the New York City area; Mia an Aquarian, born February 9, 1945, in Los Angeles, at 11:27 A.M. Their meeting and marriage were almost inevitable. "The special planetary ruler of Frank's seventh house, governing marriage," Carol advised her class, "is the activating planet of Mars. For marriage to take place in

Frank's life, Mars must be set in motion. In Sinatra's chart, Mars is in the tenth house, governing publicity, so he would always be a controversial subject, especially regarding marriage and love affairs."

Then came a discussion of the singer's chart at the time of his marriage—his third—to Mia, on July 19, 1966. "Progressed Jupiter was involved in an aspect with Mars, the planet governing Sinatra's marriage house. Since Jupiter is always considered a benefic, good-luck influence, the tie-in of Mars and Jupiter indicated that the actual wedding would take place under propitious astrological stimulation, though if they had looked ahead astrologically, they could have seen an unfavorable combination of planetary aspects in six months. They would never have married then—not if they had wanted a marriage destined to last. But nobody did a progression of the planetary aspects, and they probably wouldn't have listened, anyway. Lovers never do."

Wedding-wise, the stars were compulsive: "The moon in a man's chart governs the effect of women in his life. At the time of Sinatra's marriage, his moon was activated by its link with Neptune, triggering a particularly exalted frame of mind, though Neptune does sometimes indicate a cloud of underlying illusion."

Now for Mia's marriage aspects:

"The special planetary rulers of Mia's house of marriage and partnership are Mars and Pluto. Mars is located in Mia's tenth house, governing the career, just as it is in Frank's, indicating that her career would be strongly emphasized by their marriage."

The celestial forces joining the disparate pair in matrimony were unique. "Mars, the great stimulator," she stressed, "was not only in their respective tenth houses, but also ruled their respective seventh houses dealing with marriage. They couldn't have stayed apart, if they had wanted to, with these conditions driving them on. Additionally, Mia had her Pluto, indicating personal change through the avenue of a partner, in the fourth house influencing homelife. Mars was also in aspect favorable to the sun, further emphasizing the marriage. In a woman's horoscope, the sun rules the men in her life. At this time, the sun was sextile (favorable for opportunity) to her moon in the ninth house—the department governing the legal aspect of marriage and travel. She was all set for the honeymoon. And Venus, the planet of love and romance, was tied in with jovial Jupiter in her fifth house—ruling love life."

And so, with all these wonderful aspects, why did this auspiciously omened marriage go to pot so fast?

"The three most important signs in any chart are the natal sun, the moon affecting subconscious desires and motivations, and the rising sign, the position of the sun in the eastern horizon at the moment of birth. Frank's sun was in Sagittarius, his moon in Pisces, and he had Libra rising or ascending. Mia's sun was in Aquarius, her moon in Capricorn, and she had Taurus rising. The basic comparison between the two charts showed a powerful attraction and a unique blending of energies. However, these combined energies subsequently sped up the adverse planetary activity that governed disharmonious influences."

Carol insisted that any astrologer could have seen the breakup by merely anticipating the planetary activity six months ahead. "Frank's progressed sun came to a conjunction of Uranus (similar degree in the same house) in the fourth house dealing with homelife, influencing complete change and disruption in his home environment, and at the same time opening a new chapter in his life.

"The progressed moon was square (strongest opposition) to his ascendant when the marriage finally broke up. The moon rules women in his life and a square aspect also triggers a period of struggle and crisis. The moon was also aspecting Mars, the planet of strife, while Jupiter was still aspecting Mars." These aspects, while unfavorable for the continuation of a lopsided marriage, were adding a new wisdom to his life style, making a restricted relationship difficult.

Like most American astrologers, Carol is a determinist, and she now implied that Sinatra could have altered his marital destiny had he known of the obstacles ahead. "If he had had such foreknowledge of the planetary energies activated at that time, he could have remained married but utilized this energy to bring about a favorable change in their marriage."

It seemed contradictory, this almost compulsive desire to allot free will to people who seemed incapable of it.

Now Mia's divorce aspects:

"Five months after the marriage, in December, 1966, progressed Venus (ruling love) formed a square (opposition) aspect to her radical Mars (ruler of her seventh house, governing marriage) and reached its peak in December, 1967, about a week after their separation, when the progressed moon squared to progressed Mars. When a square aspect occurs by progression, it often indicates a period involving struggle and crisis. Any aspect of Venus affects the emotions, social relations, and artistic ventures. Any aspect of Mars brings strife, haste, and an increased expenditure of energy. In Mia's natal horoscope, Venus is a member of grand square—the most powerfully discordant aspect in a horoscope. So this particular progression activated the most adverse planetary configuration in her horoscope."

And so that was what happened to Frankie and Mia on the way from the altar. And Mia, obviously, is no small marriage risk in the future, while Sinatra, astrologically speaking, is going into a new cycle, in which soul-searching should eclipse peccadilloes.

Unquestionably, some astrologers draw on intuition in delineating charts. Nostradamus, discussing his own remarkable powers, once explained: "Aside from astrological calculation, one must be inspired by the prophetic spirit which is the gift of Providence." Examining a chart, he not only saw what astrology had in store, but what the horoscope itself did not encompass.

Most astrologers deny that the psychic influences their delineations. However, no other explanation seems to justify some forecasts. In July of 1958, Elaine Shepard, a former actress, consulted astrologer Isidor Oblo. He foresaw a brilliant writing career. "It is global, international—I see more success for you than you ever dreamed about."

"That's absurd," Elaine Shepard said, "I've never done any writing."

"Nevertheless," he rejoined patiently, "it's all there, and it will begin within two years."

"Suppose I stay in a room, doing needlepoint, as I have been doing," she said sourly, "what then?"

"Nothing you do will alter your destiny," Oblo responded, "it will overtake you even in your room."

One year later, telephoning a friend about a job, Miss Shepard was rerouted to another office, getting an editor by mistake. Unknown to her, this editor had been searching for a nonprofessional with a fresh approach to report on international affairs, somebody viewing the news as other women might. They talked briefly on the phone and she came in to see him and got the job, launching the remarkable career Oblo had foreseen for her. Her first assignment took her to Moscow. She interviewed Khrushchev and accompanied Eisenhower to the Middle East. Her stories ran on front pages throughout the country. Other news hens sniped at her enviously, and not knowing her destiny pattern, insinuated that her newsbeats were due to her feminine wiles.

She lectured, wrote two successful books, *Forgive Us Our Trespasses* and *The Doom Pussy*, and became in time as much of a celebrity as some of the personalities she wrote about.

It was all very strange, for had it not been for a remarkable chain of events, none of it could ever have materialized. How could Oblo have foreseen that the telephone operator would make a mistake, that an editor would be receptive at that moment because of his special interest in adding an outsider, and that Elaine Shepard, given the opportunity, would succeed as she had?

Pure astrology? Maybe, but Elaine Shepard, for one, was not so sure. And Oblo wasn't saying.

12

God, Fate, and Free Will

The girl was beautiful, an heiress of a great family, but she was troubled in spite of it, or perhaps because of it. There did not seem to be any substance or meaning to her life. She could not fit in anywhere. She had no family to go to, the home was broken, and she had been shipped off to school three thousand miles away at the earliest age. All her life she had lacked love, and was now incapable of giving or receiving it.

"Can you help her?" I asked Maude Robinson, who had helped thousands with her psychic insight and her faith in a provident God.

She gazed back into my eyes with a sad look.

"I can lead her to God," she said. "What more is there?"

That afternoon, Mrs. Robinson sat across from the lovely girl, who was little more than a child, and talked to her about God. I listened a bit impatiently, as I felt the girl's problems were immediate, and that a psychic reading, offering a hopeful turn in the road, could have been sound therapy.

Instead, Mrs. Robinson quoted from the Psalms: "Deliver me, O my God, out of the hand of the wicked, out of the hand of the unrighteous and cruel man. For thou art my hope, O Lord God, thou art my trust from my youth."

Tears filled the girl's eyes, and Maude's own eyes were moist.

"Put yourself in God's hands," she said huskily, "only He can help you."

For a half hour she spoke quietly to the girl, seeking to instill a feeling that she could always turn to the God within her and reach the distant stars.

As we left, the girl seemed grateful for the psychic's interest, but the message had not got home. She had tried God before, and He had failed her.

As I drove Mrs. Robinson to her home in Norfolk, I spoke frankly, as an old friend. "I wish you had told her something about the future that would have given her a lift."

She answered quietly, "Her future lies with God."

I looked at her sharply. "What do you mean by that?"

"She will not be here long." She shrugged. "But this earth is not all there is to life."

"What do you see for her?" I asked quickly.

She spoke softly, almost in a whisper. "She will take her own life, and nothing we can do will change that. It is God's will."

My hand started on the wheel. "Oh, don't say that," I said with a sinking feeling.

She kept staring ahead, as at a distant scene unfolding. "She is in torment, and in death she will find the peace she is seeking."

I was stunned. "Do you mean this beautiful girl will commit suicide?"

She regarded me solemnly. "There is great sadness in this girl. I feel it, it is so strong, and then I feel it leaving her. She will be with God."

Shortly thereafter, the girl got involved with the marijuana and LSD set. She telephoned one night, under LSD, and reported shrilly that she finally knew where it was at.

"LSD," she said, "is the answer. You see everything, and most of all, yourself."

When I cautioned her, she laughed indulgently. "No older person understands what it's all about."

I did not hear from her for a week, and then one afternoon I got a call from her roommate.

At the tail end of the LSD experience, on what was known as a downer, she had slashed her wrists. She had been taken to Bellevue Hospital, where she was presently recovering. Help had got to her just in time.

I breathed a sigh of relief.

"Doesn't it shock you?" The roommate was puzzled by my lack of surprise.

"I'm just relieved it wasn't any worse," I said.

That night, I made a phone call myself, to Maude Robinson in Norfolk, Virginia.

"You'll be pleased to know," I said, "that what you foresaw didn't end up that badly."

There was a pause at the other end, and Maude's voice came back slowly. "That is not what I saw. I saw her finally finding the peace she will never find here. It is only a matter of time, and not much time at that."

"Are you sure?" I asked.

"I wouldn't see it if it wasn't there to be seen." Her voice faded and came back. She was quoting now from her favorite book: "Thy days are numbered like the hairs on thine head."

Deflated, I put down the phone.

In the next few months I lost sight of the beautiful young girl with everything—and nothing. And then one day, her roommate was on the phone again. This time, I could detect the distress in her fumbling hello. "I just learned yesterday," she gasped, "that she killed herself. She had gone back on LSD."

I kept asking myself what I might have done that would have helped. But Maude kept assuring me that there was nothing that anybody could have done at that time. The life pattern is set, and so is death. As Thoreau pointed out when a caller shed crocodile tears over his sickbed, life and death are only a hairline apart. And perhaps as Tolstoy—and a Greater —has said, death is but the beginning. The psychics, with their confidence in reincarnation and the everlasting life, are sublimely hopeful of the future, regardless of the dreary past.

"To accept God's will is not to be fatalistic," Maude Robinson said with a glint in her eye. "All it means is that, like Job, we accept the situation and keep going."

As Maude pointed out, life is more inside than outside us. We suffer and are hurt only as we give others the power to hurt us. I remember my grandmother once saying that it wasn't living that was so hard, but thinking about it. Actually, how much does man contribute to his own life pattern? How many projects launched by him work out as planned? Perhaps our happiness or lack of it lies in acceptance, not resignation.

Edgar Cayce, perhaps, reconciled fate and free will best. While he once held that a future event was foreseeable because it was fixed, it was still the choices one makes and one's reaction to events that karmically laid the groundwork for the next life experience.

Fate versus free will is one of the oldest philosophic problems. Do we have free will in one set of circumstances and not in another? It seems hardly likely that a mere change in time or place can alter natural principles or laws inherent in a constant universe. Some fifteen million Americans, thrust into World War II, exercised little free will as they were shunted to the far corners of the earth on missions they had never even dreamed of. In acceptance of their roles lay their only freedom of choice. They could complain or remain cheerful; they could be defeatist or optimistic, holding, as so many did, that the bullet wasn't made with their name on it.

With the end of war, did man assume a freedom already relinquished? Obviously, war is different only in that it imposes a controlled state, and its massive events highlight man's fragility in the face of destiny's steamroller. In civilian life there are many diverse activities free of the stereotypes imposed by military regimentation, and hence there are more ways of reacting, providing an illusion of free will.

The discussions between the determinists and the fatalists are endless. At a psychic session presided over by a highly spiritual sensitive, Kay Croissant of Pasadena, California, two protagonists entered into a revealing exposition of the relative merits of the rival philosophies.

"Of course, we can change things," a determined little determinist said, "otherwise life would be meaningless. We would just float along aimlessly."

"Perhaps we are instruments of God in the ceaseless evolving of evolution," the other countered, "and we do not know what that instrumentation is unless we do our utmost to find purpose in life."

The determinist was unimpressed. "Without free will," she repeated, "we wouldn't be free to make of ourselves what we want."

The discussion was interrupted by a friend who asked the

determinist if she could attend a psychic seminar that weekend.

"I would like to, more than anything I know," the determinist said with a sigh, "but my husband insists I go to Palm Springs with him, and you know my husband."

The apostle of free will had no choice over her own weekend!

If there is a fate ordering our lives, does it help to know what that fate is? If an individual knew he had but a year to live, would he spend his days on earth more wisely, by getting ready for the plunge into oblivion, or a new life, as some maintain? Or would he go his own way as before, or worse, become so fearful that he would wither away in the time allotted him?

Few are able to remold their personalities overnight. Yet the opportunities are there, if the individual will but exercise the free will that is his to make the best of an event presumably inevitable because it is clearly foreshadowed.

The case of a Norfolk schoolteacher, who had consulted Maude Robinson about a marital problem, is very much to the point. She had separated from the husband and kept their sixteen-year-old son, an epileptic. Maude Robinson told the woman she had acted out of pride and should make the first overture toward healing the breach. "Never," the woman said, "he must beg me to come back."

As weeks went into months, the wife became increasingly concerned about the separation.

"Don't be afraid to love," Maude Robinson told her. "Manifest your love and he will love you."

The advice fell on deaf ears. And when her son said he would like to live with his father for a while, the mother grimly packed his bags, drove him to her husband's place, and said, "You've made your choice—don't come back."

Later, the boy wanted to go back, but she stubbornly refused. "You made your choice," she repeated. "Stay there."

She consulted Mrs. Robinson intermittently. "When will my husband come back to me?" she kept asking.

Maude surveyed her calmly. "You will be reunited in six months, but it will be in sadness and sorrow." She regarded the woman narrowly. "I am asking you," she said, "to take your son back. He needs you more now than ever."

The woman's mouth tightened. "He chose," she said.

Maude shook her head wearily. "You will be sorry one day." The woman looked back coldly. "You said my husband would come to my home, so how can I be sorry?"

Maude Robinson, like Cayce, believed in reincarnation and in leaving freedom of choice to the individual, as an opportunity for the karmic buildup for the next life experience. Nevertheless, or perhaps because of this, she renewed her efforts to soften the mother's pride, but all the mother thought about was her victory.

"When he comes back," she said confidently, "my son will be with him."

Maude solemnly quoted from Scripture: "Though I give my body to be burned, and have not charity, it profiteth me nothing. Charity suffereth long, and is kind; charity vaunteth not itself, is not puffed up, doth not behave itself unseemly, seeketh not her own, is not easily provoked, thinketh no evil."

The woman got up to leave.

"Yes," Maude said, "the boy will be with him. But if you care anything about him, reach out and give a mother's love."

The woman stalked out, unrelenting in her pride.

In six months, almost to the day—the husband was indeed back in her home—for the funeral of his epileptic son, who had died unexpectedly.

Maude Robinson had seen it all. But like other psychics, she seldom told of a death.

The mother was inconsolable. She called Maude Robinson repeatedly, blaming herself for not showing the love her son had needed so desperately.

So what had the psychic accomplished? Actually, very little, but had she been heeded, the mother could have taken comfort in having given her son the love he needed, instead of being plagued by guilt.

The husband, now as irreconcilable as his wife, returned to his own home. Neither had learned, even in sorrow.

"Without giving love," Maude observed sadly, "how could they find it?"

While a psychic may be helpful in guiding one over hurdles, the individual cannot live by it. For he never knows whether the psychic is correct until the event itself materializes. It is much more satisfying to make one's own mistakes. A good psychic, like a good doctor, may be a jewel, but running from psychic to psychic, in the frantic hope of finding a ray of light, can be demoralizing.

Consulting various psychics, I learned peripherally that I was to be married again—almost immediately, in the distant future, never—to some dazzling redhead, blonde, or brunette. It can be altogether confusing, once one has lost the direction of his life, regardless of that direction.

"Let events take their course," a psychic researcher suggested, "and profit through remaining calm and detached as the predictions unfold."

Even more intriguing than precognition, as heady as that is, is the thought of the life everlasting. Curiously, Edgar Cayce had subconsciously dredged up past lives for people in Egypt, Greece, India, Persia, and legendary Atlantis before, as a Fundamentalist, he could begin to accept the startling concept of rebirth. Reexamining the Bible, he found allusions to the reappearance of the ancient prophets that he now felt could only signify rebirth.

Cayce died in 1945. However, other psychics, notably Betty McCain, who recently died herself, and Maria Bleiker in New York have discussed past lives as if they were discussing last week, stressing the karmic conditions these have imposed in making choices in this life. Like Cayce, psychic Leonard Montone, having no interest in reincarnation, began anticipating major events in the current experience and attributing them to an earlier karmic pattern—and often hit the events if not the cause.

Montone's emergence as a psychic seemed almost fore-ordained. As a student in a monastery, he developed an interest in the mystical but was discouraged by superiors. Disenchanted, he gave up his studies but could not seem to find a niche in civilian life. He moved from Philadelphia, his home, to New York, and there had his horoscope drawn, as a vocational guide, and was advised of his psychic potential and need to help people.

He was also told he would soon be offered a job in a publisher's office, and he was. This impressed him, and shortly thereafter came further confirmation of the astrologer's insight. One day he happened to pick up a wristwatch a girl had momentarily removed, and he started to get sharp visual impressions. He saw, incongruously, an infected, bleeding lower gum, with a running abscess. He brushed a hand across his eyes in bewilderment, but the picture would not go away. He told the girl what he had seen, and she gasped. It was her sister's watch. And only the day before her sister had been to an oral surgeon to have her lower gum treated for an abscess.

The next day Leonard saw a ring on a girl's finger and got a sudden impression of an abortion. He couldn't ask her about it, but he did check with her brother. The brother came back with partial confirmation. "A friend of my sister's," he said, "had an abortion two months ago."

Leonard smiled acquiescence, but the intuition which told him about the abortion also told him who had had it.

As he continued his readings, first with friends and then strangers who had heard of his ability, Montone began to get other impressions. For instance, consulted by Manchester Jack Lubow's friend, George Teichner, he suddenly began speaking about Teichner's previous existence in Germany, and said that in this life, to fulfill a leftover need, he would require a German wife.

The news hit Teichner like a shot. Not long before, he had taken a German airline hostess as his wife, feeling compulsively drawn to her. It was necessary, Montone said, that he have a child by her to complete a childless role in his last life.

Teichner, an accountant, was impressed by certain other revelations about himself. He was told that he was restless in his work because of an artistic temperament that was the legacy of several previous life experiences. He would not be happy until he left his accounting for the field of art, letters, or music, in which he had been schooled. He was also told to stop eating steak—which he ate three times a day—as it would make him overly sensual, dangerously attractive on a purely sexual level to women.

It all suddenly made sense to Teichner. He had a German wife, he longed for a career in the theater or the arts, which he loved, and 90 percent of his clients were women. They just seemed to flock to him.

Montone himself did not know what to make of his gift, nor what he should do with it. "Unless I can help people," he said, "there doesn't seem to be much point to it."

Certainly, there is room for help. As never before, multitudes of all faiths—and no faith—are turning uneasily to the approach of a new millennium. They are casting an eye to the Bible—and to modern prophets—for understanding of the prophecies of doom and destruction and of the dawn of a new and better day. But actually, in the sublime order of things, what is there to fear? Despite predictions of climactic disaster before the turn of the century, the future stretches on virtually endlessly, with a few possibly unpleasant interludes. The order is already established. Nothing will likely change it. The best we can do is to know what is coming and to prepare for it. God has His own way of influencing man's behavior: "I have declared the former things from the beginning, and they went forth out of my mouth, and I showed them; I did them suddenly, and they came to pass."

Man is as much a part of the natural law as are the planets that contain him and other life. Even in his disorder, there is a certain order in his relationship to the world about him, and this some call destiny.

As Thomas Aquinas said centuries before, there is a divine providence and through this an orderly disposition of all creatures. And what is foreseen through prophecy, in tune with this providence, is neither fortuitous nor mere chance. Belief in the prophets buoyed generations of Jews separated from their homeland: "Fear not, for I am with thee; I will bring thy seed from the east, and gather thee from the west. And I will say to the north [Russia], keep not back; bring my sons from far, and my daughters from the end of the earth."

Today the world awaits the fulfillment of other prophecies it only vaguely understands. The restoration of Israel, a promised forerunner of Armageddon, heightens the feeling that we are on the brink of great things. The English Bible scholar, Dr. Grattan Guinness, saw indications long ago that "the cleansing of the sanctuary and the restoration of Israel were not too distant." And with this prophecy, Guinness emphasized the prophesied war to end all wars: "Then the last warning bell will have rung; the last of the unfulfilled predictions of Scripture as to events prior to the great crisis will have received their accomplishment. Then the second advent of Israel's rejected

Messiah to reign in conjunction with His glorified saints as King over all the earth will be close at hand."

Guinness was perhaps mistakenly assuming that the ensuing struggle would be physical rather than spiritual, but the shining alternative is always there:

For as the lightning cometh out of the east, and shineth even unto the west, so shall also the coming of the Son of Man be. . . . Immediately after the tribulation of those days shall the sun be darkened, and the moon shall not give her light, and the stars shall fall from heaven, and the powers of the heaven shall be shaken.

And then shall appear the sign of the Son of Man in heaven; and then shall all the tribes of the earth mourn, and they shall see the Son of Man coming in the clouds of heaven with power and great glory.

In this heralded second coming, there is hopeful recognition that the greatest life ever lived, has not been lived in vain. Obviously the Prince of Peace brought a message two thousand years ago that the world was not ready for. What would make it ready? Perhaps Edgar Cayce knew when he foreshadowed destruction in 1998, as had Nostradamus centuries before:

> In the year 1999 in the seventh month
> A great king of frightfulness will come from the skies
> To resuscitate the great king of Anguomois,
> Around this time Mars will reign for the good cause.

For more than three hundred years this quatrain has baffled experts. But space travel, some think, provides the answer. The men from outer space will descend, even from Mars perhaps, and help the civilized forces—Anguomois meaning France, and to the great French seer, France meant civilization.

Also coming to focus at century's end are the Malachy prophecies, the Prophecies of the Popes, passed on for four hundred years and presumably dating back another four hundred years. Malachy, born Mael Maedoc us Morgair, was Archbishop of Armagh. He supposedly penned the prophecies, identifying each pope by a characteristic slogan. They were not published until 1595, the five hundredth anniversary of his birth, by a Dominican friar who said they had been gathering dust in the Vatican. In all, there are III terse Latin mottoes, one for each pope, from Celestine II of Malachy's time to "the time of the end." They often seem to hit. Paul VI was heralded in the prophecies by the fleur-de-lys, and this was his family crest. He is the one hundred and eighth pontiff on the Malachy list, leaving three to go. This limitation, some say, led to an obvious forgery at the conclusion: "During the last persecution of the Holy Roman Church," the alleged prophecy ends, "there shall sit the Roman Peter, who shall feed the sheep amid great tribulations, and when these are passed, the City of Seven Hills shall be utterly destroyed and the awful Judge will judge the people."

False prophets, obviously drawing on the Cayce prophecies, have emerged with predictions of earthquakes, tidal waves, atomic disasters, and sundry cataclysms. California has been washed repeatedly into the sea by charlatans preying on the fears of the unwary. Cayce's own predictions are modified by a belief that a spiritual awakening is an inevitable corollary of any great holocaust. Believing in reincarnation, he hopefully foresaw the end of great cities and countries as a mere ripple in the sea of time. "Don't worry so much where you live," he constantly enjoined, "but how you live."

The future stretches boundlessly for humanity. One day soon we will put our people on the planets and begin man's exploration of a universe without time or space but only with perpetuity. With the speed of thought, infinitely faster than even the incredible speed of light, extraterrestrial psychic communication will become a commonplace in a world in which necessity is ever the mother of invention. And in time, as the psychic effort does become routine, we may learn enough about how it works to solve not only the riddle of the universe but our very being.

As Hollywood's well-known psychic Jule Johnson—Madam Juno to the motion picture world—once pointed out, the psychic force works through God, and God works in his own mysterious way. "We ask for strength," she said, "and God gives us difficulties, which make us strong. We plead for courage, and God gives us danger to overcome. We ask for favors, and God gives us opportunities."

And blessed was the prophet who saw all this—and gave us hope.